THE WAY AMARILLO

A Musical Odyssey Across The USA

George Miller

KNOW THE SCORE BOOKS TRAVEL PUBLICATIONS

TITLE	Author	ISBN
CHASING THE EIGHTIES	Spencer Austin	978-1-84818-951-5
DOING THE WAINWRIGHTS	Steve Larkin	978-1-905449-34-7
THE FOUR-LETTER COUNTRIES	David Jenkins	978-1-905449-99-6
NEW BOOTS IN NEW ZEALAND	Gillian Orrell	978-1-905449-40-8
THIS IS THE WAY TO AMARILLO	George Miller	978-1-905449-98-9

THIS IS THE WAY TO AMARILLO

A Musical Odyssey Across The USA

George Miller

www.knowthescorebooks.com

First published in the United Kingdom
by Know The Score Books Ltd, 2008
Copyright George Miller

The right of George Miller to be identified as the author of this work has been asserted by him in accordance with sections 77 and 78 of the Copyright, Designs and Patents Act, 1988.

PORTSMOUTH
CENTRAL LIBRARY
TEL: 023 9281 9311

Know The Score Books Limited
118 Alcester Road, Studley, Warwickshire, B80 7NT
01527 454482 info@knowthescorebooks.com www.knowthescorebooks.com

A CIP catalogue record is available for this book from the British Library
ISBN: 978-1-905449-98-9

Jacket design by Ellen McIntosh

Printed and bound in Great Britain
By Cromwell Press, Trowbridge, Wiltshire

Mixed Sources
Product group from well-managed forests and other controlled sources
www.fsc.org Cert no. TT-COC-2082
FSC © 1996 Forest Stewardship Council

Lyrics reproduced by kind permission of:
EMI, SGAE, Blackwood, Novalene, Alley Music, Arc Music, Combine music, Universal and Sony/ATV

Disclaimer:
Despite every effort, some copyright owners of lyrics reproduced in full in this book have not been traced. Any rights holder involved is cordially invited to contact the publisher in writing providing proof of copyright ownership.

ACKNOWLEDGEMENTS

I have many people to thank for giving me encouragement and support in writing this book – friends, acquaintances, neighbours and relatives, all of whom have been superb. I am grateful to you all for your forbearance and patience, I hope you find the end result worth the suffering.

I am indebted to my trusty review team Peter (Graham) and Frank (Balloch). It is fair to say that this book would not have happened without their contribution and support from the outset – thanks boys.

The daunting logistics of this excursion were eased by the efforts of Julie Cloe at Dawson and Sanderson in Hexham. Tamsin Austin at the Sage Gateshead likewise provided assistance beyond the call of duty. Thanks to Tony Christie and Sean Fitzgerald for their interest and moral support. Ron Harman at the Country Music Hall of Fame in Nashville provided an enormous boost during my travels and his ongoing commitment to the cause has been exceptional. Also Stateside, I am grateful to Stanley Marsh for permission to use the Cadillac Ranch image and for a fascinating day in Amarillo, and to Pifas Silva in El Paso, Wink Rodriguez in Tucson, Priestess Miriam in New Orleans, the management team at Hooters Las Vegas, Julie Dodson and Justin in Chattanooga, Eric Miller in Amarillo, Rachel Pace in Clarksville and, for their hospitality and friendship, Dan and Tabitha Lavacot, Hoppy Williams and many more who helped me on my way.

Thanks to Simon Lowe of Know the Score Books for having faith in my venture and for providing continuing support and professional advice, and to Tony Lyons for his cheerful and able contribution.

Special thanks to my wife Julia for her patience and support and to my daughters Stephanie and Laura for their unstinting belief. Also, I owe a special thank you to my six year old granddaughter Lucy for helping me with my spellings and to new arrival Sam who lifted my spirits when the going was tough.

And a thank you stretching across the Atlantic to all the people in the States who made me feel special and to all the new friends I made on the way to Amarillo. I could not have anticipated the warm reception I was given wherever I went on my travels. Rest assured I will be back.

ge Miller, April 2008

This Is The Way To Amarillo - A Musical Odyssey Across The USA

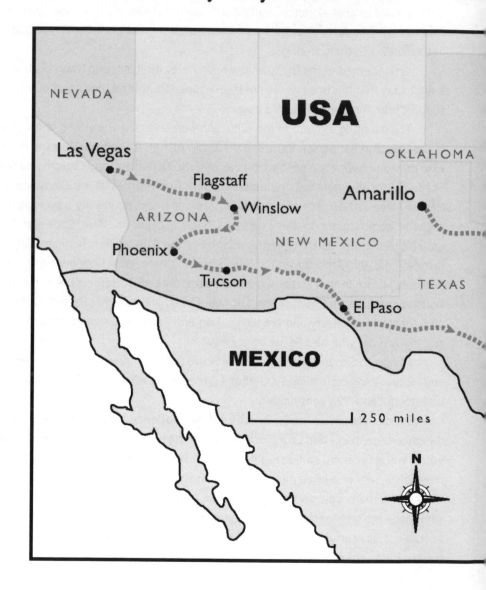

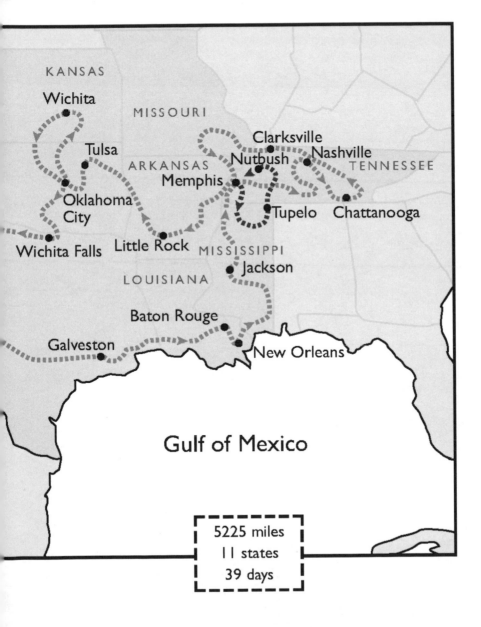

KANSAS

Wichita

MISSOURI

Tulsa

ARKANSAS

Clarksville

Nutbush

Nashville

TENNESSEE

Oklahoma
City

Memphis

Tupelo

Chattanooga

Wichita Falls

Little Rock

MISSISSIPPI

Jackson

LOUISIANA

Baton Rouge

Galveston

New Orleans

Gulf of Mexico

5225 miles
11 states
39 days

For Mam and Dad

'It seems to me that the occupation of Unbiased Traveler Seeking Information is the pleasantest and most irresponsible trade there is.'

Mark Twain, *Following The Equator*

CONTENTS

Introduction

"Well, I'm a standing on a corner in Winslow, Arizona . . ."

THE EAGLES HAVE A LOT to answer for, I decided, as I stood alone in the middle of the desert watching the Greyhound bus disappear along the highway in a cloud of red dust.

As I surveyed the desolate landscape I asked myself whether I might be being unreasonable in expecting to get dropped off somewhere near civilisation. The advice of Glenn Frey and Jackson Browne to *Take it Easy* seemed rather ironic as I stood there in deepest Arizona at three o' clock in the afternoon, the temperature in the eighties and a heavy pack on my back. Running down the road and loosening my load was definitely out of the question and I certainly had a world of trouble on my mind. Seemingly miles from anywhere and not a building on the horizon, I wondered if I would ever find Winslow. And, if I did, would I find accommodation? Or would I end up negotiating with the nearby Apache or Hopi tribes to rent a tepee for the night?

As I set off in what I hoped was the direction of town I reminded myself this was just day three of my journey in search of musical enlightenment, a pilgrimage which would carry me more than 5,000 miles through numerous southern American states; from Nevada to Texas, Louisiana to Mississippi, Tennessee to Oklahoma. I had no idea what might be in store for me over the coming weeks as I travelled through towns large and small in my mission to unearth the mysteries of US musical folklore. It was to be a magical mystery tour which would throw up all sorts of surprises, perilous episodes and more than a sprinkling of bizarre characters as I explored the places made immortal through the art of the songwriter.

IT HAD ALL STARTED BACK home in England, in a bar somewhere in Newcastle, with my drinking accomplice and music enthusiast, Pete. Fuelled by numerous beers and a generous quantity of red wine, I had suggested that I quite fancied visiting the States and tracking down towns which are the subject of well known songs, researching the lyrics and performers along the way. Never one to display a lack of enthusiasm, Pete had immediately seized on the idea and given me all the inebriated encouragement I needed. In a more abstemious moment I might have questioned why he didn't volunteer to accompany me on such a trip.

We'd kicked around some of the places this hare-brained venture might take me to: Vegas, New Orleans, Memphis, Nutbush, Tulsa, Chattanooga and, of course, Amarillo. But the more places we came up with, the more we realised how little we knew about them. That meant I was hooked on the idea. Out came the Atlas and the credit card and before I knew it I was booking myself on a trip which, I think I can safely say, no-one had ever embarked upon before.

And so, many months and many pints later, here I was in the Arizona desert thinking about Pete, probably comfortably asleep in his comfortable bed back home.

Was he dreaming of locating the *Wichita Lineman*, missing the *Last Train To Clarksville* or being stranded *Twenty Four Hours From Tulsa*?

Somehow I doubted it!

Chapter One

"Bright light city gonna set my soul . . ."

I KNEW THIS WAS MY sort of place the minute I saw the sign; 'Cold beer, dirty women, mud wrestling, bikini bull-riding and a BBQ chicken dinner for $5.95'.

My interest in the sign was, of course, purely historic as it stood outside the famous Frontier Hotel. I was in Las Vegas, the indisputable world capital of hedonism and it was here at the Frontier, on 23 April 1956, that Elvis made his Vegas debut soon after coming to prominence with his first number one single *Heartbreak Hotel*.

The King didn't exactly take the town by storm on this occasion as he was unable to distract the clients from their slot machines for long enough to gyrate his way into their hearts, or even their minds. It was more than a decade later that he came back, breaking all box office records and holding centre stage between 1969 and 1976, whilst performing an incredible 837 shows.

But before then, in 1964, he had filmed *Viva Las Vegas*, spawning the song of the same name which gave me my excuse to put Sin City at the top of my list of destinations for my trip:

Oh, there's a blackjack and poker and the roulette wheel
A fortune won and lost on ev'ry deal
All you need's a strong heart and a nerve of steel
Viva Las Vegas, Viva Las Vegas

Vegas was the first port of call on my six week mission – a tour of the southern states, an area which by now I had established was the hotbed of American musical history. Sure, the North has lots to offer in this respect but I had decided it would have to wait its turn. For now, the heritage of the South was the key; it was clear the region positively oozes Rock and Roll, Country, Blues, Jazz and more besides. And what better place to start than the epicentre of Nevada decadence, the infamous Las Vegas?

I SOON FOUND THAT ELVIS'S impact on Vegas can't be exaggerated and that he still has a King-sized presence more than 30 years on. The guide books waste no time in telling you there is a bronze statue in front of the Las Vegas Hilton, formerly the International, where he staged his all-conquering comeback in 1969, his 1976 Eldorado car is on display in the Imperial Palace, and his white caped suit (the 'Adonis') is on display at the Hard Rock Café. On top of this, the Aladdin can boast it is the hotel where Elvis married Priscilla, and the Flamingo and Sahara hotels were both used in the filming of *Viva Las Vegas*.

And let's not forget, slightly less salubriously, the Elvis Wedding Chapel, where you can choose from a variety of Elvis weddings. 'Each starring the King himself' . . . 'Elvis will perform your wedding ceremony and sing a selection of his greatest hits. Choose from a range including the Elvis Blue Hawaii Wedding package, featuring lush tropical sets, smoke effects and hula hula girls,' enthuses the promotional literature, before going on to suggest you might want to hire a Priscilla impersonator as a Matron of Honor!

It had been Elvis's boyhood dream to be a comic book hero or a movie star, but I doubt whether he would have anticipated making 31 films, most of them, it has to be said, fairly dire money-making exercises satisfying the demands of his manager, the infamous Colonel Parker (or Colonel Sanders as Elvis once referred to him). However, it can't be said that Elvis was a bad actor and he had considerable screen presence as well as a lot of acting ability. Viva Las Vegas was actually one of his more highly-regarded films and his undoubted talent is demonstrated by the fact that in the film he sang the title song in one uncut take, shot through the lens of a single camera. No mean feat. The single, when released, had moderate success, reaching number 17 in the UK charts and number 29 in the States, where it was the B side to *What'd I Say*.

But Elvis was not the only performer to have a hit with a song about Vegas, there have been many other songs about the town, one of the best and most successful being Tony Christie's *Las Vegas* ('Hey Las Vegas, the devil gave us to you-oo') which was a huge hit in 1970, selling over 6 million copies. As Tony features prominently later in the book, I'm sure he'll forgive me for not dwelling on his success at this point, but let's have a look at some of the words anyway, it's a great song:

The Lord above made the world for us, but the devil made Las Vegas

Oh Las Vegas, you'll be the death of me, city of sin
oh what a mess I'm in, look what you've done to me
Oh Las Vegas, I'm losing everything,
why do I stay when every game I play, I just get deeper in
Hey Las Vegas, can nothing save us from you,
night after night, watching the wheel go round
Hey Las Vegas, the devil gave us to you,
one of these days, I'm gonna burn you down

A rousing song, but somewhat in contrast to Elvis's more upbeat message about Vegas:

'a thousand pretty women waiting out there.........' 'and I'm just the devil with love to spare.'

Although Elvis didn't write 'Viva' I would guess that the lyrics fairly accurately reflect his optimistic outlook on life at that stage of his career, when he was in his prime, and he no doubt wouldn't have wanted 'to sleep a minute away' and would definitely have had that 'strong heart and nerve of steel' to which he refers!

Other Vegas-related songs I uncovered include Sheryl Crow's *Leaving Las Vegas* ('Life springs eternal on a gaudy neon street') from her *Tuesday Night Music Club* album. The song caused some controversy as Sheryl went on live television and claimed the song was autobiographical, even though she didn't actually write it herself, thus infuriating the writer David Baerwald.

If it is autobiographical she seems to be bit of a girl if you consider the meaty lyrics:

> *Used to be I could drive up to*
> *Barstow for the night*
> *Find some crossroad trucker*
> *To demonstrate his might*

Fairly raunchy stuff.

Other performers who have sung about Vegas range from the Stereophonics to AC/DC and from Dean Martin to Chumbawumba. But the prize for fewest words must surely go to Who da Funk and their *Shiny Disco Balls*:

> *Drugs...*
> *rock 'n' roll...*
> *bad-ass vegas whores...*
> *late-night booty calls...*
> *shiny disco balls...*

What can I say, such beautiful lyrics, put together and presented in a tender and romantic manner. If you're not impressed with the poetry of these thirteen words you should try listening to it!

But perhaps the most relevant song from my point of view, considering the travelling escapades I was just about to launch into, is Billy Idol's 1984 hit *Eyes Without A Face*, the song which won him the accolade of Songwriter of the Year:

> *Steal a car and go to Las Vegas oh, the gigolo pool.*
> *I'm on a bus on a psychedelic trip...*

I may not have been planning a psychedelic trip but the bus was going to be a dominant feature of my life over the next six weeks. Would I survive to tell the tale I wondered? One thing was certain – I was not going to embark on six weeks on the Greyhound circuit without first regenerating my batteries by plugging into the multi-million mains voltage of Vegas.

I HAD ARRIVED IN THE States after a fairly uneventful twenty-one hour, three plane journey from England to Vegas (this would be my last uneventful journey for some time) and coming in to land at McCarran International airport was an interesting experience. Somewhat surprisingly for the virgin traveller to Vegas, just before the plane hits the runway the famous 'strip' appears, with the names of the 'resorts' clearly visible – the Luxor, the Mirage, Bellagio, Caesar's Palace and so on. The funny thing is it looks like you could just walk to your hotel from the runway.

The reality is very different, of course, and it was with great amusement that an hour later my taxi driver enjoyed relating the fact that every summer many newcomers, saving their dollars for the gaming tables, would attempt the walk from the airport into town. It is apparently a common sight to see people dragging suitcases the two miles or so along the highway in searing 114F temperatures before they realise their mistake.

In return, I amused the driver by telling him about the entry requirements demanded of visitors to his country, in particular the visa waiver form I'd been compelled to complete on the plane. For those readers about to go to the States for the first time – think hard and be prepared to answer the following questions: 'Are you or have you ever been a member of a terrorist organisation?' 'Are you entering the United States for purposes of a terrorist act?' 'Have you ever been engaged in genocide?' 'Were you a member of the Nazi party prior to 1945?' 'Have you ever been convicted of moral turpitude?' If you answer 'yes' to any of those questions, answer this next one – are you a complete head case to be flying to the United States? Don't bother responding, the answer will be quite apparent.

The taxi dropped me at Hooters Hotel just off the main strip. I had no idea what it would be like – it didn't sound a particularly up-market place with a name like Hooters, but I'd given it the nod over 'Terrible's' which sounded even worse. Still, for thirty dollars per night, the equivalent of fifteen quid, it would have to be pretty bad for me to complain. Definitely a better choice than The Blue Moon Resort, 'Vegas's only all-male hotel' where 'clothing is optional.'

There aren't too many nice surprises in life, but as I walked in and saw the waitress in orange hot pants and a slogan on the back of her T shirt 'Tacky but delightfully unrefined', I knew I'd be at home here. The reception area was a sea of gaming machines as well as blackjack, poker, roulette and craps tables, all in a healthy state of action. The girls in hot pants were everywhere, there were even pictures of them on the wall entertaining the troops in Iraq. These were all calendar girls, apparently, and very easy on the eye of the weary traveller. By the way, I must confess to a little naivety here – I hadn't realised that 'Hooters' is a North American colloquialism for a certain (generally) attractive part of a woman's anatomy. I do now recall a rather strange look from the lady in the travel agents when I was booking my flight and I told her that I had booked into Hooters. Now, the key question: 'tacky but delightfully unrefined' – was that referring to the hotel or to the girls? Not that it would matter to me, I just wanted to get my head down and prepare my plans for the next day. This was a mission, not a holiday.

Waking up the next day I looked out of the window and, forgetting where I was for a moment, was somewhat surprised to see, on my left, the Sphinx, and just behind it one of the Great Pyramids, but built out of glass – the Hotel Luxor, of course. Once I had adjusted my confused and weary mind to this impressive, if somewhat garish, awakening I looked straight ahead and was confronted by an array of even more garish orange and blue turrets in the fashion of King Arthur's Camelot – the Excalibur Hotel. To my right I had the Statue of Liberty and the entire New York skyline and further away the Eiffel Tower and Arc de Triomphe, I was truly an international traveller this bright and sunny morning.

Having assimilated my new surroundings, I had a shave, got dressed and ventured downstairs to try the hotel coffee bar and café. After managing to eat some of my breakfast – American food is an acquired taste, I looked at the pictures on the wall. On seeing the Grand Canyon and Hoover Dam posters I suddenly developed pangs to go on a visit. How could I be so close and not go to the Canyon? Having said that, there's still a few hundred miles between Vegas and the Canyon and it's therefore a full day out. I reminded myself that such indulgences would have to wait for another occasion.

I settled for amusing myself over coffee by reading about the construction of the Dam. Did you know it was completed in 1936 and that the concrete is still hardening every day? The construction was completed two years ahead of schedule – now that's what you call project management; Scottish Parliament and Wembley Stadium eat your hearts out! But, before you get carried away, consider this – the official death toll during construction was 96. And that's not including those who died from carbon monoxide poisoning from the machinery and vehicles inside the tunnel. The reason for their exclusion is that the contractors claimed these deaths were from pneumonia, therefore they carried no responsibility. Another example of the contractors' worker-centred approach was displayed when there was a strike because of dangerous conditions. This was quite easily fixed – it involved representatives from six contractor companies and an undisclosed number of guns and clubs. I must remember to pass this on to the Institute of Personnel for their next survey on 'employee engagement'.

An interesting but unfortunate quirk in respect of the death toll was that the first person to die was a JG Tierney and the last to die was his son Patrick Tierney, thirteen years to the day later. I seem to remember something similar happened during construction of the Forth Rail Bridge. God moves in mysterious ways, but leaves plenty of food for thought. On the bright side I was fascinated to discover that one of the bonus features to emerge from the Dam's construction was the invention of the hard hat. This came about as a result of (obviously necessary) creativity by some workmen who dipped two baseball caps in tar and allowed them to harden. I couldn't help wondering, somewhat forlornly, whether they remembered to take out a patent.

Although my schedule was not fixed – the only reason I had pre-booked a hotel in Vegas was because US border control will deport you on landing if you cannot provide evidence of overnight accommodation – I wanted to be on the move the next day, which left me roughly 24 hours to get to the bottom of what makes Las Vegas tick and how it came to be here in the first place.

I decided to read up on the local history, thinking that a city which in the twenty-first century bases its entire wealth on entertainment (regulars in town are Elton John, Celine Dion and Tom Jones) must have had something of an interesting past.

With a little effort I managed to establish that the area was discovered by Spanish traders en-route to Los Angeles along the 'Spanish Trail'. They referred to the route as the 'Journey of Death'. A young Spanish scout called Rafael Rivera veered from the main trail one day and became the first person of European descent to set eyes upon the Las Vegas valley with its abundant wild grasses and plentiful water supply, created by water from rivers which had long since disappeared below the surface. This relatively luxuriant landscape led to the name Las Vegas – Spanish for 'The Meadows'.

In the late 1800s, when the mining industry was at its peak, Vegas became an ideal re-fuelling point as a railway town, with its link to Salt Lake City in Utah to the North. It became a city, of sorts, in 1905, with 800 inhabitants. In 1931 gambling was legalised in Nevada. Divorce laws had also been liberalised in the state, making residency easier to obtain and after six weeks of residency, a 'quickie' divorce could be decreed. This proved quite a draw. The short-term residents stayed at the engagingly named 'dude ranches', which were effectively the forerunners of the strip hotels.

The construction of the Hoover Dam, which started the following year, brought an influx of construction workers who boosted the valley's economy still further (the funeral parlours will have done a nice little business for instance). By 1940 the population had grown to just over 8,000 and then the onset of the Second World War brought the defence industry to the valley and the opening of what would eventually become the Nellis Air Force Base. Vegas never looked back.

Following the war, 'resort hotels' were developed and tourism became the main industry. This was followed in the '60s by huge capital investment, led by Howard Hughes, resulting in the building of many more resorts. When Elvis had his second coming in 1969, resort owners realised for the first time that money could be made from entertainment shows as well as from gambling. This was to be a watershed in the development of Vegas to its present status – Elvis had entered the building!

There was a huge population explosion between 1985 and 1995 with the number of residents actually doubling in that time to 368,000. The city celebrated its 100th birthday on 15 May 2005 and, by 2006, population figures had reached 570,000, with growth of 7,000 inhabitants per month across the Las Vegas valley as a whole. Add to this the 38 million visitors per annum and you get some idea of the commercial opportunities in the area.

Having previously been a magnet for divorce seekers, the situation was turned on its head in the 1950s when, due to lenient state laws, Vegas became a haven for weddings with licences being available on the spot – 'anywhere, anytime'. In 2004, 5.5% of all weddings in the States, an impressive relative percentage, were conducted in Vegas. It doesn't compare, though, with the day the wedding industry in Vegas reached its peak. This happened on 26 August 1965 with 171 weddings – this being the last day to get a draft deferment for being married during the Vietnam war. A rather drastic alternative some might say.

I had hoped to meet the mayor of Vegas, Oscar Goodman, whose website seemed to encourage contact from the public. He describes himself as the 'happiest mayor in the world.' He was, however, probably too busy meeting the media in order to explain his latest faux-pas if his recent history was anything to go by. Following a gaffe where he outraged parents (and probably his wife) by suggesting at a high school talk that his ideal desert island companion would be a bottle of gin, he surpassed this, reasonably in my opinion, by suggesting that 'punks' who deface the town with graffiti should be televised having their thumbs cut off. To show his reasonableness, he did explain they would get a trial first. I would expect no less from one of the top criminal defence lawyers in the States.

DURING A DISCUSSION WITH the Hooters 'Bell Captain', the rather quaintly-named concierge at the hotel, I became interested in the apparently secret (but obviously well known) 'Area 51'. This is a top-secret military base in grid number 51 of the vast Nevada nuclear test site (at 1375 square miles the test site is bigger than some small countries). Area 51 was set up in 1954 to test the U2 spy plane and has continued to test interesting and sinister new craft including, more recently, the Stealth fighter (even a flying saucer has been tested it has been suggested). It has a runway six miles long and is so sensitive that its buildings are not even shown on the map. The place, not surprisingly, is a magnet for UFO freaks and the area is the subject of much filming and reference in sci-fi films including the *X Files* and *Independence Day*. This is reputed to be the place where all the captured aliens end up for interrogation/dissection, including, it is rumoured, the aliens from the 'crashed alien spacecraft' at Roswell in 1947.

The location has a reputation as the world's hotspot for UFO sightings (fair enough when you consider what is going on inside the site) and the 100 mile highway accessing the site has been officially re-named the 'Extraterrestrial Highway' by the state Governor. With a road sign pointing up into the sky and a speed limit in places of 'Warp 7' I suspect someone in the Governor's office is not taking this at all seriously. I look forward to his abduction.

Equally secretive, at least to begin with, was the nuclear fission industry. Vegas was right in the firing line when the Nevada Test Site was opened in

December 1950 as the nation's 'On continent nuclear weapons testing area'. Prior to 1950 most tests had been conducted in the Pacific, Bikini Atoll being a prime site, but this had been a costly and time-consuming issue, not to mention 'logistically' difficult. No mention, though, of the problem of frying Pacific Islanders in the process.

So, it was now to be the outlying lands of Vegas for future tests. Between 1951 and 1962 no fewer than 126 atmospheric tests of atomic weapons took place at the range, a mere 65 miles from the city. Nothing to worry about, of course. In fact in Vegas the tests became tourist attractions. People came from all over the States to watch the blinding flash and the mushroom clouds. Clark County, in which Vegas is located, even incorporated a mushroom cloud into its official emblem.

All this reminded me of a track called *It's Good News Week* by a band called Hedgehoppers Anonymous which reached number five in the UK charts way back in my relative youth in 1965. The band were made up of Air Force personnel from RAF Wittering in Cambridgeshire and got their name Hedgehoppers from RAF slang for a low-flying plane. The infamous Jonathan King took them under his wing, so to speak, and became their producer, adding 'Anonymous' to their name – perhaps in a gesture indicating they shouldn't make themselves known to their Commanding Officers as *It's Good News Week* included lines such as:

> *It's good news week*
> *Someone's dropped a bomb somewhere*
> *Contaminating atmosphere*
> *And blackening the sky*

Not a particularly good career move if you were involved in the military in the 1960s. Interestingly, a young Jimmy Page played on the record as a session musician, only a year before he moved on to greater things with the Yardbirds.

The lyrics and the tune to *Good News Week* had always stuck in my head and they came readily flooding back, reminding me of the impact the song had made at the time. The topic of nuclear testing, and its relevance to Vegas, quite fascinated me and I was intrigued by the headline on a Vegas public safety booklet issued in 1957: 'Beware – irradiation can be inconvenient.' This classic understatement quite appealed to me somehow and I decided to investigate what was behind this.

It's out of the way, it took me an hour's walking to find (perhaps I shouldn't be so tight in avoiding taxi fares), but there it was – the Atomic Testing Museum on East Flamingo Road. Now if you think this is a sad way to spend a sunny afternoon in Las Vegas I can't argue with you. You wouldn't be alone either, as evidenced by the fact that there was only one other visitor. I studiously avoided eye contact with this individual on the basis that he had to be a complete weirdo, a feeling which I'm sure would have been reciprocated. Anyway, for ten dollars it wasn't a bad couple of hours and was probably summed up by my comment to the very nice lady on reception as I left. "Scary," I offered as I tried in vain to tear off the plastic wrist tag with which I'd been adorned on entry. "Yes," she volunteered as she came to my rescue with a pair of non-atomic, old tech, metal scissors.

The museum told me much more about the nuclear testing in the desert. In addition to the above-ground explosions mentioned earlier, 828 underground detonations have left the test area looking like a moonscape and still radioactive 50 years on. The most impressive, if that's the right word, of these subterranean tests was the explosion that left a crater, the Sedan Crater, a quarter mile in diameter and 320 feet deep, having displaced 6.6 million cubic yards of earth. This was a 104 Kiloton bomb, equivalent to 104,000 tons of TNT and five times the power of the atomic bomb dropped on Nagasaki in 1945, as if that wasn't big enough.

What amused me was the advice given to an unsuspecting public. In 1957 schools were given a green booklet entitled *Atomic Tests In Nevada*, liberally sprinkled with light-hearted illustrations. Remember this was six years into the test programme: 'You people who live near the Nevada Test Site are in a very real sense active participants in the Nation's atomic test program.' That's a reassuring start. 'Some of you have been inconvenienced by our test operations, but have accepted them without fuss or alarm. Your co-operation has helped us achieve an unusual record of safety' (I couldn't help wondering what constituted the usual safety record). 'Experience has proved the adequacy of the safeguards which govern Nevada test operations. Be aware that the devices fired before dawn have produced a flash visible 400-600 miles away and produced light 100 times more powerful than the sun.'

'Potential exposure is low', it went on to say, whilst explaining that it is best to turn away from the blast. It also goes on to mention how 'inconvenient' fall-out can be and how it can interfere with industrial equipment. It describes in a friendly, matter of fact way, that fallout is carried on the wind and can occur thousands of miles away (but only little bits). For troops on the test site this was fairly academic – they didn't have much choice in the matter as they were routinely asked to sit on the ground a mere six miles away and advised to turn their backs (there are some amazing photos of this in the museum).

I am unhappy, but not surprised, to now report some little known facts: in a report by the National Cancer Institute released in 1997 it was determined that 90 atmospheric tests deposited high levels of radioactive iodine-131 across a large portion of the 'contiguous United States' – doses large enough to produce 10,000 to 75,000 cases of thyroid cancer. As of February 2006, around 9,600 claims for compensation had been approved, for a total amount of over $480 million.

The test site offers monthly tours, but I'm relieved to say that there wasn't one available while I was there. As I left the museum and wandered out into the bright non-nuclear sunshine I shuddered as I recalled the words of J Robert Oppenheimer 'I am become Death, the destroyer of worlds.' I suppose that sums it up neatly.

IN THE EVENING I decided to go downtown to Fremont Street to watch the light show in the shopping arcade. If George Bush wants to sign up to saving the world he could perhaps switch this off for a couple of nights a week. If I tell you that the hourly show features 12.5 million LED lamps in the barrel-vaulted ceiling it will give you an idea of the profligacy. Very colourful, but I must mention to my youngest daughter the futility of constantly harassing me for wasting electricity by over-filling the kettle.

Back on the strip I entertained myself by touring the free attractions, in the grounds of the major hotels, which included exploding volcanoes, dancing fountains and fights between pirate ships. All very entertaining. With so much on offer, at no cost to myself, I was not tempted to see a show, particularly *Menopause The Musical*. What with this and *The Vagina Monologues* showing all over the world I thought perhaps it was time for we men to retaliate with something like *Prick's Prologues* or *Testicle Tales*. Unfortunately I later discovered I have been beaten to it by a show already running in the States and which has had a successful five month run in London's West End. *Puppetry of the Penis* as a title doesn't leave much to the imagination, neither apparently does the show which features two guys, Australian naturally, displaying their various 'penis installations'. They are now recruiting more 'artists' in order to franchise the show. Despite the advert stating that they are an equal opportunity employer (that is circumcised or uncircumcised considered) I have decided not to apply.

The other main feature of my walk along the strip was the constant acceptance (you don't have much choice when they are thrust into your hand) of glossy coloured cards with pictures of attractive looking girls on them. The going rate appeared to be $35 for one girl, $80 for two or $99 for three girls back to your room. Just to look, of course. Prostitution is illegal in Vegas strangely, although it is permitted in many counties in Nevada. Nevada is actually the only State in the US where prostitution is allowed, but for some perverse reason it is not legal in cities with a population of over 400,000, thus ruling out Vegas.

In case the pavement touts somehow miss you there is backup to help out in the form of trucks driving around town with huge 'A' boards advertising 'Girls to your room in 20 minutes'. An added refinement is the proliferation of automatic dispenser bins along the pavement with little booklets sporting titles such as *Alternative* and *LV Best Blondes*. In the interest of research I decided to pick up a couple of these (the books not the blondes) and saw that the girls had exotic names like Sumi, Tia and Alexis. I wasn't so sure about Sybil – I think it reminded me too much of *Fawlty Towers*. For female readers (presumably) there was Jake, Luke and Jason, all suitably muscular and tanned. It was when I saw the picture of an attractive female who advertised herself as 'Beautiful body with an 8 inch surprise' that I realised I'd read too much. That and the 'Attractive 70 plus – wanting to make you very happy.'

Back at Hooters I decided I would have my one and only flutter of the trip. With a track record like mine on the gambling front, that's one flutter too many. Anyway, I cashed in the princely sum of $20 and decided to adopt a positive attitude. I'd heard stories about people who had put their last quarter in the slot and ended up winning huge amounts. Even some of my friends back home, not renowned gamblers, have had considerable success making their money last till four in the morning in Vegas and even, in some cases, coming away hundreds of dollars better off. I acquired the chips at 10.45pm and went to bed at 10.55pm. Say no more. Still the girls at the table were very friendly and helpful (obviously not helpful enough) and seemed genuinely interested in helping me lose my money.

Resisting the temptation to glance again at the girlie literature, I instead went to bed with my *Collins USA Map for the Independent Traveller*. Onward travel beckoned and I had to work out a route to my major targets on the musical map of the USA such as Galveston, Memphis, Chattanooga and Nashville.

Next morning during breakfast I couldn't resist a little glance at the table next to me to confirm what I thought I had seen on a fellow guest's plate. Yes, I was right. It really was a chocolate muffin sitting in the middle of a plate of bacon and eggs. Mouth-watering.

As my chosen bus wasn't due to depart Vegas until 1.30 pm I had the luxury of a free morning. I decided to be a nuisance and introduce myself to the management of the casino thinking that I might berate them for making me destitute within the space of ten minutes the previous night. Well, perhaps not, but they might give me an insight into their operations. I felt safe in the knowledge that since Howard Hughes came and bought up half of the properties in Vegas from his hotel room, where he incarcerated himself for four years, that the mob no longer controlled the casinos. Hughes never once left his room, but spent an average of $178,000 per day buying up the casinos and hotels. Although it made him generally popular the sentiment wasn't shared by the Justice Department, who eventually stopped his expansion through a monopolies lawsuit.

Safe in the knowledge that I was unlikely to meet a direct descendant of early Vegas luminary, renowned gangster Bugsy Siegel, I waited with only a small degree of apprehension for the management to appear. To my surprise I ended up in the company of three directors of the casino who were extremely helpful. One of them, David Demontmollin, Executive Director of Marketing, took great delight in telling me has had a book published – *The Las Vegas Little Black Book: A Guy's Guide to the Perfect Vegas Getaway*. A little late for me to be meeting someone who knows all the places to go as I would be on my way to a different world in a couple of hours.

I was enthusiastically informed that Hooters is a chain of 450 restaurants and that this is their first venture into the hotel/casino business. I was further enlightened that the whole Hooters ethos is fun, the idea being that they want their clients to have a good time whilst losing their money. In addition to 650 slot machines, available for gambling 24 hours a day, there are 30 table games at which people can entertain themselves. Apparently, Hooters operate 'loose' slot machines – in other words they pay better odds than the casinos on the strip. Punters then get a better run for their money. I particularly liked the customer-friendly sign above the exit door, 'If you're leaving here with any money left you haven't tried hard enough'!

When I asked if they get anyone famous staying, bearing in mind that they've only been open for a year, I was advised that Jean Simmons is a cus-tomer. I thought this a rather unusual environment for an 80 year-old female film icon. It was only later it clicked with me that he was probably referring to Gene Simmons the singer from KISS, the rock group whose performances include fire-breathing, blood spitting and pyrotechnics and who have been known to have occasional substance abuse issues. Not to mention the make-up, womanising and Simmons setting his hair on fire many times. Yes, definitely a more likely Hooters fan.

All told, I was impressed by the ethics of the company, particularly when they offered to take me round the floor and introduce me to some of the girls. On one of the tables I was introduced to Matt, training manager for all the 200 or so staff.

"What a job for a handsome young guy," I said. "Have you any funny stories to tell me?"

"What could be funnier than a gay training manager training hundreds of gorgeous calendar girls?" he offered with a wry smile. Really, I do need to be more observant.

There are apparently 15,000 Hooters girls around the world, so this is pretty big business. When I asked about the prizes on offer I was surprised to learn that it is possible to win $10 million, this through a state-wide link every three months. More realistically the in-house top prize was $25,000, which I have to say I wouldn't turn my nose up at. The team were proud of the fact a "$1 machine holds 3 cents", which effectively means they pay out 97% of the takings. Sounds pretty fair to me. I obviously should have played the slots with my $20, instead of the tables.

Going back to my naivety about the Hooters name, the chain has been at times beset by problems, facing challenges about their alleged sexism. The defence that the Hooters emblem features an owl so that's where the name comes from I take with a pinch of salt. They also ran into problems a few years back with the Equal Employment Opportunities Commission who brought forward a charge claiming that the Hooters' hiring practice discriminates against men. I ask you, who would want to see men running round with trays of drinks, dressed in orange hot-pants, tights and skimpy T-shirt? Apart from the training manager, I suppose. After a four-year battle, which included a march on Washington by hundreds of Hooters girls, and support from 500,000 Hooters customers, the action was not exactly dropped, but instead put into a sort of hibernation where it has remained for the last five years. I think someone sensibly decided this was not a vote winner.

Whether you agree to the concept or not, there is plenty of evidence to show that Hooters is a good employer and a fun place to work. They also contribute a lot to the community, so I am comfortable that at least part of my $20 is going to a good cause. The final word on this issue has to be the response to my question, "Do you ever have problems with 'big girls' seeking employment?"

"Those orange hot pants are tight and unforgiving," was the concise and eloquent reply.

On the way back to my room to pick up my bags I talked to a couple of the customers and they both seemed to be enjoying themselves during their mid-morning gambling spree. Bill, a driver from Chicago, was enjoying a complimentary one night stay (which I suppose you could say was almost the case for me considering how little I paid). He wasn't the 'stay at the table for three days' type, his limit being $100, and he freely admitted that, like me, he doesn't win very often. Still, he looked happy enough and so would I be, given the choice between sitting in a casino or in the cab of a 40 ton juggernaut thundering its way down the Interstate.

The other punter I spoke to was Sheila from New York who had been brought here for her 40th birthday by her sister. Whilst she was struggling to keep her end up, if you pardon the expression, she told me her sister had actually had a $1,200 'hit' on the slots that morning. Just shows how generosity pays in the end. I hope they had discussed beforehand whether they were sharing or sisterly love could yet be severely tested.

I JUMPED INTO A CAB and discovered that, like the evening before when I was taken downtown, the taxi driver was from Ethiopia. I'd had a bizarre conversation with the driver the previous night, so I thought I might have better luck this time. This guy was clearly a sports fan and a keen Liverpool supporter for some reason. So I decided to be friendly and talk to him about the only Ethiopian sports person I know. Like the previous night the conversation fairly quickly turned strange and we started talking politics, which I don't enjoy discussing so much – particularly with taxi drivers. My chauffeur began to express his goodwill towards England for supporting the Emperor in his struggle against the Italians back in the '30s. I soon realised where I had gone wrong, but it was too late to claw my way back – what I had meant to say was not Haille Selassie, the former Emperor, but Haile Gebreselassie, the world Marathon record holder! Very close you have to admit.

While sitting waiting for the Greyhound bus I wondered if I had done justice to Elvis during my stay. After all I hadn't done the 'Elvis Tour' or been to the Elvis Museum. But I was fairly relaxed about it as knew I would be saying hello to him again in Memphis and would be hopefully fitting in a visit to Graceland. And, as you say Elvis – 'How I wish that there was more than 24 hours in the day'.

Viva Las Vegas

Bright light city gonna set my soul
Gonna set my soul on fire
Got a whole lot of money that's ready to burn,
So get those stakes up higher
There's a thousand pretty women waitin' out there
And they're all livin' devil may care
And I'm just the devil with love to spare
Viva Las Vegas, Viva Las Vegas

How I wish that there was more
Than the twenty-four hours in the day
'Cause even if there were forty more
I wouldn't sleep a minute away
Oh, there's black jack and poker and the roulette wheel
A fortune won and lost on ev'ry deal
All you need's a strong heart and a nerve of steel
Viva Las Vegas, Viva Las Vegas

Viva Las Vegas with your neon flashin
And your one armbandits crashin'
All those hopes down the drain
Viva Las Vegas turnin' day into nighttime
Turnin' night into daytime
If you see it once
You'll never be the same again

I'm gonna keep on the run
I'm gonna have me some fun
If it costs me my very last dime
If I wind up broke up well
I'll always remember that I had a swingin' time

I'm gonna give it ev'rything I've got
Lady luck please let the dice stay hot
Let me shout a seven with ev'ry shot
Viva Las Vegas, Viva Las Vegas
Viva, Viva Las Vegas

Words and music by Doc Pomus and Mort Shuman

Chapter Two

"It's a girl, my Lord, in a flatbed Ford . . ."

THE ORIGINAL PLOT HAD been to head for Phoenix. It just seemed too straight-forward somehow. I had noticed on my map that I wasn't too far away from a town called Kingman which is mentioned in the classic song *Route 66* ('Get your kicks on Route 66').

So, it was on board the 1.30pm Oklahoma bus, which would take me to Kingman, a mere 123 miles away, that I took my foul-smelling, and even worse-tasting, sandwich. This was my first experience of the catering facilities at Greyhound bus stations. The idea, at this station anyway, is that you buy a sandwich, put it in a communal microwave over in the corner, press a button and wait two minutes. It may have been due to my culinary skills, or lack of them, but the result was a soggy combination of bread and meat (don't ask me which sort, I haven't a clue – by the time I had finished it tasted as if it could well have been greyhound).

The ticketing system meant that although I had purchased a ticket the night before, it didn't guarantee a seat. The first come, first served policy means it is always advisable to get there an hour beforehand and join the queue, obtaining provisions at the same time. The bus was only half-full and I managed to get a double seat to myself, so it wasn't too uncomfortable, though I was surprised at how basic the facilities were – perhaps I had been expecting too much given the iconic stature of the Greyhound name. It did have air-conditioning and one toilet, but the niceties of UK coaches such as coffee-making facilities were conspicuous by their absence and I was reminded of the bus on which Dustin Hoffman and Jon Voight had travelled to Miami in *Midnight Cowboy* 30 years earlier.

We meandered for two hours across mountainous roads surrounded by dry and dusty desert scenery. It was with some surprise that, after about an hour, in the middle of nowhere, I observed the sign for Don Laughlin's Golf Resort. I didn't expect to see a golf course in the middle of the Mojave Desert, but suddenly there were signs for Don Laughlin's this and Don Laughlin's that. Then we arrived at a town called, yes, you've guessed it – Laughlin.

As a young man in the 1950s, Don Laughlin was apparently 'invited' to leave his college because of illegal gambling activities. After chancing his luck, literally, in the world of gambling, he built the town now carrying his name as a gambling resort. Laughlin is the last settlement in Nevada before crossing the Colorado river into Arizona and, as a refuge from the hurly-burly of places like Vegas, has grown from its original 95 inhabitants to over 9,000. Crossing the bridge over the river you enter the town of Bullhead City, a town which in turn owes its existence to the gambling empire built by Laughlin.

If you are looking for peace and tranquility make sure you do not come here when the big event of the year takes place – the Laughlin River Run. This annual event constitutes a motor cycle rally with over 50,000 devotees and, judging by the photos I saw of some of the participants, it looks a bit dodgy. In fact, a few years ago three people were killed in a huge brawl between Hells Angels and a rival gang called the Mongols. This was, in fact, just a bit more than a brawl – it was described in the press reports as a 'gunfight', but it also involved knives, wrenches and hammers. At the resultant trial the Assistant US Attorney mentioned that one victim effectively 'had his skull crushed with a wrench.' Amazingly, after a four year trial and much plea bargaining, only two people got jail sentences and even then comparatively short ones. I got the feeling that if it hadn't been for press interest it may have gone virtually unnoticed and been written off as high jinks in the country. I was glad I wasn't stopping and it did make me wonder what might be going on in other out of the way places, quite possibly some that I would be visiting.

IT WAS AROUND 4.30PM when the bus arrived at Kingman. The sun was shining and I thought I might enjoy a nice half-hour sitting in the sun as soon as I had sorted out a hotel. I had been taken by surprise at the sudden arrival at Kingman as I thought I had another hour on the bus. Racking my brain to work out how this was the case I eventually discovered that I had crossed a time zone, something which in the UK we tend not to have to worry about. So, if you are one of the many who get up at the wrong time when the clocks change and turn up late (or early) for your Sunday morning golf, or whatever, consider this. The United States has nine Standard Time Zones – Atlantic Standard Time, Eastern Standard Time, Central Standard Time, Mountain Standard Time, Pacific Standard Time, Alaskan Standard Time, Hawaii-Aleutian Standard Time, Samoa Standard Time and Chamorro Standard Time. In case you are wondering where Chamorro is – forget it, there's no such place. Chamorro refers to the native language of the Northern Mariana Islands and Guam, in the Western Pacific. As if this wasn't enough, there is the complication of Daylight Saving Time (the equivalent of British Summer Time) and, at certain times of the year, Atlantic Standard Time becomes Atlantic Daylight Time. However, just to make sure we are on our toes, not all states observe Daylight Saving Time (Arizona being one of the exceptions). That's cleared that up, then.

The bus had drawn up outside the Kingman Greyhound building, a bleak-looking affair just off the highway, alongside a railway track. I thought about taking some pictures for posterity, but when I looked at the characters hanging around the outside of the building I decided against letting them know I had a camera. The bus was scheduled for a twenty minute stop here, which is just as well because I made a very quick decision that there was no way I was going to spend the night in this place. I may be doing the town a disservice, but my initial scan around the locality indicated little more than a truck stop with one main road and some fast food restaurants such as the ubiquitous Denny's. Why would you want to include a place like this in a song I asked myself, but to be fair it is a sad fact that many of the Route 66 towns have become somewhat derelict since the route was replaced by the Interstate system.

I dived straight into the Greyhound office and asked where the bus was headed next and ended up purchasing a ticket to Flagstaff, which was apparently another couple of hours away. To be honest, the only reason I had fancied Kingman was the fact that it had a Route 66 museum. I decided, however, that there were limits to my dedication, and bravery. Besides, I was also aware that Flagstaff, like, Kingman, is mentioned in *Route 66*, so I'd still be keeping the faith.

By the time we got to Flagstaff it was dark and I hadn't noticed that we must have been climbing steadily. What is impossible to tell from your everyday road map, is that Flagstaff is at an altitude of 8,000, almost twice the height of the UK's highest peak Ben Nevis. So the air was a bit fresh, it was nine o'clock at night and I hadn't a clue where I was, really. It was my first day travelling and the plans had gone to pot already.

I had rapidly come to the conclusion that the Greyhound stations are often not too close to the town centre, a conclusion which would be reinforced by subsequent experience. Although there were one or two motels nearby, they didn't look very welcoming and, despite being somewhat weary, I didn't want to be stuck in a motel with nothing to do, nowhere to go, and nothing to eat but Whopper-Burger and fries, so I decided to trek the mile or so into town.

After about twenty minutes I came across Flagstaff railway station which was a good sign as railway stations are generally a better indication of where the town centre lies than the Greyhound depots. At that very moment I nearly jumped out of my skin as a freight train bellowed out its warning on approaching the public crossing I was standing alongside. This was my first encounter with BNSF (the old Santa Fe Railway – now Burlington Northern Santa Fe), the freight train service which would become a feature of my travels, keeping me company at all hours with its thundering rolling stock.

I wandered through the deserted streets of Flagstaff, searching for accommodation. The first people I came across were two girls (I use the term loosely), having a laugh about something in the middle of the street. It could have been the sight of me approaching, when I think about it. I asked them if they could suggest a decent hotel and they obliged by pointing to one of the larger buildings in the next block – the Monte Vista Hotel. "It's haunted though. Even John Wayne saw a ghost there," they kindly volunteered. 'If it was good enough for John Wayne it's good enough for me,' I thought. I didn't give a hoot about ghosts as it was getting on for 10 pm and I needed somewhere to stay.

Fortunately, there were rooms available at the Monte Vista and I secured one for $85 which wasn't bad for the 'best hotel in town'. My room, though, turned out to be unlike the pictures of the rooms displayed on the noticeboard in reception, which also proudly chronicled the stars who'd stayed at the hotel over the years whilst filming in the region, a favourite for movie locations it seems. But what did I care? It was refuge. I needed refreshment and decided in next to no time that alcohol would be the best bet. Dropping my bag, I headed straight for the bar. The hotel obviously had its priorities sorted, it had a bar but no restaurant – the same decision I would make if I had to choose.

In the atmospheric old bar, old by American standards that is, the landlady asked me what I wanted to drink and in response to my question about what they had on offer she surprised me by mentioning Newcastle Brown Ale, among other things. I knew my local brew travelled well, but I didn't expect to find it in John Wayne mountain country. She was amazed when I told her that I came from Newcastle and she immediately pointed me in the direction of two young Indian girls whose attention she had attracted.

"He's from Newcastle," she shouted as she disappeared into the cellar to fetch my beer. I felt obliged to wander across and talk to the girls to see what the fuss was about. It turned out they had both just turned 21 and this was their first ever drinking session and for some reason they had started their drinking careers on Newcastle Brown. I thought It a little bizarre to be 8,000 feet up in Indian country, watching two locals, probably from one of the nearby reservations, cutting their teeth on Newcastle Brown. I didn't want to spoil their night, so decided to move on after warning them about what my dad said to me when he discovered I'd been drinking the same brew when I was sixteen – "Be careful, it'll put hairs on your chest," he'd told me, rightly as it turned out. I hope the girls appreciated the advice.

I had a little walk around town, little being the only walk available unless you wanted to do a couple of laps. From what little I could see of Flagstaff it seemed to be about the size of a typical rural English market town, and just as pleasant. Unfortunately it seemed that most of the restaurants had closed at 10pm. The only potential life-saver for me in terms of food seemed to be an establishment called Pita Pit which looked like a kebab house. This might have been half-decent news if it hadn't been for the vagrant sitting in the doorway who immediately wanted to be my friend (I didn't take this as too much of a compliment as he wasn't spoilt for choice). I couldn't see any way of eating without undesirable company so went to bed hungry.

I woke up the next morning feeling somewhat confused. The previous day I had been in the desert and now I was 8,000 feet up in the mountains. As the hotel didn't have a restaurant I decided to check out and go in search of some bacon and eggs, but, before I left, I decided to ask the young man on reception about the ghost stories. He kindly gave me some literature to read and I sat down in the very grand art deco reception area to have a look at the stuff while he sorted out the bill.

I learned that the 'historic Hotel Monte Vista' is officially listed on the US Register of Historic Places and that during the '40s and '50s over a hundred movies were filmed in and around the area. As lodgings were in short supply, the hotel became the favoured haunt for the stars and there was an impressive list of previous guests, including Bob Hope, Bing Crosby, Jane Russell, Carol Lombard, John Wayne, Alan Ladd, Clark Gable, Spencer Tracy, Humphrey Bogart, and, more recently, Michael J Fox and Anthony Hopkins. From the world of music, past guests have included Jon Bon Jovi, Freddy Mercury and Michael Stipe. Other dignitaries included Wild West author Zane Grey and whiskey magnate Jack Daniel. Not bad credentials for an $85 per night pad.

What I was most interested in, though, were the ghost stories. Fortunately I had been too tired the previous night to bother with them, but it seems the hotel has been featured on many television programmes and is the subject of numerous books. Apparently, different ghosts carry out varying activities in or outside different rooms, John Wayne's encounter being with a figure of a bell boy outside room 210 after a knock on the door and a muffled sound of "room service". The Duke reported that the figure seemed friendly enough and that he didn't feel threatened by it. Well he wouldn't would he?

My favourite story related to an incident in the 1970s when a trio of bank robbers held up a nearby bank and a guard shot one of the men. They then stupidly decided to stop off at the hotel for a drink and the wounded man died in the process of celebrating the successful raid. Since then, both guests and staff have reported an anonymous voice saying "good morning" and there have been reports of bar stools and drinks that move on their own. Another of my favourites is the one involving two prostitutes who were brought back to the hotel by a guest in the 1940s and ended up being thrown from their third floor window (room 306) onto the street. Many guests in room 306 have reported the feeling of a hand placed over their mouth and throat in the middle of the night and waking up unable to breathe.

I paid the bill and asked the young chap how long he had been working there and whether he had personally heard any stories direct from guests. He replied that he'd been there eight months and in that time he had been advised by quite a few people of strange happenings and that some had been aware of the ghoulish history of the hotel, while many had not. The cases I mention are just a small sample of the documented events, so it does make you think.

Pleased that I hadn't been fully briefed about the ghosts the previous evening, I left the hotel with a shiver running down my back. I passed the Pita Pit, which was now devoid of vagrancy and I found a nice little café which looked extremely welcoming. And it was. Bacon wasn't on the menu, but that didn't matter, they did have coffee and eggs. The dilemma was choice. I know the States is an English-speaking country, but try ordering eggs in a restaurant and you are faced with 'sunny side up', 'over easy', (or is it 'easy over'), 'over hard', 'basted', 'scrambled' and more. What I really wanted was poached, but there was no way I was going to start that discussion.

Having decided on scrambled, I then had to cope with the coffee, which even in England I struggle with. In addition to the better known brews, I had to contend with doppio, lungo, macchiato and ristretto to name but a few. Black coffee with cold milk was the simple answer. But I did get adventurous with the meal – I opted for corn beef fritters to go with my eggs. And very nice they were too, doubly welcome as they would avoid me having to buy less appetising fare at the bus station.

While I was eating I flicked through an old issue of a free local magazine which sported the headline 'Gerald Ford finally dead', which I thought was a trifle harsh, and then a magazine called the *Echo Mag*. That is until I came across the advert offering a '150lb full-bodied Hispanic' and something called the 'Hard Choice Awards', which I think probably speaks for itself. I tried to put the mag down in a non-ostentatious way in a place where no-one could see what I'd been reading. It's not that I'm narrow-minded, but I wouldn't want anyone in a remote, strange place getting the wrong idea.

I spent the rest of the morning browsing around Flagstaff popping into one shop and then another trying to keep myself occupied. I wandered into a mini shopping arcade and spent some time looking at the authentic Indian goods and admiring the cultural offerings. The effect was spoilt somewhat when I came across a big display basket which had a sign saying 'Cheap plastic shit'. It was good fun looking at the cheap shit, though, and I could have had a Ninja Launcher, powered by rubber bands, for $1, or a bike horn in the shape of Elvis's head, complete with sideburns and shades, for $3. Was this a sign of the musical memorabilia I would find in these places I had come to seek out?

I was amused, after the licentiousness of Vegas, to see that the nude mannequins in the shop window were censored, with little bits of material protecting their private parts. I was even more amused to see, in the middle of the precinct, a sign saying:

> No loitering, dogs left
> unattended will be cited
> and towed at owners' expense.

I wondered if perhaps I should hang around for a few days in the hope of seeing a Rottweiler appear in the dock? As for being towed, that would be an interesting sight, with quite a bit of howling I would imagine.

Fairly quickly running out of things to do, I wandered across to the railway station, a fine old building with large pitched roof and two attractive symmetrical gable ends. A sign at the front of the building announced its address as '1 East Route 66', a slightly more evocative salutation than the dreaded ZIP code I think you'll agree. There is little in the way of passenger services these days and the building now doubles as a visitor centre, so I picked up a few brochures and went out on the platform to read a bronze plaque I had noticed. It explained that the Transcontinental Railway was formed in 1866 to construct a railroad between Springfield, Missouri and the Pacific coast, a distance of 2,000 miles, and that in 1882 the railroad effectively gave birth to the city of Flagstaff. Just as I was digesting this information I was jolted once more by my friends from BNSF who I am sure were looking out for me. Flagstaff has a problem in that it has two level crossings, one either side of the station. It seems there is a morse-code type horn blasting system in operation on the railway, the signal for crossings being three long blasts, one short, then one long. Unfortunately for the residents of Flagstaff, where crossings are in close proximity, the driver is allowed to keep his hand on his horn continuously as he passes through, something I'm sure he enjoys very much.

I came across some public relations blurb which extolled the virtues of BNSF, I would like to share this with you:

'The people who built the BNSF railway are a unique breed, blending the forward thinking of dreamers with the pragmatism of results-oriented business leaders'.

My Father in Law, if he'd still been alive, would have had one word for this – "Shite". I couldn't put it better myself. I waited while the train passed, which was quite a wait. I counted 104 wagons, mostly double-decker shipping containers, pulled by no less than five locomotives. I was suitably impressed.

Ten minutes later, when the train had gone and my body had stopped rumbling in sympathy, it was time to walk to the Greyhound station, crossing a still operational bit of Route 66 in the process.

This was one of the remaining sections of the historic route which was certified in 1926 and became probably the most famous road in the world, stretching 2,400 miles from Chicago in the North, down through Illinois, Missouri, Kansas, Oklahoma, Texas, New Mexico, Arizona and then California, ending up in Los Angeles. It became known as 'The Mother Road', 'Main Street USA' and officially the 'Will Rogers Highway', after the famous Vaudeville performer.

By the time the road was usurped by various Interstate Highways and de-classified in 1985 it had been embossed on the memory of everyone in the States, having been a major factor in the migration of masses to the West, as immortalised in John Steinbeck's classic novel *The Grapes of Wrath*, and was a key factor in the movement of troops and supplies in World War II. The famous song *Route 66* ('Get your kicks on Route 66') was written, with help from his wife, in 1946 by Bobby Troup, a war veteran stationed in California, who used the road to move there after the war, and was made into a hit by Nat King Cole. This song, more than anything else, created the atmosphere and legend of the route of adventure across the States and it has been recorded over the years by around a hundred artists. Whilst it hadn't been on my original plans, the detour to Flagstaff had injected an added dimension to my trip and I was excited to be pottering about a town on the famous route.

At the bus station I bought a ticket to Winslow, Arizona, which I had decided would be my next stop. It wasn't exactly en route to Phoenix – to be honest it was in quite the opposite direction, but being something of an Eagles fan I just had to make the effort. It was also another Route 66 town which was a bonus.

This would be my second trip on the Greyhound – I couldn't wait. When the bus arrived I took my turn in the queue to get on board, but unfortunately the woman in front had two small children with her and she was the only adult. She also had enough luggage with her to suggest she was moving house, and that was only what she was taking on board, never mind what she had stored in the hold. I made the mistake of helping her get the kids up the stairs and for my efforts I got lumbered, for the 20 minutes or so it took the lady to get sorted out, with the most snotty-nosed kid you can wish to imagine. I've seen plenty of candle displays in my time but this was exceptional – worthy of the *Guinness Book of Records.* It did take my mind, to a small degree, off the aroma on the bus, a rare bouquet of stale sweat and other bodily odours.

The good news was that it was only an hour and a bit to Winslow and I might get a glimpse of the Meteor Crater, formed when a huge meteorite hit the earth 50,000 years ago, creating a hole one mile across and 550 feet deep (the impact was 150 times that of Hiroshima/Nagasaki). As it turned out, I didn't get to see the crater and the scenery was pretty sparse and dusty, explaining how Arizona got its name – from the Spanish for 'Arid Zone', which in this area, at least, is fairly appropriate.

ON ARRIVAL AT WINSLOW I got off the bus and was immediately struck by the heat. It was only an hour from Flagstaff, but I was now effectively in the desert rather than in the mountains. I seemed to have been abandoned in the middle of nowhere – there was no bus station, not even a bus stop sign, just barren waste ground and a nearby Holiday Inn Express. On asking the bus driver where on earth the town was he slyly grinned and pointed to the Highway underpass muttering 'Follow the signs, it's about a mile.' But I had a good idea by now what a mile is to an American giving directions. Even following the sign wasn't easy as it didn't seem to be pointing in any specific direction. Trudging along the road with wilderness on all sides, I began to sweat profusely – it was 3pm, the temperature was somewhere in the 80s, and my rucksack was weighing heavily and digging into my shoulders.

Approaching a road junction I could see that there was an unusual structure set in the side of the road at the corner. It turned out that this marked the approach to Winslow and was a remembrance garden to 9/11. The monument was actually formed from two girders each approximately 15 feet high, salvaged from the Twin Towers and given to the people of Winslow by the city of New York. The memorial sign erected on a stone plinth carried the words 'United We Stand', which I later found out was the caption given to a famous picture of Abraham Lincoln, standing on a Confederate flag and congratulating a Union soldier during the Civil War in 1864. The Stars and Stripes flag which presides over the garden was donated by the Pentagon and the associated inscription on the brickwork reminds the world of Northern Arizona's promise 'We Will Never Forget'. I stood for a few moments in thoughtful mood and paid my respects.

Across the road, at last, stood a 'Welcome to Winslow' sign and a large map showing where the town lay on Route 66. The map even made reference to 'Standin' on a Corner Park'. Brilliant stuff – I really felt my journey was beginning to take off. On top of that at least I now knew where I was,

An hour later I was still looking for the corner. I think part of the problem was my interpretation of the word 'park'. That's what I was looking for – a park, the type with trees and paths and playgrounds and perhaps even a boating lake. What I wasn't looking for was a paved area of about twenty yards by five. To be fair it did have a couple of park benches, but that was about it. Anyway I found it. Apart from a few seats, the 'park' consists of a two-storey mural depicting the reflection of a girl driving a truck ('it's a girl, my Lord, in a flat bed Ford') plus a life-size bronze statue of a guy with guitar leaning against a lamp post.

The purpose of my visit was to pay homage to one of the iconic songs of the '70s and here I was doing just that and feeling very satisfied too. But what was behind *Take It Easy* apart from a girl in a truck? I have had some difficulty getting to the bottom of the origins of this. It is acknowledged that Jackson Browne, the renowned singer/songwriter, wrote the song, or at least most of it, and that it was completed by his friend and neighbour Glenn Frey of the Eagles, who then sang lead vocals on what became the band's first hit. It would seem by all accounts that Browne was quite generous in suggesting co-ownership of the credit for the song as he wrote 90% of it before it was finished by Frey, who added the line about 'standing on a corner'. If this is true it dismisses the theory that Jackson Browne wrote that line because his car broke down in Winslow which left him 'standing on a corner'.

However, another version of events suggests that Frey's contribution was that classic line 'it's a girl, my Lord, in a flatbed Ford' (incidentally, I understand that a girl in a truck in America is now regarded as highly erotic). I have it on good authority, from someone I later met in Tucson, that an alternative story about Browne being arrested for vagrancy in Winslow and writing the lyrics while in the cells is completely false and that the truth is that he was in the area because he's a friend of the Hopi Indians, whose reservation stands to the north of Winslow and Flagstaff. The same source advised me that originally it was going to be 'standing on a corner in Flagstaff, Arizona', but it didn't have quite the same ring to it!

My interpretation of all of this is that Frey added the best part of the second verse and generally lightened up the mood of the song, bringing more of a country feel to it. Whatever the truth, it's a classic tune and, apart from being their first hit single, *Take It Easy* featured on the *Eagles Greatest Hits*, which became one of the best-selling albums in history. Incidentally, rumour has it that the statue on the corner looks more like Jackson Browne than any of the Eagles. Bearing in mind what an impact the song had on the band's career this would not seem an unreasonable recognition of his input into what is a quite seminal song.

I couldn't leave the corner without a photograph, so I dragged a woman out of a souvenir shop across the road to take my picture. She wasn't able to offer any further information about the lyrics, but suggested that, as a visitor to town, I might like to visit the Old Trails Museum about 50 yards away. I immediately set off and when I got there looked at the sign in the window – 'closed at 4pm'. I looked at my watch – 4pm exactly. A kind lady inside must have seen me peering through the window and obviously felt sorry for me, so opened the door and said I could come in and have a look around for a few minutes while she closed up. I don't want to sound ungrateful, but a few minutes was all I needed. I can't say I can get too excited about old sewing machines or collections of old bottles. Still I did appreciate her gesture.

Across the street from 'the corner' was the Tourist Information Centre, which I felt was rather optimistically named as there didn't seem to be a surfeit of tourists. In fact, I was the only one – perhaps I should feel flattered that they had a centre just for me. To describe how inundated with customers the centre was let's just say I had to ring a bell to get some attention and then the excited assistant got me to sign in the visitors' book. To be fair, I do understand that visitors come from all over the world to visit the corner and, like me, drag the lady out of the shop to get their photo taken. I suppose it's sad really, but it keeps people like me happy.

The lady in the visitor centre also couldn't throw any light on my quest for knowledge about the song. Now, if I was the tourist chief, I would give all the staff special training on what to tell the visitors; even if it was rubbish I'm sure it would be well received. What she did say was that I should stay over in Winslow as there was an excellent hotel, the La Posada. I wondered about this and decided to take the advice not too seriously as I had seen a couple of examples of 'hotels' on the walk into town. Both places looked like ramshackle chalets and one in particular looked as if its owner had built the advertising sign himself, probably after a liberal sample of moonshine. It really did look like something out of a Hitchcock movie and I would rather have slept in room 306 at the Monte Vista and taken my chances with the ghost with the suffocating hand.

Weighing up my options, I calculated that the next bus out of town wasn't till 10.30pm and if I got that I'd arrive in Phoenix at 3.30am, so I wasn't spoilt for choice. I therefore set off for the edge of town looking for the La Posada, which, I had been reliably informed, is a great old railway hotel built in the 1930s as part of the Santa Fe to Los Angeles railroad. After about a mile I spotted what looked like a grand hacienda with stucco walls, soft orange rooftiles and subtly-arched windows on the upper floor. It looked more like a superstar's residence than a hotel and I wondered if I had got the right place. But this was indeed the La Posada Hotel and, yes, they did have rooms available and, even better, not too expensive. I forked out the $100 for the room and went outside to have a look around the grounds, which were quite extensive although, would you believe it, situated alongside the main BNSF railway line. In fact, had I read the literature I had obtained from the visitor centre, I would have seen that one of the attractions of Winslow was 'As one of the major hubs of the BNSF railroad, train enthusiasts can watch the engines roar into town from the patio of the newly restored La Posada Hotel.' Just what I wanted.

The railway track was pretty impressive, if you like that sort of thing — it had about six sets of tracks and it was not hard to imagine the trains stopping right outside and the passengers enjoying tea on the lawns, which is actually what used to happen. The hotel was apparently once the showpiece of the whole Santa Fe passenger system and had been 'An oasis of trees, gardens and fountains welcoming rail travellers, with bar service on the sunken patio.' During World War II an incredible 3,000 meals a day were served, with troop trains picnicking around the clock on the south lawn on their way to war. The fact that

Route 66 ran outside the other side of the building wouldn't have harmed trade either.

The Santa Fe network and, indeed the whole concept of rail travel in the States, was revolutionised in the 1930s by a businessman called Fred Harvey who transformed the system from a utilitarian service to one of luxury travel with 'fine linen and china and fresh meats and vegetables'. The women who worked for him were called 'Harvey Girls' and the whole thing became so famous that Judy Garland starred in a movie musical of that name. La Posada was designed by the famous American architect, Mary Colter. She designed the building as if it was the house of a Spanish Don and filled it full of Spanish, Russian and Chinese antiques.

Unfortunately, La Posada fell into disrepair in 1957 when passenger rail traffic receded and it was converted into the Santa Fe Regional Headquarters. Whilst this was somewhat sacrilegious, and many of the fine features were ripped out, it also probably saved the hotel from the same fate as the other Santa Fe railway hotels, which were consigned to oblivion. The hotel has since been bought and restored by the Affeldt family, as a labour of love, and is highly impressive, featuring wonderful architectural features and an extensive and varied art collection. Well worth a visit.

Like the Monte Vista in Flagstaff, the hotel has hosted many famous personalities – Howard Hughes was a regular when he owned TWA airlines, who had an airport at that time in Winslow. Charles Lindbergh and his wife also stayed there, as well as a host of famous names including Shirley Temple, James Cagney, that man John Wayne again, presidents Roosevelt and Truman, as well as Albert Einstein, just to add a bit of scientific interest to the list. I was beginning to feel quite important in such illustrious surroundings and I was pleased to note that, also like the Monte Vista, La Posada has been designated as a National Historic Landmark. I seemed to have developed quite a knack for picking up lofty accommodation. I wondered how long it could last.

I saw an advertisement for a country folk dance, downtown, in the evening and I thought I might be tempted to join the proceedings just for the experience. However, a combination of fatigue and the prospect of unusual luxury meant that I succumbed to an early shower and a visit to the Turquoise Room restaurant ('An oasis in the High Desert'). I had a very enjoyable and reasonably-priced meal in unique surroundings featuring wood panelling and chandeliers in the style of the 'grand dining salons of the '30s'. This room was a favourite of the big studio chiefs of the '30s and '40s and over a couple of glasses of beer, not to mention the odd glass of wine, I let my imagination roam free, ruminating about what it must have been like seventy years earlier.

By half past nine I was done for and I retired to my room – the John Huston room. I was very impressed, particularly for $100, and I thought that before I crashed out I really ought to read some of the literature splashed around the room about the man it was named after. I have to say that, whilst I didn't really know too much about him before, I now have a sneaking admiration for the legendary film director whose credits include *The Maltese Falcon*, *The African Queen* and *Annie*, although I'm not sure he was a particularly nice person. In fact it seems he was a cantankerous old devil with a wicked sense of humour. What appealed to me most and which put him in my book of heroes was the story about him flying over a championship golf match and dropping 5,000 ping-pong balls. That's what I call class. When his autobiography came out it failed to match up to his extravagant lifestyle, to the extent that one of his associates quipped "Good book John, who is it about?"

Huston had the last laugh – Clark Gable warned him about his drinking and smoking habits and told him he'd be dead soon if he didn't mend his ways. Gable died three weeks later and Huston went on for another 27 years before dying at the age of 82.

Route 66

Well if you ever plan to motor west
Just take my way that's the highway that's the best
Get your kicks on Route 66

Well it winds from Chicago to L.A.
More than 2000 miles on the way
Get your kicks on Route 66

Well goes from St Louie down to Missouri
You'll see Amarillo and Gallup, New Mexico
Flagstaff, Arizona don't forget Winona
Kingman, Barstow, San Bernardino

Would you get hip to this kindly tip
And go take that California trip
Get your kicks on Route 66

Well goes from St Louie down to Missouri
Oklahoma City looks oh so pretty
You'll see Amarillo and Gallup, New Mexico
Flagstaff, Arizona don't forget Winona
Kingman, Barstow, San Bernardino

Would you get hip to this kindly tip
And go take that California trip
Get your kicks on Route 66

Words and music by Bobby and Cynthia Troup

Take It Easy

Well I'm a running down the road
trying to loosen my load
I've got seven women on my mind
Four that want to own me, two that want to stone me
One says she's a friend of mine

Take it easy, take it easy
Don't let the sound of your own wheels drive you crazy
Lighten up while you still can
Don't even try to understand
Just find a place to make your stand and take it easy

Well, I'm a standing on a corner in Winslow, Arizona
And such a fine sight to see
It's a girl my Lord, in a flatbed Ford
Slowin' down to take a look at me

Come on baby, don't say maybe
I've got to know if your sweet love is gonna save me
We may lose and we may win
But we will never be here again
Open up I'm climbin' in to take it easy

Well I'm a running down the road trying to loosen my load
Got a world of trouble on my mind
Lookin' for a lover who won't blow my cover
She's just a little hard to find
Take it easy, take it easy

Don't let the sound of your own wheels drive you crazy
Come on baby, don't say maybe
I've got to know if your sweet love is gonna save me
You know we got it easy
We oughta take it easy

Words and music by Jackson Browne and Glenn Frey

Chapter Three

"By the time I get to Phoenix . . ."

AFTER A REFRESHING NIGHT'S sleep, interrupted only by my friends from BNSF, I was up at 6.30am to get organised for the next leg of my trip – destination Phoenix, immortalized in the celebrated song *By The Time I Get To Phoenix* written by Jimmy Webb, one of the world's greatest songwriters. I managed to arrange a cab for seven o'clock, to get me to the rendezvous point and to my surprise, it actually turned up on time. Unlike the bus.

The scheduled pick up time was 7.30am, but when the bus hadn't turned up by eight I decided to enquire inside the Holiday Inn which was effectively acting as a surrogate Greyhound office, even selling tickets, so they obviously had a formal arrangement. The receptionist made enquiries with Greyhound HQ, who reported that they had no contact with the missing bus. I found this rather ironic as the driver on the way down to Winslow the previous day had spent a great deal of the time on his mobile phone. Standing around it was quite cold, despite the sun gradually lifting itself over the horizon and I reminded myself of a fact that I had unearthed the night before – despite descending significantly from Flagstaff I was still 4,850 feet above sea level. I found this difficult to comprehend as I had always thought the desert was low-lying, like Death Valley which is actually below sea level. This explained, I realised, why the Turquoise Room is referred to as the 'Oasis in the High Desert'. The bus finally turned up at 8.30am, an hour late. I should have enjoyed the fresh air while I could because for the next five hours I was going to be stuck on a crowded and unpleasant bus.

I was the only passenger waiting to get on at Winslow, so I quickly deposited my bag in the luggage hold beneath the bus and exchanged pleasantries with the driver. Actually, I'm not sure that's the right word, and he certainly didn't offer any explanation for the hour's delay. There again, I suppose he had been driving through the night and I tried not to think about whether he might be tired. On climbing up the steps and into the aisle of the bus I was greeted by a sea of faces and people sprawled out all over the seats. As usual the smell was ripe, which considering everyone had been on the bus overnight, and in some cases longer, is fairly understandable. There were only a few seats available and most of those were occupied by people's legs, everyone having spread themselves out during the night. I rapidly developed a feeling that everyone was watching me, trying to guess where I would try to sit, so I decided the nearest empty seat, around three rows from the front, would be the most appropriate, particularly as it was in close proximity to the driver. The occupant, however, a mean-looking individual in his late twenties, did not seem inclined to give me a hearty welcome.

"Excuse me is that seat taken?" I found myself asking in the most assertive manner I could manage for that time of day.

"Yuup," came the response. Silence from the crowd. I looked around to see if there was anything to substantiate his claim, but, as expected, saw nothing.

"Excuse me is this seat taken?" I repeated.

"Yuup." This guy was decidedly evil-looking, his hood pulled up and his eyes covered by wrap-around sunglasses. Wondering what to do and feeling a little hot under the collar, I pondered the chances of him having a lethal weapon, even if it was just his fist. As it was early in the morning I decided that I could justify cowardice as the best approach and moved on up the bus till I came to the next available seat. This was occupied by a large man who had more than a passing resemblance to Mike Tyson. I asked my standard question and was mildly encouraged by the lack of a verbal response. The body language, though, let me know that this guy also didn't want me as a friend. However, he gradually moved his legs across enough for me to perch on the edge of the seat which was a start. I could see I was now the centre of attention and he too probably realised that everyone else was watching with interest. He muttered something like "Wassup, he kick you out?" in a tone which I decided wasn't really worth responding to, so I just took a chance and sat down as best I could.

I thought that perhaps everyone might now return to their slumberous state, but my hopes were quickly dashed.

"Are you the chaplain?" the lady behind me on my right said loudly enough for the rest of the passengers to become party to the dialogue.

"Not me," I answered, trying hard not to include the rest of the bus in the conversation.

"He is not the chaplain," she exclaimed loudly to all around, to much amusement and general mirth.

"We two are sinners," she pronounced looking at the female sitting beside her. "But we still love the Lord".

"He's not the Greyhound Brethren," pronounced a big black lady, whose head was decorated by a turban with a knot at the front, as she pointed a finger in my direction.

The woman who had first addressed me was a rough-looking lady in her forties, but at least she seemed friendlier than the other acquaintances I had made in my first ten minutes on the bus. The woman next to her was even tougher-looking and I couldn't help noticing a lengthy scar across her neck. "Someone has tried to kill her," I thought – the truth was to come out later. It transpired over the course of the next couple of hours that these girls didn't know each other till they got together during the bus journey.

By this stage of the journey they had decided to refer to one another as Thelma and Louise and I could see why. There was some discussion about who was who, but I felt it didn't make a big difference as in the film one carried a gun, but the other one used it, so that particular debate was probably academic.

They never shut up for the five hours I was on the bus, which was great entertainment, but a bit scary. They had obviously formed an alliance with some people at the back of the coach and some robust dialogue was shouted down the aisle from time to time. At one stage a middle-aged man came down the bus and kneeled alongside 'Thelma' and sought marriage guidance advice, which was a bit bizarre considering that it appeared both the ladies had an itinerant and volatile lifestyle.

After two hours the bus stopped for a break at Flagstaff, the very place I had left just the day before. I got off to buy a sandwich from the dreaded Greyhound shop, there being little else available as town was a mile or so away and the bus only had a 10 minute stop. The young girl on the ticket counter looked some-what bemused to see me again, particularly as I was obviously going to get back on the bus once more. I bought another sandwich just to prove that I never learn and, climbing back on to the bus, settled in my seat and unwrapped the egg-and-something concoction. Having not suffered the indignity of being microwaved, at least this one was cold, so I thought it might be slightly less offensive. As the sandwich consisted of two pieces of bread cut in half, and I knew I would only be able to eat one of these, I offered the other piece to Thelma and Louise.

"The preacher is a man of God," they shouted as they lost no time in accepting my celestial offer. Wanting to change the subject fairly quickly and in an attempt to enter into a conversation that would be broadcast to fewer people, I asked Thelma where she had got on the bus. She told me it had been at Oklahoma, 18 hours earlier. When I expressed my surprise at the length of her trip she said I should speak to Louise who had been on the bus for 49 hours, having started her journey in West Virginia. She (Louise) had only another 23 hours to go before reaching her destination in California. That would be a total of three days and three nights on the bus, and I began to understand why these coaches have their own distinctive aroma. I wondered why she was taking the bus for such a long journey, but I didn't like to ask, which was probably a rare piece of good judgement on my behalf.

After a while we passed a county jail in the middle of nowhere and Louise gave a wave and shouted "God bless y'all". I had little doubt she had a close affinity with the occupants of that sort of establishment. I had learned by then that she had cut her own throat in an apparent attempt at suicide and had recently come out of 'psyche' as she put it. Meanwhile, Thelma was obviously no stranger to the land of bars either, even if it was just in the capacity of visitor, as she kept talking about "when Jimmy gets out."

"I want him to say hello to God again," she had explained to everyone who had ears that functioned, probably including any passing motorists. "At the moment he's a devil worshipper," she went on before being interrupted by Louise, "Look up there in the hills," she exclaimed pointing towards a small town about three miles away. "Be careful if you go up there everyone – it's a swingers' town. Everything and anything goes!" However she declined to enlarge on how she knew this village, some two days distant from West Virginia.

Having left Interstate 40 at Flagstaff we were now heading down Interstate 17 towards Phoenix, the countryside was pretty barren, but at times attractive in a desolate but natural sort of way. This seemed to be the land of National Monuments with exotic-sounding names like Tonto National Monument,

Montezuma's Castle, Tuzigoot National Monument and Walnut Canyon. These mainly represent the remains of cliff dwellings left behind in the 12th and 13th centuries by the Sinaguan people who moved to the area following an eruption of Sunset Crater volcano near Flagstaff.

Author and movie scriptwriter Zane Grey used to hunt mountain lions from his hunting lodge around here, in the process gaining inspiration for his Westerns – over half of his novels were set in the nearby Tonto Basin. Before Zane Grey, the area was a hotbed of activity in the Indian wars with battles between the Tonto Apache and the US Cavalry based at Fort Verde. This was Geronimo country, leader of the Chiricahua Apache Indians and scourge of the white man until his capture at Skeleton Canyon in 1886. Geronimo was a nickname given to him by Mexican soldiers who named him after the Spanish Saint Jerome to whom some of their unfortunate comrades had made pleas as he repeatedly attacked them with a knife, ignoring a hail of bullets. Geronimo understandably had a deep hatred of the Mexicans after a band of soldiers killed his wife, mother and children in a raid in 1851 while he was away trading. It is interesting to note, while not wanting in any way to dissipate the Geronimo legend, that his original name Goyathlay actually means 'He who yawns'. It doesn't do the image justice somehow.

By the time I got to Phoenix (I just had to say that) Thelma and Louise were gasping for a smoke and they dived off the bus and disappeared round the back of the building before I could give them a goodbye kiss – I'm pleased to say. OK, they were rough and ready, but their company had enlivened my journey. Certainly more so than the surly moron who wouldn't let me sit down and who stayed pretty much in the same position for the entire journey.

A taxi driver I spoke to later, when I was telling him about the characters on the bus, enlightened me:

"People travel by bus for a reason in the States," he offered. "Think about it. You can fly internally pretty cheaply and in a fraction of the time. The thing is, anyone wanted by the law doesn't want to go near an airport because they'll get picked up by the security checks." Things started to make sense.

I WAS BECOMING ACCUSTOMED to Greyhound depots not being where I would wish them to be, i.e. somewhere approximating the town centre. On this occasion I found myself well out of town opposite Phoenix Skyharbor airport.

This was where I made a mistake I undertook not to repeat on the rest of the trip. Getting a taxi in America can be a tricky business at times and often entails a long wait. After trying for 25 minutes outside the bus depot and not even getting a sniff of a cab, I began to wonder what the alternatives might be. At that point I was approached by a chap who started talking to me and asked if I was waiting for a taxi. When I answered "yes" he said that he worked for the Yellow Cab company and that he was waiting for a friend who wouldn't be arriving for around 20 minutes and that in the meantime he could give me a ride into town. There are times when you just have to make a quick decision and as I didn't feel too comfortable standing around on my own, and not a single taxi had turned up since I had got off the bus, I thought this might be a good offer. His car was round the corner of the building and I should have realised when it wasn't a yellow cab that the situation could be dicey. Anyway, I climbed in and asked him to take me to somewhere in town where I'd be able to find a hotel.

I can't say I'm heavily into cars, but it didn't take an expert to tell that this was a piece of junk. The windscreen had a number of cracks, which definitely wouldn't be considered acceptable or legal in the UK and I found myself thinking that one of them looked consistent with being hit by a bullet. The inside of the car was a tip and all the fittings, including the door handles, were in a decrepit state. We pulled away and got into the middle of a huge junction with traffic lights at which point the car started to splutter and wouldn't accelerate. He muttered something about the car not being warmed up, but I found this strange as he had obviously driven to the Greyhound station in it and it was a very warm sunny day so there were no temperature issues. He started to head downtown and it was at this stage I became more than a little concerned – what had I done getting in this wreck with a complete stranger? Was I mad?

The driver introduced himself as Norm. "Nice name for a psychopath," I thought to myself, as I suddenly realised he could be taking me anywhere. All of a sudden he looked to me like one of those hillbillies from *Deliverance*, with the buck teeth and the wild eyes. Perhaps I was getting carried away, but the fact remained that as a tourist with a backpack it would have been pretty obvious that I would have some money on me and probably a camera and mobile phone.

As we approached the town, Norm veered off in a completely unexpected direction and my worst fears seemed to be coming to fruition. As he muttered something about roadworks I thought 'likely story' and looked closely at the interior handles on the doors to see if an exit route was available if necessary. There was no way – the handles were effectively inoperable and if the doors were centrally locked it was going to be very difficult to get out in a hurry. We seemed to by-pass the town centre and he was telling me he was looking for the Holiday Inn, but every time I saw a hotel I said, "That one looks fine, thanks". He wasn't interested, though, and I thought we were headed for the mountains, where he would dice me up and serve me as soup to his relatives.

Fortunately, he did eventually draw to a halt outside the Hilton. "Darn, changed its name since I was last here," he muttered. When I asked how much I owed him he suggested $20 might be appropriate and whilst that seemed a bit on the steep side I considered it a bargain to arrive safely. So it was with a big sigh of relief that I walked in to the foyer of the hotel muttering to myself 'I won't do that again in a hurry' to strange looks from the hotel staff.

The Hilton, predictably, was far too expensive for me, so I set off to look around for somewhere to stay. I was a little on the miffed side for this was not an area bristling with hotels, it was the commercial area of town, all office blocks with not another hotel in sight, just empty offices and deserted streets, with this being a Saturday afternoon.

In the end I found a hotel called The Artisan, a strange, dark place but quite upmarket with interesting décor and lots of art, which I was by now getting quite used to. It was outside of my budget, but it wasn't bad for $140. The room was large and comfortable and, as I still felt a sense of relief at not being kidnapped, robbed, strangled and perhaps even worse, I decided to relax and enjoy it.

It was still early afternoon, so I decided I would head for the city library which I had ascertained wasn't too far away. But, as I intimated earlier, my experience of Americans giving directions and distances was not good. If they tell you it's a five -minute walk, try multiplying that by four and you might be nearer the truth. I think it's because they tend not to walk anywhere themselves, so they have no idea how long it takes in anything other than a car. (Later in the trip, I watched a girl get in a four wheel drive vehicle, drive 30 yards across the car park, park up and get out again to go in a shop.)

As I sweated my way in the general direction of the library, I heard what sounded like the rhythm of war drums, it reminded me of when I used to go to the pictures on a Saturday morning to see such stuff such as Massacre at Red Rock. I followed my ears and the drumming got louder, it seemed a little spooky as this was, remember, in the commercial heart of the city, deserted at weekends. Eventually I tracked down the drums and I was amazed to find hundreds of Native American Indians wandering around, resplendent in their tribal colours.

I walked across to a little tent at the entrance to what was obviously a private park. The girl at the trestle table by the entrance tent grabbed my wrist and put on one of those plastic wristbands that you can't get off, as at the atomic museum, and in I walked – I found out later that the entrance fee was $10, but somehow I missed that bit! I picked up a programme (free with the $10 admission) and discovered that I was at the 17th World Championship Hoop Dance contest featuring tribes from across the USA and Canada. This was in the grounds of the Heard Museum for Native Cultures and Art, whose gardens I was now in as a non-fee paying guest.

The contestants rejoiced in such names as Starr Chief Eagle from the Rosebud Sioux, Bear Akachuk from the Cree/Assiniboine tribe in Canada, and Nesbah Yellow Horse from the local Dine tribe. My favourite, however, was Anthony Whiskey Jack of the Cree in Alberta, Canada. You can see what sort of family he comes from.

It was a very colourful spectacle, but I have to confess that after about half an hour of watching young girls swinging hoops around it did get a little repetitive, so I decided to move on and get back to my original objective of finding the library. It was a pleasant diversion, though, and I'm sure I won't be able to contain my derision when I next go to the gym and witness the rather pathetic attempts of individuals trying in vain to get a hula hoop to rotate three times around their waste before it falls to their ankles.

The library was a hugely impressive building, but if I hadn't asked a workman across the road where it was I would have walked straight past it. It just didn't look like the sort of library I know. I went into the building and up to the second floor where the reference room was located. The first thing I did at the reception desk was to compliment the attendant on the fine library they had, asking if it was new.

"12 years old," she answered. Well, I wouldn't have guessed it. Being obviously flattered by my comments, she handed me some literature on the building which, to paraphrase and abbreviate, went something like:

Inspired by Monument Valley, the building resembles a curving copper mesa (flat-topped hill) split by a stainless steel canyon focusing on light and illusion. Among other things, the building has a five-storey atrium, the 'Crystal Canyon', with nine skylights to track the sun. Its pièces de résistance are the round skylights covered by lenses creating an illusion of flames at noon on the summer solstice, June 21st.

I must time my return carefully.

My purpose for going to the library was to see what I could find out about renowned country musician Glen Campbell, of *Rhinestone Cowboy* fame, who is a resident of Phoenix, and also to research a bit about the city itself. I knew Glen was going to feature strongly in this book as he has a tendency to sing songs about places, usually written by Jimmy Webb, and I reckoned there would be no better place to investigate his life than his adopted home town (he was actually raised in rural Arkansas, near a delightful sounding town called . . . Delight). He has now been accepted as a son of Phoenix and is probably their best known resident.

Campbell is now 68 and there's quite a lot to report. To summarise: he was one of 12 kids (the seventh son of 8 boys), has 8 kids himself, fathering his first child at 17. He married the mother, has been married three subsequent times, had an addiction to cocaine, been convicted for Driving Under The Influence (and kicking an officer in the groin when arrested). He has starred in a film with John Wayne (*True Grit*), had his own TV show, has paid $7 million in alimony, survived a light plane crash, spent time in the Betty Ford clinic for addictions, had 27 top ten hits, sold 45 million records, been a member of the Beach Boys, played with Elvis and Sinatra and is now a Born Again Christian. Apart from that he's had a quiet life.

What first put Phoenix on my list of destinations was, of course, Glen's smash hit *By the Time I get to Phoenix*. The song was released in 1967 and reached number. 26 in the US charts, becoming his first top 40 hit. But what was it all about? Firstly, it was written by Jimmy Webb who played a major part in Campbell's career. There is a suggestion that Webb was writing about a love affair with a girl called Susan, although there isn't much evidence to support this. The track was originally recorded by Johnny Rivers in 1965 and Campbell was in a recording studio in LA when he heard the Rivers version. He was intrigued by the title, but even he didn't know what the lyrics were about. He was apparently taken by the "fabulous melody and chord progressions" and decided he wanted to record it himself. The rest is history, as they say.

Testing the feasibility of the lyrics for a moment, firstly it is apparent that the person making the trip is either self-deluded or very conceited, or both, but let's take a look at the logistics:

'By the time I get to Phoenix
She'll be rising'

It is clear from subsequent destinations that the trip is from west to east — with a starting point somewhere west of Phoenix. It is not unreasonable to assume the starting point might be Los Angeles, particularly as that is where Jimmy Webb was based at the time the song was penned. (It is also worth noting that Webb was raised in Oklahoma which is where the song ends up). Los Angeles is 390 miles west of Phoenix, so, if the girl in question rises at 7am, the driver will have been on the road for about seven hours. It could well indicate he stormed out after a late night row.

'By the time I make Albuquerque
She'll be working'

Phoenix to Albuquerque is around 460 miles, so let's say that would take around eight further hours. She'd by now be well into a day's work. It would probably be about 3pm. But that would suggest a very late lunch hour as the next line is:

'She'll probably stop at lunch and give me a call'

Then we have:

'By the time I make Oklahoma
She'll be sleeping'

Well, that would most likely be the case, as it's 540 miles from Albuquerque to Oklahoma, so let's say nine hours, which would take it to midnight. And that's without any sleep or breaks for the driver, unless of course he was on the Greyhound bus which would take even longer.

So, it's all a bit confusing, but what the hell, the song became a gold record for Glen and set him on his way to a glittering career and it is among the most performed songs ever written.

It would be remiss of me not to say a few words about Jimmy Webb at this point, as he will be featuring again before long. One of the world's most respected popular songwriters, he is the only person ever to have been awarded Grammys in all three categories of music, lyrics and orchestration. His hits include *Up, Up and Away* (in my beautiful balloon), one of my least favourite songs but one which became a big hit for the Fifth Dimension, the multi-million selling *MacArthur Park* for Richard Harris and, of course, *Galveston* and *Wichita Lineman* for Glen Campbell. He wrote and produced for, among others, Joan Baez, Joe Cocker, Elvis Presley, Bob Dylan and Frank Sinatra. Not a pedigree to ignore.

One of Webb's most popular songs, certainly in the States, is *The Highwayman*, which has been recorded by an assortment of legends including Willie Nelson, Johnny Cash and Kris Kristofferson. The lyrics of this song are again intriguing. Effectively, the subject of the song dies in all four verses, in four different epochs, always to return. In previous centuries he dies as first a highwayman, then as a sailor, and in the future he dies as a spaceman. In the verse referring to the 20th Century his manner of demise is interesting:

> *'I was a dam builder*
> *Across the river deep and wide*
> *Where steel and water did collide*
> *A place called Boulder on the wild Colorado*
> *I slipped and fell into the wet concrete below*
> *They buried me in that great tomb that knows no sound*
> *But I am still around*
> *I'll always be around, and around, and around, and around, and around.'*

This clearly refers to the building of the Hoover Dam which was originally known as the Boulder Dam. Fortunately, I have been able to deduce that the demise of the individual in this verse is purely fictional and that none of the 96 workers killed in the construction met their end in this gruesome way, although I can imagine that in reality there were some pretty nasty alternative endings.

AFTER MY AFTERNOON EXCURSION, I returned to the hotel knowing that, as there was no restaurant, I would need to go out for a meal in the evening. After a welcome shower and a just as essential change of clothes, I got the receptionist to call a taxi for me to go downtown. Unfortunately, the cab took an hour to arrive. While I waited outside the hotel I couldn't help noticing a drab, rectangular, flat-roofed building adjacent to a car park on the opposite corner. 'Adult Store' the sign proclaimed. This I found a little strange. It wasn't the sort of neighbourhood where I would have anticipated finding such a shop. This was clearly a business area and I couldn't imagine too much custom for this outlet, particularly at a weekend, as it didn't seem to be close to any residential area. I would find out more later.

The taxi driver, when he eventually showed up, suggested I should go to Alice Cooper's bar in town, Alice being a resident of Phoenix, a fact which up until now I hadn't realised. When I got out of the taxi I asked him which direction I should head in if I didn't fancy 'Cooper'stown'. "Well sir, don't turn left," he said somewhat mysteriously. "I wouldn't even dare go down there in my taxi." Not wishing to ask why, I tried to reassure myself that he wasn't one of those people who get their left and right mixed up, paid the bill, and headed for the Cooper'stown sign across the street. It turned out to be a theme restaurant – the theme of course being Alice Cooper – as evidenced by the 'Welcome to my nightmare' sign on entry. The waitresses all had Alice Cooper-style make-up, which for some was a distinct advantage. Access to the restaurant was through an outdoor courtyard which was very lively, with a band performing on stage and a big screen in the background showing an American Football game. The restaurant itself turned out to the best sports bar I have come across with huge screens wall-to-wall showing different sporting events.

To my consternation I found myself becoming engrossed in a re-run of a professional basketball game featuring the Phoenix Suns which was being featured on the big screens. This concerned me for a number of reasons. One, I spilt ketchup on my shirt, and two I had always considered Basketball to be a girlie sport, a not-so-varied variation of netball. It had always seemed to me that one team scored, the other team ran up the other end and scored and then the ball was passed back to the other team to score and so on. Well, this game was a bit like that really, but when I started to get into it I quite enjoyed it, apart from being confused by all the intervals and added time. Unfortunately for me, having loyally put myself behind the local team, they lost 108-105 after they had come from behind to recover a huge early deficit. To great excitement they had gone in front with only minutes left, only to let it slip right at the end. Being a Newcastle United supporter I was used to this sort of disappointment, so I was able to take it in my stride and not let it spoil my night. Amazingly (to me at any rate) the game had been attended by a sell out crowd of 19,000, which I thought was pretty impressive for a game of netball.

Looking at the menu I couldn't resist a Stevie Nicks Burger (Stevie, the lead singer with Fleetwood Mac, being another famous product of Phoenix) but to tell you the truth I can't really remember what it tasted like as I was too busy fantasising about her picture on the cover of the 1977 *Rumours* album. It scared me to think that I could still vividly remember this and it scared me even more when it dawned on me that Stevie would now be nearly 60.

I was secretly hoping that Alice might show up but that was probably expecting too much. He was most likely out playing netball. Alice's real name, by the way, is indeed Alice Cooper. But that's only because he legally changed it in 1974 from the more mundane Vincent Furnier. You have to give him credit – as most people know, John Wayne changed his name to John from Marion (Morrison) which you have to admit was a sound career move, but to change your name from Vincent to Alice, now that's a different kettle of fish.

Actually, there is a lot to admire about the way his band became famous. They were all members of the high school cross-country team and decided to enter the college talent contest. None of them could play any musical instruments, so they dressed up like the Beatles and mimed their performance to Beatles songs. They won, and enjoyed the experience so much they decided to learn to play. It's not hard to work out who their early inspiration was, as, apart from imitating the Beatles for the talent contest, the band called themselves first 'The Earwigs' and then 'The Spiders'. Commendably the group stayed together and, with just a few changes, were the same team that went on to become famous (or infamous depending on which way you look at it) as the bedaubed monster rockers we know today. I did wonder, with Alice now being a restaurateur, how he got the licence, given his previous experiences with chickens (allegedly somewhat misreported), but by all accounts he's a very nice guy and he clearly plays a big role in the local community.

I left the restaurant feeling just a little bit guilty that I hadn't been very adventurous in my choice of food and if I ever go back I'm definitely going to try the 'Wings of Mass Destruction' - 'The heat you have been waiting for, the merciless peppers of Quetzlzacatenango, grown deep in the jungle by the inmates of a Guatemalan insane asylum.' I think I missed out.

I got a taxi back to the hotel and got dropped off on the corner; the same corner with that boring rectangular building I mentioned earlier. It looked closed, which surprised me as it was about 11pm and it was meant to be an adult shop. Then I saw someone walk across the car park, push the door open and enter the building. I was intrigued. Should I be boring and go to bed, or should I just have a little peek and see what an American adult store is actually all about? Naturally, as I was on a fact finding trip, I had to force myself to investigate. I entered the store rather sheepishly, as you would do – was I supposed to turn my collar up? Or even find some dark glasses? Fortunately, I wasn't the only person in the shop, so I felt just a little less self-conscious and was able to avoid speaking to the guy behind the counter. He was engrossed anyway, watching something on his video which appeared to be an advert for human flesh.

The first shelf consisted of girlie magazines which were all wrapped up in cellophane – pretty tame I thought. Then there was the adult toy section which was mildly interesting, though I might have benefited from some explanatory notes. But the thing that intrigued me most was the little opening to what was obviously another room. No door, no curtains, just a little internal archway. There were signs posted declaring – 'Warning, no illegal activities allowed', 'Police likely to visit at anytime.' 'We do not tolerate illegal activities' and so on. Well, I could leave and go back to the hotel and wonder forever what was on the other side of the wall. Or I could follow my investigative instincts and step beyond the threshold. Curiosity had to be satisfied; besides, after that build up, I could hardly tell you I decided not to go in.

The length of my visit was probably about the length of time it's taken you to read this sentence. I couldn't describe what I found in that room (well I could but it would probably get cut out), let's just say it was almost certainly illegal, it didn't involve women and I couldn't get out fast enough.

I walked across the car park trying to look nonchalant and making sure I didn't look in any direction other than straight ahead in case I attracted the attention of anyone who might be lurking around. I reached the sanctuary of the hotel, wishing they had a bar, as a stiff drink would have gone down very nicely. I went to bed trying not to think of what I had just seen, instead I tried to conjure up that album cover again hoping it might lead to more pleasant dreams. I thought I deserved them.

Unfortunately, Stevie didn't visit me, but a good night's sleep without any nightmares, was much appreciated and I awoke reasonably refreshed. It was Sunday morning and I checked out of the hotel and headed off in the general direction of town. I had decided to head for Tucson, near the Mexican border as it features in the Beatles song *Get Back*; this would be another unplanned diversion but it seemed a shame not to call in when it was only 120 miles or so away. But first I needed a refreshment. I came across a little shopping precinct and took the opportunity to enjoy an alfresco coffee in the sunshine, something you can't get in the North of England very often, not without getting very cold anyway.

Over coffee, and looking around at my surroundings, I pondered on the information I had established, whilst at the library, about my host city, Phoenix. Where did the name come from I wondered? There are various theories about this, but the predominant one is that it was, as the name suggests, a city resurrected. In 300 BC the Hohokam people were the first to settle, building an elaborate 135 mile canal system. After the somewhat mysterious disappearance of these settlers, roving Indians arrived on the scene and named the previous occupants the Ho Ho Kam — 'the people who have gone' (no-one knows what happened to them). White settlers didn't arrive until 1865, after the Civil War, and the city was founded by a Confederate soldier, Jack Swilling. It was given the name 'Phoenix' by Phillip Darrel Duppa, a local dignitary, because the city's irrigation system was developed from the Hohokam ruins. "A new city will spring up phoenix-like from the ruins of a former civilisation," he declared.

It is now an impressive city with a population of 1.5 million, or nearer 4 million if you include the adjacent townships of Scottsdale, Chandler, Glendale, Mesa, Paradise Valley and Tempe which together form the 'Valley of the Sun'. As a place to live, it seems to have a lot going for it and, whilst I realised I had only scratched the surface of the city, I had researched the song which had drawn me there and I did enjoy the place. While I enjoyed my coffee I decided I was pleased that Mr Duppa gave the city its name, as I don't think that Jack Swilling's alternative of 'Stonewall' (after Stonewall Jackson) sounds the same somehow.

By The Time I Get To Phoenix

By the time I get to Phoenix she'll be rising
She'll find the note I left hangin' on her door
She'll laugh when she reads the part that says I'm leavin'
'Cause I've left that girl so many times before

By the time I make Alberqerque she'll be working
She'll prob'ly stop at lunch and give me a call
But she'll just hear that phone keep on ringin'
Off the wall that's all

By the time I make Oklahoma she'll be sleepin'
She'll turn softly and call my name out loud
And she'll cry just to think I'd really leave her
Tho' time and time I try to tell her so
She just didn't know I would really go.

Words and Music by Jimmy Webb

Chapter Four

"Jojo left his home in Tucson, Arizona . . ."

ON THE WAY TO THE GREYHOUND station the taxi driver was keen to regale me with complaints; "$2.1 billion down the drain on the new tram system", "water supply running out", "$2.3 million for a 30 second advert during the Superbowl" etc etc . I smiled and thought about London taxi drivers, I suppose it's the same the world over.

I got on the bus to Tucson and noticed that its final destination was El Paso in Texas, another place on my list. 'Out in the West Texas town of El Paso, I fell in love with a Mexican girl', but hang on, better save Marty Robbins for another chapter. I spent the next couple of hours Saguaro-spotting, this being the chief entertainment when travelling across the desert. The Saguaro is the giant cactus found in the Sonoran Desert and is a much-beloved prop of makers of Western films. These immense plants can grow to 50 feet and weigh up to 8 tons. They take 75 years to develop their first arm and they live for more than 200 years, humans permitting. I have to say that cactus-spotting as a hobby can be a bit wearing after an hour or two, a bit like hoop dancing really. I amused myself by recalling an interesting story about the Saguaro; apparently it is illegal to harm them, including indulgence in a pursuit known as 'cactus plugging'. This refers to the practice of cutting open the cactus, draining it, filling the insides with explosive and then blowing it up. In another variation the perpetrator simply tries to cut the plant down by firing bullets into the trunk. This had unfortunate consequences for a character called David Grunfdman in 1982 when he attempted the latter mode of destruction. Unfortunately for him one of the huge arms fell off and impaled him, crushing him at the same time. He did not survive to tell the tale.

On arrival at Tucson I immediately sensed a Mexican feel about the place, though the town centre commercial office area was very modern. I liked it instantly, it just felt good.

The downside was the sign I saw on leaving the Greyhound depot; 'International Gem and Mineral Exhibition – the World's largest.' For anyone looking for accommodation, the last thing you want is a major expo in the town. Not only does it mean accommodation is tight, but the prices invariably shoot up too. When you're on a limited budget that can be very bad news indeed, and I didn't know where to start. I was saved by the fact that in Tucson they have a really good Tourist Information Centre, and it was nearby, situated in a lovely little square of adobe buildings which conveniently housed a coffee shop as well.

Accommodation really was short and it was only through the efforts of the lady in the office that I managed to find a hotel. Even then it was quite a hike out of town and was going to cost $150 for what was basically a motel room. But I did enjoy the full hour I spent in the office chatting to the very helpful and friendly ladies who did me all sorts of favours (please don't take that the wrong way). So much so that I felt obliged to spend even more money by purchasing one or two knick-knacks from the gift shelf, it was the least I could do.

So off I trudged to try to find the University Inn. Once again I was advised that it was only "a mile or so", I guess the 'or so' should have given me a clue. An hour later I wearily reached the hotel and booked in. It was civilised enough, looked clean and had a small outdoor pool area. As the temperature was a very pleasant 80F and I had just walked two miles with a heavy pack on my back I figured I could indulge myself for an hour or so with a clear conscience. As I stretched out by the pool it gave me the opportunity to think about my quest in Tucson. The task was to track down the reference to the famous Jojo in the Beatles' classic 1969 number one *Get Back.*

'Jojo was a man who thought he was a loner
Jojo left his home in Tucson, Arizona'

My research had indicated that the Beatles had come up with the name 'Jojo' from a bar in Tucson which used to be frequented by Linda McCartney, then Eastwood, in her days at the University of Arizona nearby. I was aware, however, that no bar of that name existed any more. Some detective work would be required. But first some serious relaxation, if just for an hour.

I was spoilt for choice in Tucson and I could well have stayed for a week and sampled some of the interesting things I had read about in the tourist shop. I was particularly interested in 'Biosphere 2', a space age site about 30 miles out of town. Constructed in the late 1980s, and used to test whether it would be possible to colonise space, it consisted of an airtight bubble where scientist types were able to try growing food and other essentials of life in a synthetic atmosphere.

There have been a number of missions over the years, but the centre is effectively out of commission now and is no longer airtight. The cost of the project was $200 million, a sum met by oil magnate Ed Bass. Ed is apparently worth $1.2 billion, so I don't think he'll miss it. Mission 1 was launched in 1991 and involved eight people staying in the bubble for two years. If you like banana and peanuts you might have enjoyed your stay as these seem to have been the only things that flourished. It would hardly make up for low oxygen levels damaging your health and the continual hunger experienced by the participants. They eventually fell out and split into two groups, with people who had been close friends becoming implacable enemies amid allegations of such skulduggery as the smuggling of food packages.

Mission 2 in 1994 didn't fare any better, lasting barely a month before there was a serious dispute with the management, leading to removal of the on-site management team at gunpoint! Four days later two members of the first mission deliberately vandalised the project, opening all the doors and violating the closed atmosphere. So all told, a good way to spend $200 million.

I also liked the sound of the Titan Missile Museum. At the height of the cold war there were 54 Titan II missiles in underground silos around the States, waiting patiently for their chance to blow the world apart. In 1987 the last site was deactivated and the only remaining silo, complete with missile, is in Tucson. This is open to the public, but I decided I'd had enough of Doomsday scenarios with the Vegas experience and decided to give it a miss. One frightening fact that I did discover is that in 1980 a technician dropped a wrench which broke the skin of a missile and blew an 8,000lb nuclear warhead clean out of its silo, landing a hundred yards away. I don't remember that being very well advertised at the time.

In the early evening I got prepared for my mission. I had established, or so I thought, that the bar which used to be Jojo's was now called Grumpy's. The lady at the tourist office had kindly done a bit of digging for me and had come up with an address for Grumpy's – 4844 East 22nd Street. East 22nd Street wasn't on the city map I had acquired, so I knew it was going to be out of the centre. I sensibly decided to get a taxi, which was just as well as it must have been four miles from my hotel. When I arrived at 4844 I was flattened to find that it was not, and apparently never has been, Grumpy's. The sign said loud and clear Hector's Oasis and, what's more, it was apparent from the oriental structure in the car park that until recently it had been a Chinese restaurant.

The taxi drove away leaving me in the car park and I thought "bloody hell I'm in a crap neighbourhood" (not necessarily dangerous looking but quite industrial), "my taxi has gone, I know how long it can take to get another, the town's a good hour's walk away and I haven't eaten yet." Come to think of it I hadn't eaten all day really.

I walked into the bar and found it frequented by one barmaid, one chap who appeared to be in charge and one customer. I ordered a pint, which was at least some comfort, and began my enquiries.

"Was this once Grumpy's Bar?" was my opening gambit.

"Nope, never," came the response from the chap in charge. This was Don and it turned out he wasn't the boss. He was a retired accountant who was helping out in his spare time to get the bar into better shape as it was in need of refurbishment following the recent takeover by his friend Hector.

"Your best bet will be to get a taxi, go a couple of miles down the road to see the previous owners, Scott and Jim, and see if they can help you."

I got the feeling this was going to be a long night.

I asked the barman to book me a taxi and I bought Don a pint, then felt obliged to do the same for the girl behind the bar. "An expensive night too, if it carries on this way," I thought. I was just about to ask why they had a blow-up doll, fully inflated and posing seductively behind the bar, when a little, dark-skinned character about 5 feet 4 inches suddenly appeared, sporting a pork pie hat. Despite his minimal stature it was clear he was a larger than life character and he came straight over to shake my hand. This for just being a customer I gathered. He introduced himself as Hector Rodriguez, the owner of the Oasis. This was going to cost me another drink I could tell, so I might as well get one for myself while I'm at it. Hector's arrival turned out to be a real stroke of luck as he knew everyone and everything. He was, or had been, a professional musician and knew his way around. This lifted my spirits considerably and I suddenly felt much more optimistic.

"Grumpy's? You want to be just down the road," he offered. "It's not Grumpy's anymore, it's a bar owned by my brother Raul, it's called Al J's bar. He's been in around a year now."

Cancelling the taxi and finishing my pint, I said goodbye and set off for the relatively short walk to Al J's bar. I walked inside not sure what to find and was confronted by a set of pool tables with some pretty serious-looking games going on. Everything ground to a halt as I walked in and I felt like one of those cowboys who has just walked through the swing doors of the saloon. I went to the bar and ordered a drink, the pool games gradually picking up their momentum again as people lost interest in me. I spoke to a lady who was clearly in charge of the bar and asked her if I could speak to Raul Rodriguez. The reply was curt. "Don' know him."

"A likely story" I thought. "You must do."

"Who are you?" she demanded. I tell you this girl was not to be messed with. I'm sure she thought I was from the Revenue or something, she certainly wasn't making me feel overly welcome. In fact, given the general climate, I was beginning to have thoughts like "I'm 5,000 miles from home, will anybody ever find the body". I'd heard plenty of stories about strangers in the Deep South going missing never to be seen again, but this was usually in Alabama or Louisiana, not the South West. Perhaps I hadn't done my research thoroughly enough.

After a while I won her over, sort of, and she finally offered "That's Raul over there playing pool, we call him Wink". I waited for the game of pool to finish and the money to change hands (I was right in thinking the games were a bit serious), then plucked up the courage to approach Wink and introduce myself.

To my surprise he was very welcoming. We got talking, I told him his brother had sent me, and we got on like a house on fire. I even got a free meal of burgers and salad! Amazingly, Wink was unaware of the connection with Jojo's, but I confirmed the theory through a customer called Lorenzo Lopez, who had joined us in conversation at the bar. "I moved here in 1969," he said. "And at that time it was Jojo's bar." A satisfying moment for me and I guess a potentially rewarding one for Wink. "Why doesn't he check the story out, rename the bar Jojo's and trade on the connection," I thought. After all, the Beatles are still huge in the States.

We were joined at the bar by a chap called Abel Paredes, who insisted on buying me a Micholada, which is a mixture of beer, tomato, lemon juice, oyster juice and tabasco sauce. It was very nice of him and I gave it my best shot, but by this time I was feeling more than a little wobbly and the whole scenario seemed a bit surreal. As I was about to leave, Wink insisted on taking me back to Hector's bar, so off we set in his motor. By this time things were a little bit livelier at the Oasis, but Hector and Don were still propping up the bar, so we joined them.

After yet more drinks, talk started coming much more freely and Don, in particular, became a lot more forthcoming, a signal perhaps that I should increase my alcohol budget in future. We got talking and it turned out that he used to date Linda Ronstadt at high school and that he shares the same birthday as she does, 15 July 1946. I later checked this out and the birthday at least was right. I had noticed that the city centre bus interchange was called the Ronstadt Transit Center and thought it must have been named after Linda, the heart-throb of the 60s and 70s (whose record sales are estimated at 75 million). Don put me right and advised me that the centre was named after Linda's family, who have been leading lights in Tucson since the 1880s. Her grandfather Federico (Fred) was an early pioneer who moved to Tucson in 1882 at the age of 14 to learn the wagon-making trade. He brought with him his musical talents and they have percolated through the generations. In 1994 the family was awarded a 'Copper Letter' from the City of Tucson for 'keeping the air of the town beautiful with music for well over a hundred years.' A fine and talented family by the sound of it.

Hector, in the meantime, wanted to tell me about his band in his early days, which included Wonder Woman Lynda Carter. Lynda is another Arizonan, from Phoenix, and another student of the University of Arizona, although she dropped out to pursue a career in acting; this despite being voted most gifted student. She was also Miss World USA, whatever that means.

At the end of the evening (it was well past Midnight at the Oasis), Wink insisted on taking me back to the hotel and offered to pick me up the next day and take me to his sister, Maria's, bar for a Mexican lunch. "Things are really picking up," I thought, and so they were.

Reflecting on the history of *Get Back*, it is worth noting that this was the only Beatles song that credited another artist – pianist Billy Preston, a good quiz question, I'd suggest. It was 1969 and The Beatles were doing a lot of in-fighting at the time and Preston's presence helped calm things down as well as leading to some good studio performances as they put together their last two albums *Abbey Road* and *Let It Be*. Trying to interpret the lyrics of the song is something of a challenge as is often the case with Beatles songs.

The first verse tells the story of a man named Jojo, who leaves his home in Tucson, Arizona, for some California grass (marijuana one assumes). He is encouraged to return.

In the second verse there is uncertainty as to whether Loretta Martin is a promiscuous woman, or making a feminist statement, or perhaps a transsexual – 'thought she was a woman, but she was another man'. Just to show how convoluted the Beatles words could be it is recorded that John Lennon at one point in the studio sang 'Sweet Loretta Fart she thought she was a cleaner, but she was a frying pan'! Loretta is also encouraged to return.

There is lots of speculation over a controversial third verse which never made it onto the final disc, but is to be heard on bootleg recordings of some sessions at Abbey Road studios in January 1969. This became known as the 'No Pakistanis' version:

> *'Meanwhile back at home there's nineteen Pakistanis,*
> *Living in a council flat*
> *Candid little neighbour tells them what the plan is,*
> *Then he tells them where it's at'*

This was not intended to be racist, but rather a satirical comment on Enoch Powell's 'Rivers of Blood' speech, which was in the news at the time. This verse was apparently dropped because Paul McCartney didn't feel it was of high enough quality, rather than for any political reason. It would have been interesting to see what the result would have been had it been left in. The song would probably have been banned by radio stations, particularly the BBC, and might not have had the exposure to make it a hit. In the event it entered the UK charts at number one on 26 April 1969 and stayed there for a phenomenal six weeks. A few weeks later it hit number one in the States and remained there for five weeks.

I think there is little doubt that Linda McCartney's link with Tucson was a key feature of the song and the Jojo verse, but where the rest comes from is anyone's guess. There again, when you consider some of the Beatles' other lyrics, such as 'semolina pilchards climbing up the Eiffel Tower' the words to *Get Back* seem positively relevant and articulate.

I went to sleep with the enticing thought of a meal at Maria's to look forward to and thoughts about the next destination. Would it be El Paso, Albuquerque or even Amarillo? Tomorrow would tell.

Get Back

Jojo was a man
Who thought he was a loner
But he knew it wouldn't last,
Jojo left his home in Tucson, Arizona
For some California grass

Get back, get back,
Get back to where you once belonged
Get back, get back,
Get back to where you once belonged.
Get back Jojo, go home
Get back, get back
Back to where you once belonged
Get back, get back,
Back to where you once belonged
Get back Jo

Sweet Loretta Martin thought she was a woman
But she was another man
All the girls around her say she's got it comin'
But she gets it while she can

Get back, get back,
Get back to where you once belonged
Get back, get back
Get back to where you once belonged
Get back Loretta, go home
Get back, get back
Get back to where you once belonged
Get back, get back
Get back to where you once belonged

Get back Loretta
Your mother's waiting for you
Wearing her high heel shoes
And her low neck sweater
Get on home Loretta
Get back, get back
Get back to where you once belonged

Words and Music by Paul McCartney and John Lennon

Chapter Five

"Blacker than night were the eyes of Felina . . ."

A GOOD SLEEP SORTED MY HEAD out and when I woke I made a quick decision that El Paso would be my next destination. I had been agonising for a while over what direction I would take at this point as the decision would shape events over the coming five weeks.

To head for El Paso would mean that I was going to be travelling due east into Texas rather than the option of travelling north to New Mexico. I knew that once into Texas and beyond El Paso I would need to be heading in the direction of the Gulf of Mexico, towards Galveston, a musical destination which could not be missed. So, the big decision was made – the direction for the rest of the trip was to be east, then south east, north and then west rather than the other way round. The exact itinerary would be influenced by events.

There was a minor snag however. To avoid arriving in El Paso in the early hours I would need to get a morning bus and that would, of course, mean missing out on the invite to Maria's restaurant. So I rang Wink and thanked him for the offer, leaving him with the thought of turning AL J's into the money-spinning Jojo's. Hopefully this was some consolation for him not having my company for the day!

At the bus station I encountered the usual chaotic scenes and in particular my eye caught a young Japanese girl who was asking at the counter whether they had a map so she might see where to go. She cut an unusual sight in 'shorts' which came down to her ankles (something of a contradiction in terms), with a T-shirt down to her knees. The shop assistant couldn't help her and, as she looked somewhat forlorn, I wondered for a moment how difficult it would be to extricate my map from the depths of my rucksack. I knew it would be a real pain to unpack in a crowded area, particularly as I was trying to negotiate a polystyrene cup full of coffee at the same time. By the time I dithered she was gone, to where I do not know, leaving me feeling a little guilty. But let's face it, if she was intent on travelling the Greyhound and didn't know the geography of the US, she would soon learn that a map might be a useful thing to have around.

This little distraction was overtaken by a young black chap in a smart suit, who had with him a baby in a push chair. He really had his hands full as he had lots of luggage as well as a little dog stuffed in his jacket. At that point a Greyhound official appeared and told him he wouldn't be allowed to travel with the dog. With hardly a blink of the eye the response was "well, you can keep him" as the owner thrust the unfortunate animal into the attendant's arms. To my amazement the attendant did just that and disappeared, taking the dog with him. "$100 dollars down the drain," said its erstwhile owner. "Just bought it for my daughter back home". It was all so casual and matter of fact, no arguing, just a simple "keep it then" and that was it. Strange.

I tried in vain to peek through the little glass window in the door behind the counter as I wouldn't have been surprised to see they were running a pet store as a side-line, perhaps a shop front on to the street outside. I couldn't help reflecting on the irony of a bus line named after a dog not allowing animals to travel, but never mind.

The bus duly arrived and I managed to get myself reasonably comfortable for the six hour journey. The route followed Interstate 10, passing close to the infamous town of Tombstone. Perhaps it was as well that we didn't call at Tombstone as I had just read that it has been the subject of some controversy recently regarding a descent into downmarket tackiness. It has even been threatened with losing its National Historic Landmark status as a result of such activities as installing neon blinking lights around historic signs, placing historic dates on new buildings (a bit on the naughty side) and building 'authentic' artefacts such as hitching rails which weren't in place in the Wild West days. I understand that remedial action is well under way.

The town apparently got its name from a warning given by a passing soldier to an early prospector, Ed Schieffelin, who was advised that the only rock he would find among the waterless hills and warring Apaches would be his own Tombstone. The town was founded in 1879, but as it did not have railroad access it was very isolated and became one of the deadliest regions in the West. Its celebrity status was, of course, a direct result of the Gunfight at the OK Corral in 1881. Although this was not the deadliest gunfight the West ever saw, it was bad enough, with three people killed in the space of a thirty second firefight in which thirty shots were fired (described as 'a lively fire commenced' in the local newspaper).

The fracas involved three of the five Earp brothers, namely Wyatt (who was not a lawman at that time), his brother Virgil, (who was the Town Marshal) and Morgan, who was a police officer. Completing the team was their colleague Doc Holliday, who probably needed a diversion from his girlfriend 'Big Nose Kate', who must have been a little strange, as well as odd-looking, as she had recently tried to implicate him in a murder plot.

Up against them were the two Clanton brothers, Ike and Billy, Billy Claiborne and the two McLowery brothers, Frank and Tom. They had formed a band of cowboys widely believed to have been cattle rustlers.

The circumstances leading to the fight are a bit hazy, but it certainly appears that it wasn't a cut and dried goodies v baddies contest as might be popularly imagined, and which was certainly presented in the 1957 film starring Burt Lancaster and Kirk Douglas. The law-enforcing participants were regarded by some as tyrants, abusing their position to enhance their business interests (namely gambling). The 'opposition' was the five cowboys who were described as 'fun-loving and wild', but who were very popular in some quarters as they brought lots of business to town. There is a suggestion of undercurrents of North v South in the confrontation (bearing in mind the Civil War had been finished less than twenty years) and in some people's minds it was a case of 'uncivilised southern gangs' against 'northern capitalists and immigrant miners'.

The whole thing was sparked off by the attempted disarming of the cowboys to comply with City Ordinance No. 9 – 'To Provide against Carrying of Deadly Weapons'. Unfortunately there were some 'grey areas' surrounding this edict, such as definition of 'city limits' and at which point of arrival guns had to be surrendered. In the event, three of the five cowboys (Ike Clanton and the two McLowerys) ended up dead and Wyatt Earp and Doc Holliday were subsequently charged with murder (the Grand Jury refused to indict them due to lack of evidence). This led to a revenge campaign which resulted in Morgan Earp being murdered three months later by a shot to his back and Virgil being shot, losing the complete use of his left arm. Wyatt and Doc then embarked on the infamous 'Vendetta Ride' during which they tracked down and killed the men they thought were responsible.

Once we got beyond Tombstone, the journey continued uneventfully, passing an endless moonscape of flat barren land – I say a moonscape, but it was punctuated with hundreds of geysers, providing a surreal landscape which looked as if it could be the set for a sci-fi movie. After passing through Fort Bowie (the scene of Geronimo's surrender in 1886), we headed through Lordsburg towards Deming and Las Cruces.

On approaching Deming I was intrigued by the roadside sign announcing 'Deming, the Home of Pure Water and Fast Ducks'. Surprisingly, in the middle of a harsh desert, the claim about fresh water is true, with water being drawn from the aquifers (water-holding rocks) of an underground river. Rivers in this region, in this case the Mimbres, tend to establish themselves high in the mountains, but disappear as they reach lower ground, simply sinking into the desert.

So, now we know about the pure water but what about the fast ducks? Well, it transpires that this is the home of live duck racing. Each autumn, owners and trainers bring their thoroughbreds to town and race along an eight lane track for prize money in excess of $10,000. What Billy the Kid would have thought of it I don't know.

The reason I mention Billy the Kid is that this was the stamping ground of Billy and his adversary Pat Garrett, the sheriff who eventually killed him after Billy had reputedly slain 21 men in his short life (21 years as it happens).

The flavour of Wild West menace, albeit contemporary, was re-inforced by the roadside signs with one huge hoarding carrying a 'Wanted' picture of a fugitive and another carrying a warning 'US Correctional Facilities in this area – do not pick up hitch-hikers'. It would appear that either they aren't convinced of their ability to 'correct' or alternatively their security arrangements need looking at.

The last town before El Paso was Las Cruces, again strong on cowboy history, this being the place where Pat Garrett in turn met his end. Aged 58 his reactions weren't as fast as a younger man, J. Wayne Brazle, a youthful ranch-hand, in a dispute over goats grazing on land leased out by Garrett. Such was the outcome of relatively trivial disputes in the Wild West.

Another claim to fame for Las Cruces is the annual Whole Enchilada Festival, which boasts the world's largest flat enchilada, about ten feet in diameter. The construction of the enchilada is the centrepiece of a three day festival which attracts 70,000 visitors. Among the more stupendous of the enchilada's credentials are the 75 gallons of red chilli sauce which provide the 'bite' for 750 pounds of ground corn.

Now we were on the home run to El Paso and my anticipatory juices were working overtime, I couldn't wait — the very name conjured up an image of Mexican magic and, to anyone who has heard the Marty Robbins classic *El Paso*, Felina whirling in Rosa's Cantina.

We arrived at around 5pm and as I got off the bus I pondered over where to start. I knew very little about the town, apart from the fact that it had a song named after it and that it was on the Mexican border. The good news was that it was still daylight and the bus station was, for once, in a safe-looking environment and only a short walk to the central square, San Jacinto Plaza. I spotted, on the other side of the road, a large hotel called the Camino Real which I guessed should be my first point of enquiry. Not that I expected to be able to afford to stay in what looked such an up-market place, but I thought they might at least be able to direct me to somewhere more fitting for my station.

Once inside the hotel I was suitably impressed by the décor, fittings and architecture. The focal point was a high, multi-coloured stained glass 'Tiffany' dome in the roof of the restaurant/bar area, beautifully carved windows in what, in ignorance, I would probably have described the Italianate Style, but I understand would more correctly be described as the Spanish Colonial Revival Style, all topped off with a huge chandelier dangling from the ceiling.

To my surprise I was informed that it would only cost $100 to stay the night, so I promptly booked in for two before they got the chance to say they had made a mistake. I felt a bit out of place standing, rather sweatily, at the reception in my shorts and with my rucksack at my feet having just got off the bus. But, if they would have me, I wasn't going to turn them down.

My room was just as impressive as the foyer — spacious, beautifully carpeted and with a superb King-sized bed. I noticed an adjoining door and, as you always do, (or should do) I tried the handle. I was taken aback when the door opened and I assumed that they had made a mistake in leaving access to the adjoining guest's room. This wasn't the case however and I was astonished to find a living room with three-piece suite and a meeting table with chairs. This was definitely a good fifty quid's worth.

IN THE MORNING I headed for the Convention Centre, which I had been advised housed the tourist information desk. I introduced myself to the two young girls on reception and asked what they knew about Marty Robbins and the song named after their town.

"Not a lot," was the answer to that question. Just as I was about to ask where the city   library was one of them volunteered that their Communications Manager, Pifas Silva, was something of an expert on the subject, but added that he would not be in till around 3.30pm. They suggested I return then and see what he could tell me. So off I went armed with leaflets about the Mission Trail town walk and a self-guided walking tour of historic downtown. But what I really fancied was a little excursion to Mexico, which I had learned was actually within walking distance. I had always fancied visiting Mexico, I had this vision of Sombrero hats, bullet belts and Pancho Villa. So I headed off in the direction of the famous Rio Grande, which I knew divided El Paso from the town of Juárez, the Mexican town on the other side of the border.

Juárez and El Paso were originally part of the same settlement, the latter being derived from El Paso del Norte (North Pass), which was the name given in the sixteenth century by Spanish explorers seeking a route through the southern Rocky Mountains. The Spanish ruled the area for almost 300 years before Mexico took over in 1821. Texas won its independence from Mexico in 1836 and claimed the Rio Grande as its southern border. The town remained, however, part of Mexico until the Mexican-American War in 1848, Texas having joined the Union in 1845 after a decade as an independent republic. El Paso del Norte was renamed Juárez (Ciudad Juárez) in 1888 in honour of President Benito Juárez, one of Mexico's great leaders who served five terms as President between 1858 and 1872.

The first store I came to on my way to the river was the Alamo Shooters Supply which gave me a gentle reminder that I was in the land of the cowboy and this was rapidly endorsed by the nearby bank building sporting the name of Wells Fargo, which to me will always be associated with the early TV westerns. I can still see the baddies chasing the stagecoach at high speed with the various characters expertly leaping from fast running steeds, climbing across the team of horses pulling the stage (which would invariably sport the Wells Fargo livery) trying to make their way up to the driver, who was no doubt also being harassed from the rear. Sorry, I'm getting carried away again, but you know what I mean.

After about a mile of walking in 90 degree sunshine I came across the border crossing and suddenly everything changed dramatically. From the nice laid back feel of up-town El Paso I could suddenly sense a change in the atmosphere and the immediate area reminded me of something like Dover or Folkestone – commercial and teeming with people.

I didn't yet have a view of the river (it's not a riverfront sort of town) and you don't see the water till you get on the bridge. Walking up the rampway I was filled with excitement at the prospect of my first view of the renowned Rio Grande. Images of John Wayne and Stewart Grainger struggling across the river, with their horses up to their neck in water, filled my head as I approached the point of the bridge where I would get my first view. To my disappointment there was a high chain link fence and I had to peer through the mesh to look down upon the famous channel.

What I saw was not what I expected. Not the fast flowing scenic river with banks sloping down to the crystal-clear water, but instead a dual carriageway of shallow brown water lying stagnant on either side of a 'central reservation' consisting of grass and weeds. There was so little water in the channels that I saw a number of quarry-type trucks driving up the river bed. The exposed concrete sides coming up to meet the road at 45 degrees were covered in graffiti work and when I say graffiti work I am not talking about the frivolous musings you see in UK underpasses but real political stuff. These included huge representations of Che Guevara and slogans such as 'Bajo Blooeoa Cuba-Alto Al Yanki-Terrorismo' and 'No Mas Bombas al Mundo'. I'm not sure what they mean, but I've got a pretty good idea. The whole scene was a little disappointing and I was beginning to think it was more like the old Berlin Wall scenario than the romantic image I had in mind.

At the mid-point on the bridge I stepped across the borderline into Mexico, simply paying a few cents to the attendant in the booth. I don't even remember if I had to show my passport. It was certainly easier than my experience getting into the States. Suddenly I knew I was in a different country, in reality it was a different world. In one footfall the scene changes from one of relative affluence on the US side to abject poverty on the Mexican side. There was plenty going on, though. Try to imagine this scene: multiple lanes of stationary traffic, people all over the roads and pavements, balloon sellers meandering in and out of the cars, buskers sitting in the kerb, people washing car windscreens or selling kites and, sadly, women beggars sitting on the pavement with their babies. Scenes like this made me realise how relevant the border control debate in the States is and I could only imagine the disparity between potential earnings on the El Paso side compared to the Juárez side. Apparently 60,000 people a day make the crossing and it isn't hard to understand why.

I had no sooner left the bridge and entered the town than I was accosted by a 'taxi driver'. When I explained I was only on a walking visit and didn't need a cab, that was his cue for offering me just about anything I could possibly want or indeed not want. This included a "beautiful woman"; "come inside and see for yourself," he encouraged me. At 10.30 in the morning he would have had a better chance of success if he had mentioned coffee and sticky buns, but there we go. This little cameo set the scene for the next hour and it was impossible to do much without getting into discussion with more taxi drivers or shop assistants. Having said that, everyone seemed to be pretty friendly.

The town itself was somewhat ramshackle and it provided a contrast to El Paso, which had quite a few smart high rise office blocks and hotels. I was confronted by a scene of single-storey buildings and shack-like shops, the whole place wildly decorated with telegraph wires and, now and again, train or tram tracks criss-crossing the road, with level crossings making pedestrianism rather dodgy. Generally, a bit of a mess, but you couldn't deny it had character.

Containing my trip to about an hour and deciding to get out while the going was good, as I was very close to getting lost on a couple of occasions, I headed back for the bridge. The long queues at the immigration control booths clearly indicated it was harder to get into the States than it was to get out, as you would expect. After running the gauntlet of beggars and street sellers on the bridge I successfully negotiated the immigration queue, completed my re-entry and was immediately amused to see a large road sign saying 'Welcome to Texas – Drive Friendly, The Texas Way'. I say amused because just at that moment I looked up the first street in El Paso and saw a fight going on between a lady in a pick-up truck and a man in a Ford saloon. The lady was definitely the one to avoid as she was shaking her fist, cursing and looked very close to planting a right hook on her unfortunate opponent. In any event I had no intention of driving and decided to do a walking tour of the town before returning to the hotel.

Although I had various visitor route maps in my possession, I decided to do my own thing. I was spoilt for choice for buildings of architectural interest, even to the untrained eye such as mine. Every building I looked at seemed to bear the name of Henry Trost, which is hardly surprising as he designed 650 identifiable buildings in Texas, Arizona, New Mexico and neighbouring states. He moved to El Paso and started the family firm in the early 1900s at a time when the town was in a growth situation, providing him all the opportunity he needed to stamp his style on the landscape. He was a pioneer of reinforced concrete buildings and constructed most of the tall buildings (considered skyscrapers in their day) still standing in El Paso, many constructed in the Chicago Art Deco style as Trost had previously practised in the North as part of the famous Chicago School of architects. I discovered that he had designed the Camino Real and that it was built incorporating lessons learned from the San Francisco earthquake in 1906, a detail which pleased me. I also learnt that I had been preceded in my visit to the Real by such distinguished guests as Pancho Villa and Richard Nixon.

Whilst I found the architecture interesting and attractive I did feel a bit of a fraud and thought it was somewhat wasted on me. I enjoy looking at interesting buildings, but I am not sufficiently competent in this respect to appreciate the finer points of, say, the historic Palace Theater, another Trost building, which displays a 'Spanish colonial format with Moorish influence, with a delicate overall tracery of Arabesque'. The building is now used as a night club, so its finer points would probably not be appreciated by the late night clientele either, so perhaps I shouldn't feel so bad about my condition of advanced ignorance on this subject.

I decided to make a detour to have a look at the Pancho Villa 'Stash House', I had seen mentioned on the map. This was on Leon Street, which took a bit of finding. As this was off the beaten track I had to be a bit careful, but I couldn't avoid the two down and outs sitting outside a mission on my side of the pavement. In return for a small donation to their cause (I didn't need a lot of thought as to what that might be) I was offered the opportunity of a lifetime – "Hey brother. Wanna hit on this?" said the speaker as held out a 'cigarette' which he had just removed from his lips. I declined the offer.

The Stash House, when I found it, consisted of a corrugated tin single-storey building with a pitched, corrugated roof and turquoise painted iron railings out-side. The building itself wasn't very exciting, but it did stir my imagination. The US Customs Office had raided the building during the Mexican Revolution and found $500,000 in cash, plus jewellery belonging to Pancho and his brother Hipolito. Quite a sum in those days I would guess.

My visit to the Stash House reminded me that I was in one of the hotbeds of the revolution and in this context I was interested to come across the Plaza Hotel, previously the Hilton Hotel, which was the first high rise hotel built by Conrad Hilton. (It was also the hotel where Elizabeth Taylor lived for a while after her mar-riage to Nicky Hilton in the 1950s). This stood on the site of the old Sheldon Hotel, which burned down down in 1929 having been the unofficial headquarters for many of the participants in the revolution.

I wandered back to the Camino Real about 2pm in order to freshen up for my appointment with Pifas at the tourist office. On reading some further information about the hotel I discovered that its rooftop ballroom had been a favourite place to watch the progress of the revolution during the battles taking place in Juárez across the river. Yes, I was going to have to find out more about the revolution, but first what about Marty Robbins?

I WENT TO THE TOURIST Information Office at 3.30pm as arranged and was intro-duced to Pifas Silva, a very amenable chap, who I guessed was in his late mid-late 30s and who possessed annoyingly good looks. I asked him what he knew about Marty Robbins and *El Paso*. Boy, was he in his element! Before I could say 'Black as the Night were the Eyes of Felina' he was on the phone cancelling his arrange-ments for the evening and telling me to meet him at 5pm. "We'll go out to Rosa's Cantina for something to eat," he said. I was amazed at this as firstly, up until this point, I didn't know whether Rosa's actually existed and secondly I didn't expect such hospitality to be offered to someone who had just turned up on the doorstep.

Delighted at this unexpected turn of events I returned at 5pm, when Pifas took me into his office and filled me full of facts about Marty and the El Paso connection. Marty is a hero in El Paso and has done more than anyone else to put the town on the map, actually recording a trilogy of songs based on the Felina story (the other two being Felina and El Paso City). His status in the area is immense and Pifas explained that, among other things, the University of Texas El

Paso (UTEP) have adopted the tune to *El Paso* as their 'fighting song', there is a prominent street named after him and, very timely, just back in his hometown that day was Danny Olivas the astronaut. Having just returned triumphant from a space mission, Danny was at that very moment speaking at the University, explaining that as he carried out his space walk NASA played through his headphones the sound of Marty singing *El Paso*. This must have been, quite literally, an out of this world experience.

Another memorable occasion, and I wish I could have been there, must have been when the Rolling Stones gave an improvised performance of the song during their concert at the El Paso Sun Bowl in October 2006. Mick Jagger belting out a cowboy song is something you don't see every day. Pifas went on to say that CMTV (Country Music TV) voted *El Paso* runner up in the poll to find the best ever country song, second only to Glen Campbell and *Galveston*. I felt I was being spoilt here as I knew that Galveston was to be my next destination. This was certainly meeting my expectations of what I had come for.

Legend has it that Marty was passing Rosa's Cantina in 1959, with his wife driving, when he got the inspiration for *El Paso*. Basically the song is about Marty's character falling in love – 'Out in the West Texas town of El Paso, I fell in love with a Mexican girl'. One night a 'wild young cowboy' made the mistake of making advances to Felina, the lady in question. When challenged, the cowboy allegedly made the mistake of going for his gun – 'In less than a heartbeat the young stranger lay dead on the floor'. Marty's character then makes his escape on horseback into the badlands of New Mexico, only to eventually succumb to his overwhelming desire to see Felina again. Needless to say, on his return he gets chased and shot by a posse and he dies, as he would have wished, in Felina's arms.

The song is typical of Marty, whose songs tend to tell a story rather than just repeating verses and choruses. However, the storytelling did cause some initial problems as the record was four minutes and forty five seconds long and the record company thought many radio stations would not play it because of this. They therefore put a shorter three minute version on the B side, but the full length version proved the winner in this particular contest. The song won a Grammy for best Country and Western recording in 1961 and topped both the country and pop music charts. It is still a classic today and the melodic tune, evocative story and Spanish guitar make the four and three quarter minutes fly by. And now, unbelievably, I was on my way to Rosa's Cantina for tea!

I didn't know what to expect or where we would be heading. To my surprise I was taken well out of town and into the hills surrounding El Paso, where at last I observed the Rio Grande with a decent amount of water flowing through it. All of a sudden I saw the sign 'Rosa's Cantina', in big red letters standing out against the white background of a white, single-storey, flat-roofed building.

When we went inside we were surprised to find there was no-one else around except the lady behind the bar and there were no tables set for meals and no delicious smells of fajitas sizzling away behind the scenes.

"We only do food at lunchtime," we were quickly informed. This was a bit of a blow, but the mission was more important than food, so we decided on a beer only diet and ordered a couple of Coronas. These came complete with a piece of lime and salt on the rim of the bottle. The lime I got a taste for, but unless you enjoy swallowing sea water you might agree with me that the salt is one refinement too many.

The bar was about seven yards wide by fifteen yards long and there were plenty of tables, indicating that perhaps this was a popular place at lunchtime. There was also a pool table which I noted with interest. In the corner stood an old fashioned juke box and Pifas went to examine the playlist. The next thing I knew the strains of Marty singing *El Paso* filled the room. Each time we got a beer we played the record. Needless to say the record was well aired by the end of the night.

Around 7pm the front door opened and three newcomers came in. They were speaking Spanish and seemed to regard us with some suspicion and I felt as if I was something of an intruder. These guys were clearly regulars as two of them headed straight for the pool cues while the other got the drinks in. Anyway, the three of them started playing pool and I watched intently, always on the lookout for the opportunity to join in anything competitive. After my fourth, or was it fifth, Corona, I decided that I wouldn't embarrass myself if I suggested making up a foursome for doubles. Even if I did embarrass myself I probably wouldn't remember, so I had nothing to lose. Pifas professed himself to be a non-player, so he elected to remain at the bar and enjoy his beer. Through a process of sign language I managed to get the message over that I would like to play and with a little bit of fuss we got started, even though I still couldn't quite work out who I was supposed to be partnering.

The first game went well and with my very young partner (I think he was the son or nephew of one of the older guys) managed to shade the first frame. One of the opponents, who by now I had established were Indian workers from the local reservation casino, quite fancied himself as a hustler and he didn't seem at all pleased by this development. So off we went for a second frame which, although close, went the other way and so set the match up for a deciding frame. By this time I was well relaxed and I think I must have just reached that optimum point where alcohol makes you play better, just before the inevitable deterioration and decline set in.

When I got to the table for my first shot in the final frame, following my partner sinking two balls on his turn, I sunk five consecutive balls – definitely not a feat I could achieve whilst sober. This really caught the eye of my Indian friends who seemed by this time to think I was some sort of professional. They kept trying to distract me by going on about banking, but it didn't mean anything to me and I decided to ignore them. I was totally focused on lining up the black to finish off the rout and I wasn't going to let them put me off. Down went the black with a satisfying 'plop' and I went to shake my partner's hand with a smile on my face. Unfortunately his face did not register the same degree of pleasure as mine and he started garbling away again about something to do with 'banking'.

Pifas, who can speak Spanish, came across to see what was happening and after a little discussion looked at me and explained as kindly as he could that the house rules, certainly as played by my new companions, dictate that any match-winning shot has to be played off a cushion and this is known as 'banking'. Well, I've never heard such garbage in my life, but apparently rules are rules, so the win went to our opponents for a foul shot. I never like losing, but looking on the positive side we were all so merry by now that it just turned into a bit of a laugh.

The next thing I knew the oldest of the three guys was lying on the pool table wanting me to take his picture, which I duly did and that led to a round of drunken photographs which also involved us all getting behind the bar and having our pictures taken with Vicky, the lady behind the bar, who by this time was much more relaxed. We tried to get the truth out of Vicky about the history of the bar and whether it had been there before Marty wrote the song, but our efforts proved fruitless as she wasn't the owner and her knowledge was a bit sketchy. Behind the bar there was a newspaper article about the connection, but I don't think this was conclusive either. Anyway it didn't seem to matter as the bar was great, we had Marty Robbins music all night, pictures of Marty adorned the walls and the beer and the company were more than enough to keep me happy.

Before we left, I went to the Gents and was intrigued to see a machine on the wall dispensing 'Horny Goat Weed'. I hadn't come across this before and, of course, wouldn't have been interested if I had (no need, you'll appreciate). My curiosity was aroused, that's all I wanted arousing, and I undertook to carry out some research. It didn't surprise me to find out that the origin of this concoction is China. Apparently, hundreds of years ago a Chinese goatherd noticed incessant sexual behaviour in his animals and he established that when they ate certain weeds they became extremely randy. One thing led to another and now it was on sale here in Rosa's Cantina in deepest Texas. If you're interested in the scientific side of things you will want to know that it works by inhibiting an enzyme which stops neurotransmission at cholinergic synapses and neuromuscular junctions. Or something like that.

At 11 o'clock Pifas and I set off for home. On arrival back in town Pifas dropped me off at the hotel and when I went inside I tracked down the sound of music and was more than pleasantly surprised to find a live band playing and bar meals still being served in the ornate lounge bar underneath the dome. So, I finished the night off perfectly in posh surroundings eating enchilladas and, yes, another beer just to enhance the meal and cool down my tongue. A sound ending to an ultra-sound night.

THE NEXT DAY, AFTER clearing my head with numerous cups of coffee, I worked out I had time for a little research before making my way to the airport. The reason the airport comes into the equation is because the next destination was nearly 1,000 miles away. There was no way I could afford to lose two days out of my schedule by spending them on the Greyhound bus, so I had decided, exceptionally, to fly. The destination was Galveston, 900 miles away to the south-east, yet still in Texas. Almost the equivalent of John O'Groats to Lands End and all in one State! As they say, 'everything's big in Texas', including hangovers as I found out to my expense.

My enquiries about Juárez revealed some interesting statistics – I was surprised to learn, for instance, that it has a population in excess of 1.3 million, something I would never have guessed from my admittedly limited excursion across the Rio Grande, and it is a huge manufacturing centre, standing comparison with most major USA industrial cities (one reason being that it is obviously well-located to take advantage of the American market, whilst using cheap Mexican labour). The town is mentioned in numerous songs by artists such as Johnny Cash, Bob Dylan and Tori Amos and has been used as a location for many films including multiple Oscar-winning *Brokeback Mountain* and *The Day after Tomorrow.*

Sadly, it is infamous as the place where as many as 400 women have disappeared since 1993 in 'sexual homicides'. This typically involves the abduction and rape of young girls from other parts of Mexico who have come to work in the factories (maquiladoras) of Juárez and whose bodies are then dumped in a ditch. This has earned Juárez the title of 'Capital of Murdered Women' and the scandal has become something of a cause célèbre. The story is related in the film *Bordertown* featuring Jennifer Lopez, Antonio Banderas and Martin Sheen and is the subject of a Tori Amos song *Juárez* on her album To Venus and Back.

There is a suggestion that the killers will never be found and that there are links to high ranking officials and police. How true this is I do not know, but let's just say if you're reading this and you are a female backpacker you might want to think twice about crossing the Rio Grande.

Following my promise to educate myself on the Mexican Revolution, which was at this point just a cactus in my rather arid desert of knowledge, I headed for the library and spent an hour or two poring through books, leaflets and reference guides. I now know the revolution began in 1910, but when it ended is in dispute as the political situation around this time was so confusing. The official end was 1917, with the signing of the Constitution, but fighting went on well into the 1920s.

Trying to make sense of this conflict with its constantly changing alliances is extremely difficult, but, in a nutshell, the revolution was caused by the president Porfirio Díaz deciding his nation was 'not ready for democracy'. Like many other well-meaning dictators he had his main political opponent, in this case Francisco Madero, arrested and jailed. On his release on bail, or escape, depending on whose story you believe, Madero instigated a call to arms and the revolution had begun.

What followed was no little local bunfight, but a conflict which tragically resulted in the deaths of around 1 million people from a population of just 15 million. During the course of the conflict (not called a civil war so as not to be confused with the Mexican Civil War of the 1850s) there was intrigue and betrayal on a mind-boggling scale. No sooner did one leader come to power than his supporters turned against him, different alliances were made, and the assassination of key figures was the accepted norm.

Add to this the fact that the big powers were sniffing around as usual. The US changed their support to whichever side at the time would be best for American business interests in Mexico, and Germany supported whoever would cause the US most problems as they wanted to distract them from getting involved in that other little dispute of the time over in Europe.

Regrettably, most of the senior protagonists in the conflict were murdered, despite usually having good intentions. Díaz had achieved real progress in industry and modernisation, but at the expense of human rights and liberal reforms. Crucially, he presided over a policy which allowed foreign investors to take the land belonging to the peasants who were then exploited and effectively subjected to working as slaves. This was a key factor in the rise of Madero and his more famous allies, Pancho Villa in the north and Emiliano Zapata in the south.

The town of Juárez was a central location in all of this with Pancho Villa launching attacks at various stages of the war. His successful assault with his compatriot Pascual Orozco in May 1911 resulted in the resignation of Díaz at the Treaty of Ciudad Juárez on 21 May, which led to Madero becoming President. Unfortunately, Madero was slow at effecting reforms and this caused Zapata and Orozco to defect and take sides against him. General Victoriano Huerta, who had previously been Maderos' Commander in Chief, staged a coup in 1913 and Madero was forced to resign (he was executed with vice president Suarez less than a week later). Huerta, who declared himself president, was in turn deposed and replaced by Venustiano Carranza, who eventually became the first official president of Mexico under the 1917 constitution. Carranza returned much of the land to the populace. Friction continued, however, and Carranza himself was assassinated in 1920, by which time he'd had Zapata murdered in 1919.

So, to recap on the fortunes of the leaders of this ghastly affair – Díaz died in exile in France in 1915, Madero was murdered along with his collaborator Jose Suarez in the Huerta coup. Huerta died in custody in El Paso in 1916. Carranza was assassinated in 1920 having had Zapata killed in 1919. Finally, Pancho Villa was murdered in 1923, riddled with bullets as he sat in his car. The murderers were never found.

The main heroes of the conflict were of course Zapata and Pancho Villa. Zapata, who is a national hero of Mexico, certainly had the interests of the peasants at heart, but it was argued whether he and his men were revolutionaries or bandits. His enemies branded him a 'womaniser, barbarian, terrorist and a bandit'. Some elements of the media nicknamed him the 'Attilla of the South'. Pancho Villa, who operated in the north, was similarly renowned for violence and was not averse to robbing trains, kidnapping bank employees and printing counterfeit money for his cause. Again he is regarded as a national hero. Whatever the merits of their actions they were certainly instrumental in the whole confusing struggle and the result was that the exploitation of the peasants was stopped. But at considerable cost.

As for Marty Robbins I would learn a lot more about him when I reached Nashville. But it was clear from what I had gleaned so far that he was a super-hero, and one who cared for his fans, before he died in 1982, aged 57, of complications following heart surgery. I felt privileged to have followed in his footsteps, even in such a small way.

El Paso

Out in the West Texas town of El Paso
I fell in love with a Mexican girl
Night-time would find me in Rosa's cantina
Music would play and Felina would whirl

Blacker than night were the eyes of Felina
Wicked and evil while casting a spell
My love was deep for this Mexican maiden
I was in love but in vain, I could tell

One night a wild young cowboy came in
Wild as the West Texas wind
Dashing and daring
A drink he was sharing
With wicked Felina
The girl that I loved

So in anger I
Challenged his right for the love of this maiden
Down went his hand for the gun that he wore
My challenge was answered in less than a heart-beat
The handsome young stranger lay dead on the floor

Just for a moment I stood there in silence
Shocked by the foul evil deed I had done
Many thoughts raced through my mind as I stood there
I had but one chance and that was to run

Out through the back door of Rosa's I ran
Out where the horses were tied
I caught a good one
It looked like it could run
Up on its back and away did I ride

Just as fast as I
Could from the West Texas town of El Paso
Out to the bad-lands of New Mexico

Back in El Paso my life would be worthless
Everything's gone in life; nothing is left
It's been so long since I've seen the young maiden
My love is stronger than my fear of death

I saddled up and away I did go
Riding alone in the dark
Maybe tomorrow
A bullet may find me
Tonight nothing's worse than this

Pain in my heart.
And at last here I

Am on the hill overlooking El Paso
I can see Rosa's cantina below
My love is strong and it pushes me onward
Down off the hill to Felina I go

Off to my right I see five mounted cowboys
Off to my left ride a dozen or more

Shouting and shooting I can't let them catch me
I have to make it to Rosa's back door

Something is dreadfully wrong for I feel
A deep burning pain in my side
Though I am trying
To stay in the saddle
I'm getting weary
Unable to ride

But my love for
Felina is strong and I rise where I've fallen
Though I am weary I can't stop to rest
I see the white puff of smoke from the rifle
I feel the bullet go deep in my chest

From out of nowhere Felina has found me
Kissing my cheek as she kneels by my side
Cradled by two loving arms that I'll die for
One little kiss and Felina, good-bye.

Words and music by Marty Robbins

Chapter Six

"Galveston, oh Galveston . . ."

'I STILL HEAR YOUR SEA WINDS BLOWIN...'.

I couldn't resist mouthing the famous words to myself as I left the wonderful Camino Real and headed off in the taxi to El Paso airport. The airport was a very pleasant experience, which you can't say about many air terminals. It is a low-rise art deco building quite in keeping with the architectural excellence of the town itself. In fact I have to say the airport was one of my favourite El Paso buildings. The entrance hall is a sort of oyster-shell shape with a curved turquoise roof, with the main terminal buildings going off to either side. There is a nice feeling of spaciousness and a relaxing atmosphere most unusual for airline travel.

I knew Galveston was going to be by the seaside. In fact, my enquiries had made me aware that it is actually an island, situated in the Gulf of Mexico, which had surprised me. It lies just off the southern tip of Texas and is connected to the mainland by a causeway some two to three miles long. Getting there was going to be a bit of a logistical nightmare as not only was it 900 miles from El Paso, but it meant I had to fly to Houston and then find my own way the extra 50 miles or so to Galveston. So I got the plane from El Paso and a couple of hours later (as opposed to 22 hours by Greyhound) I landed in Houston. The phrase "Houston, I have a problem" cropped up in my mind, but I quickly resolved the situation by hitching a ride aboard a mini-bus which was taking some cruise ship passengers to Galveston (the port of Galveston being a significant cruise terminal). On the bus I met two lovely ladies, Wendy and Caroline, who were on their way to a Caribbean cruise, but who seemed more interested in my project than their trip, which was nice. This was the first inkling I had that the concept of what I was doing would really capture the imagination of most people I would come across on the remainder of the trip and I was quite thrilled by this realisation.

After forty five minutes or so on the bus I became excited as I got my first glimpse of the sea – it was just like that feeling I used to get when I was a kid going on a trip to Whitley Bay or Tynemouth, but here the sun was actually shining. I could see the impressive causeway looming ahead and soon we were surrounded by water on all sides and across the bay I could see the impressive three pyramid skyline of Moody Gardens. The Gardens are, rather exaggeratedly perhaps, billed as one of the 'most exciting destinations in the world', 'visit the Rainforest Pyramid, the Aquarium Pyramid, the 4D Special FX Theater and so much more'. They are named after the Moody family, who I came to learn are integral to the history of the island through their financial empire which was based on cotton, banking, insurance and ranching.

Wendy and Caroline were heading to the Gardens complex to spend a night of opulence before two weeks of luxury on their cruise ship. My fate for the night was likely to be considerably less spectacular. At least with this not being a Greyhound bus I was less likely to be dropped off in a dodgy neighbourhood and in fact I had some say in where to alight.

I suggested to the driver that he drop me somewhere where there might be hotels in the $50-$60 bracket, perhaps with some non fast-food restaurants in the vicinity, which was probably an impossible mission for him. I'm sure I could sense the sympathy filtering out from the seats in front where the two ladies were looking forward to their fillet steaks and palatial surroundings. Perhaps they would invite me over for a meal. But I would have declined, I wouldn't want to embarrass such pleasant folk.

The driver, on the journey down, had educated us with facts about Galveston, ensuring we were more than well aware of the disaster of 1900 which decimated the town and killed at least 6,000 people – probably nearer 10,000 "nobody will ever know". This disaster was apparently the making of Houston as that was a far more safe and secure location for commerce with it being fifty miles inland. I would be well briefed on the 1900 situation by the time I left Galveston two days later.

So off the bus I hopped, bidding "Bon Voyage" to my friends, and walked into the 'Best Quality Suites' or something like that. I wasn't going to mess around looking for anywhere else as I wanted to be settled in and showered before seeking sustenance. The accommodation was basic but civilised enough, so I was quite happy. What I wasn't so happy about was the fact that I hadn't a clue where I was on the island or whether it was in the kind of area I wanted to be in.

Let me give you a feel for Galveston island. It is thirty miles long by two and a half miles wide. The southern side of the island faces the Gulf of Mexico, whilst the north faces back towards the mainland and two bays, West Bay and Galveston Bay. The south side is the resort side and consists of beaches and a huge sea wall. The north side is where the port lies and to the east of the port is Pelican Island, which, like the mainland, is connected by a causeway. Protruding into Galveston Island from the west is Offatts Bayou, which is in effect an offshoot of West Bay.

I quickly established from the free map available in reception that the main downtown area including the historic Strand was on the port side. But here I was, stranded on the other side of the island. I can only assume that the bus driver felt I had a better chance of a cheap hotel on this side. You can't have it all ways it seems and it boils down to a choice between decent restaurants and a drink, but with expensive hotels, or, on the other hand, fast food restaurants with soft drinks and cheap hotels. I would have the best of both worlds I decided, after all it was Friday night and I never go without a drink on a Friday night to usher in the weekend. I would get out for a little exploration and find somewhere suitable to sit and have a drink and think about my regular Friday drinking pals back home. I wondered for a moment whether I might call them from my mobile phone to give them an update, but as it would be around three in the morning I doubt whether it would have been appreciated.

Setting off for a walk around 5.30pm I felt quite safe in the daylight and the pleasant evening sun. I headed down to the sea-front to have a look at the ocean and turned right to see what I would find. It was pleasant to see the sea, but I needed to eat and there didn't seem to be much around apart from fast food, so I turned right again, walking away from the front. I found myself in an area that was sparsely populated, with predominantly commercial buildings and a few residential properties. I kept walking, thinking that I would eventually come across the Strand if I didn't find anything in the immediate vicinity. After about 45 minutes I realised that the map I was using was not very reliable in terms of scale and perhaps my mission for food and drink was not going to be as easy as I had at first thought. I was also getting a little concerned that I was getting off the beaten track and that it was now twilight.

I passed a small supermarket on my right hand side and observed a youth walking towards me from the opposite direction. Just as we were about to pass I was disturbed to see, lying on the ground, a knife with a wooden handle and a blade about four inches long. "What should I do?" I thought, I must have looked decidedly touristy in my shorts and T-shirt and there was no-one else around apart from this guy now only about 10 yards away. Do I pick it up and risk arrest for carrying an offensive weapon (arrest in the States I did not feel to be an attractive proposition) or do I risk the chance of the other guy picking it up with who knows what consequences? In the end I decided to 'not notice it' and to increase my pace of walking by a considerable percentage. The moment passed without mishap, but it served as a reminder that I was extremely vulnerable and would need to watch my step over the coming weeks.

My immediate concern at this point was "where the hell am I?" I had now lost my bearings and my map reading skills had gone out of the window given the scanty nature of the map in the free *Galveston Official Pocket Guide*. Half an hour later and another right turn and I recognised that I was heading towards the downtown area as intended, but, judging by the map, I was only about half-way there. And now it was dark, and even fewer people around.

I decided to abandon my plans and to concentrate on staying safe and getting back to the area of my hotel, even if it meant fast food and soft drink. I realised that another right turn would complete the square and I would again be heading for the sea-front, all this after about six miles of walking. Across the street I saw a washerette and thought it would be wise to check my bearings, so I crossed over and walked in, looking for the friendliest face I could find. The chap I spoke to, in the process of sorting his laundry, gave me some directions, but he clearly thought I was in a car. When I told him I was walking he could only offer "You're kidding me!" – words which I would hear more than once over the coming days and weeks.

It was about 8.30pm by the time I came across some buildings I recognised. I was very relieved at this but somewhat cheesed off about the choice of Jack in the Box, Quisetto Sub and McDonald's restaurants I was faced with. Refusing to accept defeat in my quest for a Friday night drink, I used all my detective acumen (which is quite well developed in the context of divining alcohol) and eventually managed to find a Mexican restaurant, although it did mean walking another one and a half mile round trip. Following my earlier scare I tried to stay in well lit areas whenever possible, though this did mean risking my neck at times crossing extremely wide and busy roads. I couldn't figure out where all the traffic was going as there didn't seem to be any logical destination or attraction and it was a bit late for commuter traffic. I later learned it was a Bank Holiday weekend, with the Monday being Labor Day, so there were apparently a lot of visitors descending on town for the weekend. It turns out I did well to get a hotel and if I had arrived a bit later I could well have been stranded.

Knowing that I had nothing to read whilst I sat having a meal I picked up a free copy of the *The Police News*, Gulf Coast edition, to while away the time. This was a real eye-opener and made me realise that I had been a bit stupid wandering around the streets for three hours. To start with, the front page headlines were pretty offputting, outlining the details of two unprovoked multiple murders. But what really intrigued me were the mugshots entitled 'Rogues Gallery' in an almost fun-sounding way. There were quite a few pages of pictures and profiles of people who were wanted by the law in this and neighbouring counties. There was a total of 30 felons mentioned in the 'Fugitives' section and similarly 30 in the 'Sex Offenders' section. The latter, it went to pains to point out, were not wanted by the law, but the pictures were published for 'community awareness', listing also the offence and 'level of risk', mostly 'high' I noticed.

The contrast between this approach and the one back home couldn't be more stark, I thought, recalling a recent case in the UK where thugs who terrorised a neighbourhood were able to obtain taxpayers' money to sue the local council and the police for publishing their photographs in leaflets aimed at enforcing ASBOs. The case, which was based on an abuse of human rights, was fortunately thrown out by the High Court, but not before a quarter of a million pounds was spent on the legal costs of the imbeciles involved. The Texas approach goes to the other extreme.

The 'Fugitive' section of the paper made interesting reading and I was thankful that I was sitting in the relative safety of the Tortuga Mexican restaurant. Let me give you a flavour:

'Pena, Bobby Joe, white male, 165 pounds, tattoos both legs, burglary, habitation' (the mind boggles). 'Latoya Jackson' (this name seemed familiar, I thought, but I could see from the photograph this was not one of the musical Jackson clan, but a lady whose distinguishing features were described as 'mole on lip, tattoo right arm and pierced nose). Her LKA [Last Known Address] was simply described as Galveston, and she was wanted for Deadly Conduct. I would have been interested in more detail on that last offence, but at least I had enough information to recognise this particular beauty if she tried to chat me up.

Reading on, I came to the 'Texas Executions' section. I had not expected this and was taken aback at the extent of it bearing in mind this was a monthly publication and that these were just the executions for September. Five executions were 'advertised' for the month, each case attracting its own subsection with an account of the crime and a photograph of the perpetrator superimposed over the picture of a bed with straps. Seeing the photographs of the condemned, all male, 3 black, 2 white, did make me inclined to feel sorry for them. The oldest was 48 and the youngest 28. It was a bit sobering to look at the pictures of all five due to die, but having read the heinous and callous crimes they had perpetrated I wasn't going to feel any sympathy for them. 'Injected the three victims with a household cleaner, Tilex, before stabbing them to death'.'All three victims were beaten with a hammer and their throats slit' and so on. It was the casual way these executions were slipped into pages 18 and 19 amid adverts for Di Bella's Italian restaurant ('friendliest service in Galveston County') and 'Nobody sells more Fords than Helfman Ford' that surprised me.

I wondered if the advert on the left hand side of the page for 'West End Electric' might have been specially commissioned for this page, but on further investigation I discovered that the favoured method of execution in Texas is in fact by lethal injection rather than the electric chair. This has actually led, since my visit, to the indefinite suspension of all executions in the State due to controversy over whether lethal injection is a 'cruel and unusual punishment'. I would have thought it would be less painful than frying in the electric chair, but I'm not really in a position to make a judgement.

In my subsequent research I found that the Texas Department of Correctional Justice pride themselves on their website which has a 'Death Row Home Page'. Wow, what entertainment – you can even see what the recently deceased had for their last meal! Now wouldn't that provide an advertising opportunity for any company who sees their product being mentioned? What a marketing opportunity – it could only happen in America.

Among other proud announcements on the website is the fact that death by lethal injection takes on average seven minutes and costs $86.08 for the drugs, which I thought seemed quite a bargain. I also noted that the average time held on death row before execution is 10.26 years – that's what I call keeping someone in suspense. Perhaps the most interesting fact, though, is that the daddy of all Texas State Governors in respect of enforcing the death penalty turns out to be none other than one George W Bush, who presided over 52 executions in his five years as Governor. He was not known for his clemency and was denigrated on one occasion for apparently mocking one born again Christian lady before her judgement day. Bush became known as the The Biggest Serial Killer in Texas or alternatively as the 'Texecutioner'. Interestingly, some of the pre–presidential criticism directed at him because of his stance on the death penalty suggested that he 'only knows one way of how to do something – maximum force and violence' and that the old saying 'a hammer only knows how to do one thing' might be a way to describe his approach to things. I leave it to you to decide whether his Presidential record reflects those testimonials.

It is estimated that on average 7% of people found guilty of murder in the US are in fact innocent. If this average applies to Texas then George W will have presided over the execution of four innocent people. That's a statistic worth thinking about.

The Police News seemed a weird mixture of the serious and the light-hearted. For example, on the page before the executions I found cartoons and amusing police anecdotes. On page ten I found pictures of two contrite looking ladies who had apparently been 'plying their trade' in the Sweet Apple Club in Galveston. Kum Suk Fussell was bailed in the sum of $129,000 for being a 'very bad girl', but Sun Jex just $30,000 for being a 'bad girl, but only $30,000 worth'.

ON SATURDAY MORNING I arose somewhat jaded and, in the absence of a restaurant or breakfast room, settled down in the reception area to replenish myself with quantities of coffee and a complimentary pastry whose wrapping proudly declared that it was made by the wonderfully named Otis Spunkmeyer.

Unfortunately, the chap on reception, Waldo, had me as a captive audience, which at first I didn't mind too much as I was always looking to speak to people in order to pick up bits and pieces of information. This guy was a bit weird, though. He was very friendly, but was a bit of a bible puncher as I found out to my cost the next day. Today, however, he was interested in the service being held for Princess Diana or should I say Diana, Princess of Wales? It is amazing how people in the

States are still fascinated by our royalty – and not just Diana, though she clearly is still a key figure. 'How well do you know the Queen?' is a not uncommon question on declaring British nationality, I found. Waldo was well clued up on the Diana case and I found myself being drawn into a discussion on whether she was murdered by the establishment.

I tried to change the subject and he told me that he is learning Spanish, Russian and French, all at the same time. When I asked him the motive for this he volunteered that it was to stop senility. His means of tuition is apparently to hire videos where he can pick up on the language, the latest examples being *The Hunt For Red October* for Russian and some James Bond film for French. Somehow, the conversation then changed to his wife's legs. "I married her for her legs," he declared. When I asked if she still had nice legs he replied that he didn't know as he was now divorced!

The subject then turned to God, who, he said, had put us here to solve problems, but without any proper training. He then expressed some annoyance that God has had 2,000 years of vacation and said "it's high time he showed his face". Trying to extricate myself from this worsening conversation I looked in the direction of the flat screen TV on the wall and watched the weather forecast. It appeared as if Tropical Storm Felix was on my heels and he/she/it was quite likely to turn into a hurricane. The bulletin added that we were approaching the peak of the hurricane season, which surprised me as my enquiries before I left the UK indicated that it should have been earlier in the year. Knowing that even the mildest hurricane on the five point Saffir-Simpson scale carried sustained winds of 74-95 mph, I was not keen to experience Felix in person, but at least it diverted conversation from God's holiday plans.

On finishing my coffee I decided to head off towards the Strand which I hadn't been able to get to the previous night. I set off in the direction of the Tourist Office, which I had spotted on the map. It was in an unlikely place, not far from the washerette I had come across the previous evening, the assumption being presumably that all tourists have cars. The office was staffed by two youngsters, one boy and one girl, and they were both very pleasant. Unfortunately, they didn't know much. Didn't know Glen Campbell and hadn't heard his song about their town. After a pleasant but fruitless discussion they told me the Strand was two to two-and-a-half miles' walking distance; it would be the same distance by car I guess, but that's being pedantic.

I set off and after two-and-a-half miles it was clear I was still nowhere near. I spied a Mexican bakery across the main road and thought I would take a well-earned break. In I went for yet another coffee and pastry. The coffee was cold, the pastry was dry and the toilets were stinking. There again, the owners probably didn't think much of me either as my hairy legs were covered in burrs from the long grass I had been forced to walk through to avoid getting mown down by traffic on the dual carriageway, my white T shirt was covered in green bird shit and I was hot and sweaty as it was midday and the temperature was somewhere in the 90s.

An hour or so later I found the Strand and proceeded to scout for potential restaurants for the evening. Down by the port I noticed that a cinema was advertising two half-hour films, one about the Great Storm and the other about the famous pirate Jean Lafitte, who occupied Galveston for three years in the nineteenth century.

I decided these would be required viewing for the evening, prior to eating at the Mediterranean Café which I had spotted. The Strand is adjacent to Galveston's port, which used to have over 50 piers in the heyday of cotton, and had been largely untouched by the Great Storm. I could see why it was the central attraction on the island with its Victorian buildings and sidewalks and I looked forward to visiting in the evening. In the meantime I decided to head back to the seafront, thus completing a circular tour, and to then get the Treasure Island Tour Train, one of those little fun trains that runs on the road and rattles along through the traffic. A bit of a touristy thing to do, but it would ensure that I hadn't missed anything of note on my foot tour.

The train driver was, as he put it, a "Bald-headed, redneck Mexican", "the best tour guide in Texas" or so he reckoned. The only place he had hair was on his chin which was adorned by two little plaits with beads dangling from them. Complete with studded leather jacket, he looked more like a Hells Angel than a toy train driver. The historical tour started by him pointing out "on the right hand side you'll see a Ben and Jerry's", which I thought an inauspicious start, but the trip wasn't bad in the end. I gleaned all I wanted to know, including the fact that the UTMB (University of Texas Medical Branch), a huge campus with 13,000 employees, houses "every bug known to man". According to our guide, the facility is located on Galveston because the island lends itself to effective quarantine and the people 'on base' would be considered expendable. But that's tour guides for you. I got off the train and ended up walking again, this time back to the hotel along the sea front. It was now about 5pm and I estimated that I had walked 14–16 miles over the course of the day.

The sea front in Galveston is dominated by the huge sea wall, the island's defence against the fury of the Gulf storms. It forms a pleasant ten mile promenade representing easy walking atop the long beaches which are regularly punctuated with piers. Some of these piers are simple fishing piers, but some have more substance. On one of these stands a large hotel building, The Flagship, which looks as if it has been plucked out of some English sixties shopping centre. It is a bizarre sight, a concrete rectangular red and white building perched on a 1,000 foot long pier, and to be honest I found it a bit of an incongruous sight. I am sure it is nicer than it looks and I have to agree it's an unusual advantage to be able to cast your rod out of the window whilst having your breakfast or, even better, fish for your breakfast which I have to admit is a bit of a unique feature for a hotel.

Located on one of the wooden piers is the Balinese Room, which was an infamous club during the post-World War II era when it was run by Sam and Rosario Maceo, Sicilian immigrant barbers turned bootleggers who built up an empire in Galveston. During the years between the two world wars, Galveston had become known as the sin city of the gulf, exploiting prohibition laws by offering illegal drinks and betting in nightclubs and saloons. This was coupled with extensive prostitution and many islanders took pride in the unofficial title of Free State of Galveston.

In the '40s and '50s, The Balinese hosted big stars like Sinatra, Bob Hope and Jack Benny, long before Las Vegas, and for many years the club resisted attempts to shut down its illegal activities. The casino had been situated at the end of the pier, a long way from the on-shore entrance which gave it an advantage when the Texas Rangers tried to raid it. When the Rangers arrived a buzzer would sound and this was the signal for chips, cards and roulette wheels to be hidden in secret compartments in the walls. Tables would be set with tablecloths and the band would play. It is said that the place was raided on 64 consecutive nights without result. Perhaps the best line of defence, though, was the fact that Frank Biaggne had a long reign as Sheriff between 1933 and 1957 and he refused to raid the joint as it was a private club and he was not a member! Seems like a reasonable policy to me, particularly when it's being run by a couple of Sicilians.

The good times ended on 30 May 1957 when new sheriff Paul Hopkins inserted two detectives disguised as gamblers and when the next raid was made employees were prevented from hiding the evidence. Everything was confiscated and destroyed. The building regrettably went into disrepair and Hurricane Rita exacerbated the damage in 1961. The club is the subject of a song by ZZ Top on their *Fandango* album where the chorus includes the lyrics 'and everybody knows it was hard to leave, and everyone knows it was down at the Balinese'.

In recent years a project has succeeded in restoring the pier and it is now occupied by businesses such as gift shops and other tourist attractions. The showroom has been restored to its former glory and is now a restaurant and night club – a fitting resurrection for a club where, legend has it, the famous Margarita drink was invented when celebrity bartender Santos Cruz mixed a new drink for singer Peggy (Margaret) Lee in 1948. He named it Margarita after the Spanish version of her name and thus laid claim, among many others, to the naming of the tequila and cointreau concoction.

I TOOK A TAXI, around 6.45pm, to the Strand. Paul, the taxi driver, lost no time in telling me about the dark side of Galveston, one which certainly hadn't been apparent during the day. It seems there is a significant ghetto area and crack cocaine is a big problem in the city. I had never really considered the dangers of being a taxi driver, but when he mentioned it I could see that it could be pretty dicey. He explained that he comes across criminals quite a lot in his trade, often having to pick prisoners up from the county jail when they have finished their term. A dodgy business I would imagine and he told me he sometimes drives straight past when he sees them, relying on his judgement to decide whether it is a safe bet or not. On the other hand he has been known to take released prisoners for a meal on the way home, on the promise they would pay him back when they get there. His ambition is to write a book and when I said Robert de Niro has already done the taxi driver bit he replied rather sharply "You talkin' to me?" Well I think he did, or was it just my imagination? Seriously, he informed me that this time the taxi driver will be the hero without executing anyone. Relieved at this I wished him luck and said I'd watch for his book.

Paul dropped me at the Pier 21 Theater just in time for the last double show of the evening, *Great Storm* at 7pm and *The Pirate Island of Jean Lafitte* at 7.30pm. The theatre is part of the Great Storm Museum and the young usherette showed me into the cinema section and advised me the show would start in five minutes. To my surprise I found I was the only person in attendance. When the lights went down I had my first experience of what it's like to be alone in a darkened cinema. Pretty scary I can tell you, particularly in a strange place. What was even scarier was the prospect of just one other person coming in to join me. Now in a town with a crack problem and in a country with more than their share of weirdos that wasn't an exciting possibility.

To understand the impact of the Great Storm it is necessary to reflect on what Galveston was like before it hit. Prior to the hurricane, Galveston was one of the major towns in Texas. In fact, in 1870, it was the largest city in Texas, with a population of 14,000 people. By 1900 it had slipped to fourth, this was not due to a decline in Galveston's fortunes, but to the growth of cites like Dallas which had acquired transcontinental rail connections and extensive manufacturing capacity. Galveston's strength lay in its position on the natural harbour of Galveston Bay, making it the centre of trade in Texas and one of the largest cotton ports in the country. All that changed, however, on 8 September 1900, thanks to an event that still ranks as the United States' worst natural disaster. Worse than Hurricane Katrina or the San Francisco earthquake. No-one knows how many died but, as the bus driver had advised me on the way down from Houston, best estimates are 6,000 to 10,000, a considerable figure from a population of 40,000 at that time.

In the early morning of 8 September a high surf had indicated there might be some problems to come. By noon, low-lying areas were becoming swamped and the winds had increased. At 4pm a 16 foot storm surge hit the exposed coast and the winds were in excess of 120 miles per hour. The tidal surge swept the city from its Gulf Coast in the south to the Bay in the north, levelling practically everything in its path. Wooden buildings were swept off their foundations and smashed to pulp by the waves. Thousands of residents were drowned, some were crushed, and 85 passengers died on a stranded train. Among the dead were 90 children and 10 nuns from St Mary's Orphanage, many of them roped together for 'safety'. In the aftermath, corpses were piled onto carts for burial at sea, but unfortunately many were washed back in. Funeral pyres were set up and bodies burned for weeks after the storm, with men being forced at bayonet point to burn the washed up bodies as the stench was overpowering and their own families were among the victims.

Tragic as this event was it was hardly unforeseen. In 1858 *Braman's Information About Texas* declared: 'Within the last two or three years, people have begun to think that the islands and peninsulars along the Texas and Louisiana

Coast are unsafe for human abiding places. And Galveston Island is but a waif of the ocean, liable at any moment of being engulfed by the self-same power that gave it form.' As predictions go that's a pretty relevant one. In addition, 14 years earlier another area in the gulf, Matagorda Bay, had been hit for the second time in 12 years, destroying the town of Indianola which would later be abandoned, despite at one time being second only to Galveston in terms of Texan ports. These warnings were not heeded and the Galveston community did little to protect their city.

After the disaster, however, residents and officials decided in a matter of weeks that they would rebuild the town in the knowledge that this was the only deep water port in Texas. With a fiercely positive spirit, residents signalled their determination by voting to issue bonds to build a massive defensive seawall. There followed a building plan which not only included construction of a seven mile, 17 foot high sea wall, but also the amazing concept of raising the island, and parts of the city. Mud was dredged from the Gulf of Mexico and used to raise the level of the city by up to17 feet and more than 2,000 buildings which remained intact were also jacked up in a tremendous feat of engineering over the next 10 years.

In 1915 there was a similar storm but, thanks to the new protection, only a small number of casualties. In 1961 the city was hit by Hurricane Carla and whilst the sea wall did its job, tornadoes went over the wall and devastated some areas of the city. However, there were again only a few deaths and a full scale disaster was averted. Without the sea wall there would no doubt have been thousands of casualties.

Sadly, on the commercial front, over the years following the Great Storm, more and more business gravitated north to Houston, which offered more protection and was in the throes of an oil boom. In 1914, completion of the 56 mile Houston Ship Canal, connecting the port to the Gulf of Mexico, sounded the death knell for Galveston as the premier Texan port.

I watched *Great Storm* in splendid isolation and then the lights went up before the next show began. I was pleased to be joined at this point by a family group, so at least I knew now that if Waldo Weirdo decided to come in and target me I was not on my own. The credits rolled for the next feature *The Pirate Island of Jean Lafitte*. I recognised the name from somewhere. I had a vague recollection of him as a great American patriot, but I couldn't remember what he had done to earn his exalted status. It was no doubt something to do with defeating the British.

I learnt from the film that Lafitte was a privateer who arrived on the island in 1817, making it his base and naming it Campeche (Campeachy). In case you're wondering what a privateer is let me explain that it's effectively a pirate with a licence. Well, that's a simplistic interpretation, officially it means a 'privately owned armed ship holding a government commission and authorised for use in war'. In the case of Lafitte the distinction was somewhat blurred. He had a reputation for plundering ships after capture, but the US authorities turned a blind eye to this as he helped them in the 'War of 1812' (fought between 1812-1815) against Great Britain, particularly at the Battle of New Orleans in 1815 when Andrew Jackson defeated the British forces.

Lafitte was reputed to be a friend of some very famous people including Napoleon Bonaparte and allegedly tried to help Bonaparte escape from exile. This plan apparently collapsed when Napoleon failed to make the rendezvous point.

Though it is disputed in some quarters, it is suggested that the US authorities lost patience with Lafitte in 1821 when one of his captains attacked and plundered an American ship. He was then run out of 'Campeachy', agreeing to leave without a fight. Folklore has it that he left a huge amount of treasure buried under Campeachy and that is why the island is sometimes referred to as 'Treasure Island'. What happened to him after leaving Campeachy is the subject of much debate, but Lafitte's fortunes certainly took a downturn after leaving the island. It is generally thought that after setting up a low key base on Mugeres Island, off Yucatan on the Mexican Gulf Coast, he died of fever in the Indian village of Teljas, on the mainland, at the age of 47.

History recounts a man of many contradictions and much controversy but, whatever the truth, the legend lives on. In 1958 Cecil B De Mille made a film *The Buccaneer* in which Yul Brynner plays Lafitte, there is a Jean Lafitte National Park and Reserve in Louisiana and a there is a city named after him near New Orleans. Even Lord Byron wrote about him: "He left a Corsair's name to other times, linked one virtue to a thousand crimes".

Although one of his nicknames was the 'Gentleman Pirate of New Orleans', he was definitely into considerable wheeler-dealing and even got involved in a scam with the famous frontiersman Jim Bowie to get around the slave trading laws at the time. This included Lafitte selling slaves cheaply to Bowie, who would then receive a fee from the authorities for 'recovered' slaves.

So I left the cinema well clued up and set off to find the restaurant I had spotted earlier in the day. This turned out to be very pleasant, even if it was a lonely way to spend a Saturday evening. I had a healthy feeling of achievement having walked so many miles and seen so much of the island in one day and had also learned how the island got its current name. In 1785 the Texas coast was being charted by a Spaniard called José de Evia and he named the entire bay Galveston as a mark of respect for his boss Bernardo de Galvez, Viceroy of Mexico, who was a Spanish colonial governor and general. The name was later extended to the island, but unfortunately for Bernardo he died the following year having never set foot on the territory named in his honour.

Galveston is no stranger to conflict and played its part in both the Texas Revolution and the Civil War. During the Texas Revolution the island served as the main port for the Texas Navy and was briefly the capital and last point of retreat of the Texan Republic which was fighting for independence from Mexico.

In the American Civil War, the Battle of Galveston was fought on New Year's Day 1863 when Confederate forces expelled Union troops from the city. The previous autumn the Union forces had more or less walked into Galveston and demanded surrender from a pretty much defenceless population. But when General John B Magruder became Confederate Commander of Texas his first priority was the recapture of Galveston. On 1 January he sent a groundforce across the railroad bridge, but they met with limited success. The real battle was in Galveston Harbour where, because of their six ships against the Confederates' two, Union victory looked certain. The Confederates had converted two river steamers, the Bayou City and the Neptune, using bales of cotton as protection against enemy fire. These became known as the 'Confederate Cottonclads'. The Neptune was quickly sunk whilst trying to ram the Union ship Harriet Lane. That left the Bayou City outnumbered six to one. The Bayou managed to hit the Harriet Lane and the Confederates boarded, overpowering the crew. At this point the Union flagship Westfield had become grounded in shallow water. During a three hour truce the Union Commander William B Renshaw decided it would be best to destroy the Westfield rather than let it be captured and he boarded to lay some explosives. These did not ignite and he went back for another go. Unfortunately for him (and proving the point that you should never return to a lit firework) the explosives then went off causing an explosion that rocked the whole harbour, killing Renshaw and thirteen of his men in the process. This was the turning point of the battle and the rest of the Union fleet sailed out of the harbour without any further fighting taking place. After this famous victory Galveston remained in Confederate hands for the rest of the war.

Embarking on a post-dinner walk, I strolled down the Strand and looked at my watch. It was 9.30pm on a Saturday night and the place was very quiet, definitely not like the equivalent road in London. But it was pleasant and it was a nice evening. Having said I was in Texas I have to concede that it did have a very Victorian feel to it, including the presence of horse drawn carriages and an old trolley transportation system. As this was on the far end of the island from the Gulf Coast many of the buildings were spared the 1900 hurricane and the solid Victorian historic buildings survived intact.

I was interested to see references to 'Dickens on the Strand' and discovered that each November/December, in the first weekend after the hurricane season officially ends, a Dickens festival is held. Incredible as it may seem in deepest Texas you can 'see the streets lined with Victorian-clad Bobbies, Beefeaters, and Gentlemen and Ladies'. 'You will be taken back to the age of Charles Dickens when the British Empire was at the height of its power and glory,' promises the promotional literature.

The festival was first held in 1974 when many of the Victorian buildings were under threat of demolition. A group of local historians created the festival in order to develop a feel-good factor and, with the subsequent revival of interest, the buildings have now been restored. Not only can you see 'Her Royal Majesty Queen Victoria's Knighting Ceremony', but you can visit Trafalgar Square, Windsor Castle and Piccadilly, all on specially constructed stages. Or, if the fancy takes you, why not visit the West India Dock and take in the 'jaunty tunes from the concertina as old salts share their sea tales'. A bit corny, but well done to the Galveston Historical Foundation members who saved their architectural heritage through their efforts and indeed have succeeded in turning the festival into one of the '100 Most Fun Places to be in the World' according to one travel writer. That may be stretching things a bit, but it certainly is in the top 100 US festivals according to the esteemed American Bus Association.

WHILST IN THE MEDITERRANEAN Café I had asked the waiter whether any famous people had originated from Galveston and he surprised me by saying that Barry White, The Walrus of Love was a famous Galvestonian. I suppose that in itself is enough to give the town a romantic reputation. White, though, actually grew up in Los Angeles. He had a tough upbringing by all accounts, joining a teenage gang and getting jailed for four months at the age of seventeen for stealing $30,000 worth of Cadillac tyres and, impressively, four packets of extra safe condoms (he clearly had a thing about rubber). Music was Bazza's salvation and he credited his redemption to hearing Elvis singing *It's Now or Never* while serving his jail sentence.

Also from Galveston, Jack Johnson, The Galveston Giant, who became the first black Heavyweight boxing champion, was born in 1878. He turned professional in 1897, so I am not sure if he was around when the hurricane struck. He certainly was in Galveston in 1901 because an old pro called Joe Choynski came to town to coach him. The pair engaged in a fight and Johnson was knocked out in three rounds by the experienced man. They were then both arrested for 'engaging in an illegal contest', but Choynski continued to coach Johnson without harassment in jail.

The tribulations of Johnson, when he became a professional, give a good indication of social attitudes at the time. Firstly, Jim Jeffries the Heavyweight Champion refused to fight him as blacks were not deemed worthy to fight for such an auspicious title (though they could fight for the 'World Coloured Heavyweight Championship'). When Johnson finally got the chance to fight for the title, and beat Tommy Burns, the cameras stopped rolling just before the end so as not to show the white man getting beat.

In 1910 Jim Jeffries came out of retirement to show the world that the white man is better than the negro. Apparently the ringside band in Reno, Nevada played *All Coons Look Alike To Me* before the start of the fight. The promoters invited the all-white crowd to chant 'kill the nigger' which makes even Blazing Saddles look tame and would definitely cause a bit of a stir today. Johnson stopped Jeffries in the fifteenth round after knocking him down twice, the first time Jeffries had been on the floor in his career. This outcome sparked off riots all over the States as many whites felt humiliated by the result. In disturbances in many cities, police stopped attempted lynchings, beatings took place and at least 25 people died, mostly black. Some states subsequently banned the filming of Johnson's victories over white opponents. An interesting footnote to

Johnson's career is that when he lost the title in 1915 to Jess Willard he was knocked out in the 26th round of a 45 round contest! Those were the days when men were men.

Well, we now know about Galveston the place and, from previous chapters, about Glen Campbell the artist. But what do we know about the song that cemented his reputation in early 1969 after his other two monumental name place songs *Phoenix* (1967) and *Wichita Lineman* (1968)?

Galveston is clearly about someone at war, wanting to get home to his girl, wondering will she wait for him. He's also 'so afraid of dying'. Because of the reference to 'cannons' many people think it refers back to the Civil War. However, another school of thought is that it refers to Vietnam, as the war was in full flow at the time of its release. Also, it is reported that songwriter Jimmy Webb has made reference to Vietnam a number of times in interviews. As it is not unusual, even in modern times, for artillery to be referred to as cannon, the Vietnam explanation sounds good enough to me and I am happy to go along with this theory in the absence of Jimmy telling us any different. Why he chose Galveston can only be imagined, but I guess we'd be asking the same question about whatever town or city he decided to name the song after. My research did unearth an article which suggests that Jimmy was on a beach in Galveston when he wrote the song, but the same article proposes that the words refer to the Spanish-American War of 1898, which is at odds with my considered judgement. I find it difficult to digest that such a song could be written about a piddling little war, by American standards (it only lasted 109 days), when there are so many others to choose from. So, I'm sticking with Vietnam for the war and Galveston selected as the town simply because it has a nice ring to it and fits the melody rather neatly.

NEXT MORNING I PACKED my bag ready to move on and went to have some 'breakfast' at reception. Waldo was on duty again and he didn't waste the opportunity to take advantage of the fact that he had me as a captive audience again. I don't know whether it was because it was a Sunday or whether he had only been warming up the day before, but I got both barrels this morning. I can only describe his utterings as a diatribe and he started with something like "God said there's only one nation greater than the US and that's Great Britain". He was para-phrasing the Bible apparently. "When God comes he's gonna give India back to the British as they did such a great job there". He then berated me because "Europeans don't take religion seriously enough, but oughta." And supported this with the example "look at Pearl Harbour – alive one minute, dead the next".

In an attempt to lighten things up I mentioned that the coffee was nice but somehow he turned this into a reason to quote an entire Wordsworth poem, of religious content unfortunately. He apparently remembered this from his college days back in 1962, so I had to admire his memory capabilities. He then went on to produce quote after quote from the bible which had me finishing off my coffee a bit sooner than intended. I was relieved to make my escape, determined not to end up sitting on the bus next to anyone who wanted to talk. Today I would be happy to settle for a homicidal maniac who wanted to keep himself to himself.

Galveston

Galveston, oh Galveston
I still hear your sea winds blowin
I still see her dark eyes glowin'
She was twenty one when I left Galveston

Galveston, oh Galveston
I still hear your sea waves crashin
While I watch the cannons flashin'
I clean my gun and dream of Galveston

I still see her standing by the water
Standing there looking out to the sea
And is she waiting there for me
On the beach where we used to run?

Galveston, oh Galveston
I am so afraid of dyin'
Before I dry the tears she's cryin'
Before I watch your sea birds flying in the sun
At Galveston, At Galveston

Words and music by Jimmy Webb

Chapter Seven

"Sweet Baton Rouge . . ."

DURING MY LONG WALK AROUND Galveston the previous day, I had made it my business to find out the location of the Greyhound bus pick up point as I knew I had to be there well before 8.30 for the 9am bus. This effort was well rewarded because even the taxi driver who picked me up from the hotel wasn't able to find the place without my help. I had established that there was no such luxury as a bus station in Galveston and that a shop in the middle of nowhere was designated as the agent and surrogate bus terminal, although there seemed to be little to advertise this fact. Having worked this out, and located the premises, I had bought a Greyhound ticket to Baton Rouge, via Houston.

The bus arrived approximately 45 minutes late, which wasn't a big deal as it simply meant I had less time to hang around at Houston for the transfer. Chaos ensued when we arrived as there were too many passengers for one bus and this was only resolved by getting two buses to set off for Baton Rouge simultaneously – full marks to Greyhound for this. Unfortunately, one of the buses (not mine) broke down on the way and we then had great fun trying to get two bus loads on to one, which, of course, didn't work. We took on some of the evacuees, but left others on the stranded bus to await rescue.

WHEN WE ARRIVED AT BATON ROUGE it was 5.45pm and I had been travelling for ten hours, so I got a room at Days Inn and headed off to Shoney's restaurant, which looked to be the best bet in the immediate locality. My waiter, Everitt, asked where I was from. When I replied "England" he was extremely chuffed.

"Really, that's amazing, I'm reading *The Count of Monte Cristo* at the moment".

Make of that what you will, but I could swear Alexandre Dumas was a Frenchman and the story was set in the Mediterranean.

I soon realised that I was the only customer in Shoney's. It was 7pm on a Sunday night, the room was cold and empty, and when Everitt advised me they didn't sell beer that was the last straw, so I made my exit with apologies. I managed to find a Holiday Inn across the road and at least enjoyed a couple of pints and a steak before turning in.

Next morning was Labor Day, this being the first Monday in September. The event is similar to our May Day, but in this case it also signals the end of the summer. Five years after its inception in 1882 as a 'day off for the working man', following representations from the Central Labor Union, there was pressure from other labour organisations such as the International Working Men's Union to change it to May 1 in line with most other countries. This was resisted by President Grover Cleveland in case it was used to commemorate the Chicago riots of May 1886 and thus be used to strengthen the socialist movement, so he decreed in 1887 that it would always be the first Monday in September.

I took a taxi and asked to be dropped in the centre of town. My driver suggested the riverside area, where he guessed there would be plenty happening. He was wrong. There wasn't anything happening when he dropped me at 10am. In fact Baton Rouge was closed. I would not be able to hang around to see what materialised, if anything, as I had to be on the move again in the early afternoon to travel to New Orleans. Baton Rouge was always going to be a flying visit, more or less a staging post to New Orleans, but also worth a stop in its own right as I am a closet Garth Brooks fan and he has a track called *Callin' Baton Rouge* on his *Double Live* album.

The driver dropped me at the US Veterans Memorial Museum right on the banks of the Mississippi. This was my first experience of the famous Mississippi and I made my way up the embankment in the sunshine to take in the view. The first thing that strikes you is the width, which is presumably what gives it its nickname 'Big River' (rather than its length which would then make it 'Long River'). The river takes its name from 'Misi-ziibi' the name given to it by the Ojibwe tribe and it means, unsurprisingly, 'Great River'. Other nicknames include, 'Old Man River' (from the musical Show Boat), 'The Mighty Mississippi', which is a well deserved title as it is one of the world's major rivers, Old Blue, The Gathering of Waters and Old Muddy (which is also sometimes used to describe the Missouri River).

Let me clear up here a point of great debate. On its own the Mississippi would not feature in the Top Ten in world rankings in terms of length, at 2,340 miles. But, together with its tributary the Missouri, it totals 3,900 miles which ranks it fourth after the Nile (4,300 miles), Amazon (4,100 miles) and the Yangtze/Chang Jiang (3,917 miles). It drains most of the area between the Rocky Mountains and the Appalachians and runs through, or defines the boundary for, ten states.

The river played a decisive role in the Civil War, in particular, the Union's Vicksburg Campaign, which called for Union control of the lower Mississippi.

It also gained fame through the adventures of Samuel Clemens, better known as Mark Twain. Interestingly, Clemens got his pen name through his experience as a riverboat captain on the Mississippi. The safe depth of water for sailing was considered to be two fathoms (12 feet) and there was a mark at this point on the sounding line dropped into the water to gauge depth. 'Twain' being an old term for 'two' the safe depth was therefore at 'Mark Twain', a term shouted out by rivermen when it was safe to proceed.

Much of Twain's writing was centred on the Mississippi, notably *Life on the Mississippi* and *Huckleberry Finn*, though his career as a riverboat captain was unfortunately curtailed when the Civil War stopped river traffic. Although Twain had many tragedies in his life, including the death of his brother in a Mississippi river accident, for which Twain blamed himself, the Civil War interruption perhaps did him a favour as he might never have become a journalist and writer if his riverboat career had not been prematurely ended.

On the musical front Johnny Cash had a hit with *Big River* in 1958. I love the opening lines:

> 'Now I taught the weeping willow how to cry, cry, cry
> and I showed the clouds how to cover up a clear blue sky
> And the tears that I cried for that woman are gonna flood you big river...'

Verse four specifically mentions Baton Rouge and I was exhilarated to be standing on the banks of the Mississippi looking down at the point where the River Queen would have 'battered down' before taking his woman to New Orleans (as he sadly concludes: 'she loves you Big River more than me').

Another musical connection with Baton Rouge is Kris Kristofferson's *Me and Bobby McGee* which starts:

'Busted flat in Baton Rouge
headin' for the train
feelin' nearly faded as my jeans'

Again the journey is from Baton Rouge down to New Orleans:

'Bobby thumbed a diesel down just before it rained,
rode us all the way to New Orleans'

So I began to feel as if I was on some sort of pilgrimage, as I knew New Orleans would be my next destination. Bobby McGee was first a hit for Roger Miller, and then Gordon Lightfoot, before Janis Joplin recorded it just before her death in 1970. It became her only number one single and was only the second posthumous number one single in the history of rock and roll (the first being *Dock of the Bay* by Otis Redding). As Janis was a friend and one-time lover of Kristofferson the lyrics are very poignant and some people say they refer to the relationship between them.

The song *Moon River,* made famous by the film *Breakfast at Tiffany's,* in which it was sung by Audrey Hepburn, was reputedly also written about the Mississippi and became a massive hit for South African Danny Williams, as well as becoming a trademark song of his namesake, crooner Andy Williams. Though there is some debate about whether it is the Mississippi that is being referred to in the song, the words 'huckleberry friend' give a clue and might well be a nod in the direction of Mark Twain and Huckleberry Finn.

Turning away from the river itself, at which I had gazed in no little awe for a very long time, I concentrated on the US Veterans Memorial Museum, the centre-piece of which is the USS Kidd. This is a Second World War Fletcher class destroyer named after Rear Admiral Isaac C Kidd who was killed on board the Arizona at Pearl Harbour. The ship rests on a unique frame in the river, which provides a dry dock when the river is low, but floats on the tide when it is high, there being a 40ft variation in levels at different times of the year. In its early days, the ship caused some controversy when it was decided to adopt the pirate Captain Kidd as its mascot. After supportive representations from Isaac Kidd's widow, the Navy gave permission for the ship to become the only US Navy ship ever to fly the Jolly Roger (as well as having an image of Captain Kidd painted on the smokestack). The crew took this association with the 'Pirate of the Pacific' to heart and began the practice of ransoming rescued pilots for huge amounts of ice cream.

The Kidd's most famous, but also most tragic, day was 12 April 1945, the day before President Roosevelt died. A Japanese suicide bomber crashed into the forward boiler room killing everyone inside and 38 people in total. This did not stop her distinguished career, however, and she went on to see action in Korea and starred in the famous war film *Run Silent Run Deep* featuring Clark Gable and Burt Lancaster.

I WALKED INTO THE deserted town trying to find a place to have a cup of coffee, but that was easier said than done as everywhere seemed to be closed. I headed for the focal point in town, The State Capitol Building, which is the tallest structure around and which is similar in appearance to the Empire State Building. The building was the dream and brainchild of Governor Huey P Long, who wanted it to be a symbol of the pride, the history and the spirit of Louisiana's people, with Baton Rouge being the State Capital.

To unearth funds and authority for such a building was quite an achievement during the depression and it was completed in March 1932 in an impressive 14 months construction period. The building is 34 floors high with a limestone exterior and an impressive marble interior, the materials having being brought in on 2,500 rail cars.

Long was a powerful politician and became a Democrat senator, but he managed to alienate most of his fellow senators because of his bullying tactics. President Roosevelt apparently described him as one of the two most dangerous men in America, the other being General Douglas MacArthur, and also likened Long to Hitler and Mussolini, which I like to think was a little over the top.

Unfortunately for Huey he didn't get much use out of the new Capitol Building as he was assassinated inside it in 1935 at the age of 42. His last words were reportedly "God, don't let me die I have so much left to do". He was a controversial and ruthless figure, though well meaning, as proven by his 'Every Man a King' programme ('wealth distribution but not communism'), during the dark days of the depression. I'm not sure how this sits with his edict that every employee who depended on him for a job was expected to pay a portion of their salary into his political war chest or the fact that he would fire State employees who were relatives of his political opponents.

Long was shot in the hallway outside the Speaker's office by a medical doctor, Carl Austin Weiss, whose father-in-law, a judge, had suffered at the hands of Long's political skulduggery. As usual in cases of assassination in the States there are conflicting versions of what happened. Some people say that Long was actually killed by a bullet from his own bodyguards who were busy emptying 30 shots into Weiss, who had only intended to punch Long. Again, as usual, we'll never know. The minister at Long's funeral came up with another theory – Long was assassinated "by order of the Roosevelt gang, supported by the New York Jew machine".

It was clear that through fair means or foul, Long had achieved a lot and I was feeling quite sorry for him. You couldn't say he was modest however, when you take into account the fact that he had the inside of the Governor's Mansion designed to look exactly the same as the White House, so he would know where to find the light switches when he got the President's job, and the fact that he published a book just before his death entitled *My First Days in the White House.*

The Capitol building is impressive and inside its huge ornate doors I was greeted by very strict security, as you would expect, but it was all very smart and professional with burgundy rope cordons and security staff in pristine uniforms. I was informed that I should visit the observation deck on the 27th floor and take in the fantastic views of the city and the river. Well, I would have liked to, and I could see that the building itself was well worth a visit. But there was a snag, well two actually, the first was time, the other was my rucksack. I'd had no choice but to hump this around all morning despite the fact that the temperature was in the 90s (and today summer was supposed to be over!). The security staff were rightly insisting that all bags be searched, but having taken great pains to get my bag neatly packed that morning there was no way I was going to have it emptied out on their little table. Besides, I didn't think it was a suitable exhibition point for my dirty underwear. So, I gave my apologies and said I would try to come back another time.

On the way back to the river, where I would have a better chance of picking up a cab, I came across the old State Capitol. Over the years, right from its construction, the building has been the subject of more than a little controversy. It is actually quite bizarre, being constructed in what is apparently a neo-gothic style. It looks like a fairytale castle straight from Disneyland and sports such features as turrets and battlements. It might be better if I let Mark Twain describe it for you: 'It is pathetic – a whitewashed castle with turrets and things' . . . 'the ugliest thing on the Mississippi'. To be fair I think he's probably in the minority on this one as, whilst I have to concede it is somewhat garish, it is definitely unique and many people seem to be very proud of it.

Baton Rouge has a population of approximately 750,000 in its Metropolitan area, but this is still temporarily inflated by the influx of refugees from New Orleans after Hurricane Katrina. Services and infrastructure in the city are still stretched while the re-patriation programme continues. It has been the state capital of Louisiana since 1879 and is a major industrial and petrochemical centre boasting the largest oil refinery (Exxon), in terms of capacity, in the entire North American continent. The name 'Baton Rouge' comes from the French for 'Red Stick'. In 1699 French explorer Sier d'Iberville was exploring the Mississippi River when he came across a cypress pole decorated with bloody animal heads. This marked the hunting boundary between local tribes and became known as the Baton Rouge and was the site of the original settlement founded by the French.

The history of Baton Rouge is inextricably linked with that of Louisiana as a whole. In 1763, under the Treaty of Paris, France gave up its territory in North America to Britain and Spain. Britain took all land east of the Mississippi except for New Orleans. Spain took New Orleans and all land west of the Mississippi. The US were fairly comfortable about this, having negotiated rights for access to the port of New Orleans and the navigation of the Mississippi with the Spanish. However, in the secret treaty of San Ildefonso in October 1800, Spain agreed to transfer the area back to France. When the US found out about this treaty it was of major concern to President Thomas Jefferson, who was less than happy about French control, particularly as there had already been one or two previous problems with free access rights to New Orleans and the Mississippi. Napoleon, who took control of France in 1799, had been determined to restore French power in the region in order to supply his empire in the New World.

The formal transfer from Spain to France took place in November 1803 and had become a huge issue in the US. As it happened, Napoleon by then was suffering a few setbacks and, following his defeat in Saint Domingue (now Haiti) where there had been a rebellion by slaves and free blacks, plus the likelihood of a war with Britain, he was somewhat overstretched and did not have the resources to safeguard the Mississippi region. This led to him agreeing to sell the territory to the

US and this happened within twenty days of the formal transfer from Spain to France! The transaction became known as 'The Louisiana Purchase' and changed the face of North America forever.

The land purchased was vast and included many other present day states such as Arkansas, Missouri, Oklahoma, land further north to Minnesota and even beyond, into Canada. The total transfer covered an area equivalent to 23% of the present day US and doubled the size of the United States at that time. The purchase cost $15 million, but was something of a snip as Jefferson had been prepared to pay $10 milion for New Orleans alone. The cost per acre worked out at four cents. I did hear one story which suggested that the territory was lost in a game of cards between the French and American representatives, but I think this is a purely mischevious suggestion. Whatever, it does look like the bargain of the 19th Century.

CALLIN' BATON ROUGE IS A Garth Brooks song which refers to a trip to the city during which he ends up in the arms of a girl and then leaves the next morning. He has to stop every hundred miles to call her from a coinbox (it must have been written before the days of mobile phones, or perhaps it's a bad reception area) as he needs a 'couple of dollars change' to make the calls. The story goes on . . .

> *'A replay of last night's events*
> *Roll through my mind*
> *Except a scene or two*
> *Erased by sweet red wine'*

I would respectfully recommend to Garth that if he was this inebriated he requests a photo before getting too carried away, but let's not be unromantic. He is also a little premature, in my opinion, in giving his commitment . . . 'it won't be long until I'm with you all the time', bearing in mind it would appear that he only met the lady the night before. She must have been good.

The song certainly is and it's one of my favourite Garth Brooks' tunes. I defy anyone to listen to it and not tap their foot or nod their head like a dog on the back shelf of the neighbour's car.

It was only relatively recently that I became aware of Garth Brooks (real name Troyal Garth Brooks) and there are many people in the UK who will similarly be less that familiar with his music. However, in the States he is huge, and despite having effectively retired in 2001, at least until his kids graduate, he has achieved phenomenal success. And I mean phenomenal. There is a debate over whether he or Elvis have sold the most records, though Brooks himself willingly concedes to Elvis. Recent statistics, produced in November 2007 suggest that Brooks is in first place with 123 million album sales. This would make him the most successful solo artist in the States and he would be behind only the Beatles in terms of total sales. However, many of Elvis's sales were not documented and some estimates say that he achieved US total sales of over one billion.

Where that stands against the Beatles would be an interesting comparison when you consider that at one stage in 1964 the Merseysiders amazingly had the first five singles in the Billboard chart (*Can't Buy Me Love, Twist and Shout, She Loves You, I Want to Hold your Hand, Please Please Me*) as well as seven others in the top 100. They sold over 25 million records in the US in that year alone!

Going back to Brooks, whose music is a mix of country and rock (he claims to have been strongly influenced by Kiss and George Strait, which I find an interesting combination), let me apologise to Garth for the treatment he received from the UK media during his visit in1994. On *The Big Breakfast* Paula Yates apparently insulted Garth by mocking him about country singers always "weeping over the dead dog and things" and added "I thought you'd come in here and twiddle your pistol around and be impressed". The presenter on ITV's *London Tonight* programme greeted Garth as "a top-selling, rooting-tooting, cotton-picking, Country and Western star, yeeha!" and this while introducing one of the World's top stars. What a way to treat visitors!

Fortunately, Garth remained polite and didn't let it stop him from returning to England in 1996 unlike his country music compatriot Alan Jackson, who understandably refused to return to the UK after being similarly treated. I have to say, after listening to some of Alan's music recently, that it's our loss.

To give you an idea of just how big a star Garth Brooks is in the States, let me mention a free concert he did in Central Park, New York, not exactly a hot bed of country music. Estimates have put the crowd at 750,000 or even higher. Let's hope Garth will keep his promise to return to full time activities when his kids graduate.

Callin' Baton Rouge

I spent last night in the arms of a girl in Louisiana
And though I'm out on the highway
My thoughts are still with her
Such a strange combination of a woman and a child
Such a strange situation stoppin' every hundred miles
Callin' Baton Rouge

A replay of last night' events roll through my mind
Except a scene or two erased by sweet red wine
And I see a truck stop sign ahead
So I change lanes
I need a cup of coffee
And a couple dollars change
Callin' Baton Rouge

(Chorus)
Operator won't you put me on through
I gotta' send my love down to Baton Rouge
Hurry up won't you put her on the line
I gotta' talk to the girl just one more time

Hello Samantha dear, I hope you're feelin' fine
And it won't be long until I'm with you all the time
But until then I'll spend my money up right down to my last dime
Callin' Baton Rouge

(Chorus)

Callin' Baton Rouge
Sweet Baton Rouge, my Baton Rouge

Words and music by Dennis Linde

Chapter Eight

"Marie, Marie, da voodoo veau . . ."

I TOOK MY SEAT ON THE BUS, comfortable in the knowledge that the trip down to New Orleans was a mere couple of hours, nothing by the previous day's standards.

The journey turned out to be memorable for the mile after mile of Louisiana swampland; the highway, for a long stretch, consisting of a concrete flyover built on stilts across the swamps. I prayed that we wouldn't have a puncture or a breakdown as I didn't fancy being stranded out there for any period of time. The place is apparently rife with alligators, some as large as 18 feet long. Local literature helpfully warns that even a 'five to six footer' can cause 'severe injury'. The creatures tend to alternate between the water and the banks as a way of regulating their body temperature and they are most active during the warmer months. To make matters worse there are many varieties of snake, with at least six types being poisonous – 'watch especially for the Water Moccasin which may be under foot or in the trees above – their bites can be deadly'. I decided all I could do was keep my fingers crossed.

To divert my mind from the snakes, to which I am definitely not partial, I opened the newspaper I had bought at the bus station. 'In the last week more Americans have died in New Orleans than in Iraq' the front page shouted at me. Just what you want to read as a lone traveller about to hit a strange city for the first time, no accommodation booked and heavy pack on back. '14 murders in one week' the article went on in less than encouraging vein. I recalled that I had heard on the news the previous week that as an after effect of Hurricane Katrina there are

80,000 homeless people in or around New Orleans and that the murder rate is 30% higher than any other city in the United States, which is saying something.

'The killers are more brazen, striking in broad daylight and using assault rifles, even with police just 30 yards away. And witnesses refuse to talk.' I tried to convince myself that the murders would be mostly gang-related and all the targets would have been eliminated by now. Rather than buy myself an assault rifle I would try to make sure I didn't end up in exposed locations. So, the first thing to do on arrival was to find a hotel in a safe area and forget about the penny-pinching, out in the sticks, motel locations.

In the event, I ended up at the Holiday Inn right in the French Quarter and this proved a very handy and pleasant location. After booking in it was time to get out and have my first look around 'The Big Easy' and find somewhere to eat. It is debatable where the title 'Big Easy' comes from. Some say it was because musicians found it easy to get work here, others that it refers to the relaxed atmosphere, others that it goes back to the days of prohibition when you could get easily get a drink in New Orleans.

The 1987 film *Big Easy*, starring Dennis Quaid and the sultry Ellen Barkin makes reference to this when Quaid, a policeman, is accused by Barkin of taking a bribe and replies: 'Just relax, darlin'. This is the Big Easy. Folks have a certain way o' doin' things down here.'

The streets were strangely quiet, but there again I was fairly conservative about where I went as it was dark and I hadn't yet found my bearings. I kept pretty much to the three or four main streets, trying always to make sure there were people around. Even the famous Bourbon Street was quiet and there wasn't the Mardi Gras atmosphere that you immediately think of when New Orleans is mentioned. I settled for a little restaurant on Bourbon Street and tried the Blackened Redfish, which was white and chunky and very palatable – especially when washed down with the by now customary Corona.

Intrigued by the Creole items on the menu, including the one I had ordered, I realised that I didn't really understand what Creole – music, cooking or culture – is, or how it is defined. I undertook to fill this gap in my knowledge bank straight away.

Essentially, Creole refers to descendants of French, Spanish and Caribbean natives or anyone who derives from mixed nationalities in the Caribbean. In terms of food, staple dishes include Gumbo (stew or soup often involving sea food),

Crawfish, Shrimps, and Jambalaya (a paella-type dish often consisting of chicken and sausage) all with a typical accompaniment of red beans and rice.

After finishing my meal I walked back to the hotel, having a quick look in one or two bars on the way, hoping to pick up some atmosphere and some music in this famous musical city. The first bar I entered had a band just finishing a number and I caught the last rendition of the chorus which went: 'kiss my arse baby, I can't take this shit no more'. Obviously sung with feeling, but not quite what I was expecting to hear in one of the homes of music. The next bar I looked in had a theme night on the go, but it might have been the same every night, as the establishment was called the Pirate Bar. I didn't enter as I didn't feel inclined to acquire the necessary gear such as an eye patch (3 dollars), bandana (4 dollars) or sword (5 dollars).

Back at the hotel I came across reference to the Battle of New Orleans, which rang a bell with me and I began mentally picking up the words and tune:

> *'In 1814 we took a little trip*
> *Along with Colonel Jackson down the mighty Mississip'*

The voice of Lonnie Donegan was coming through loud and clear:

> *'We fired our guns and the British kept a comin'*

So what was it all about? Well, basically the British and the Americans fell out in 1812 due to a number of reasons, one being that Britain, who were at war with France, imposed what the US considered to be illegal trade restraints so as to prevent the Americans aiding the French. This led to a war known as the War of 1812, but which, as mentioned earlier, was actually fought between 1812-1815. A peace treaty was signed at Ghent in December 1814, but of course news did not travel fast in those days so no-one in New Orleans was aware of this till February. A large British force of more than 10,000 under the control of Sir Edward Pakenham assembled in the Gulf of Mexico in January 1815 and prepared to attack New Orleans, which was defended by Major General Andrew Jackson and 4,000 men. The attack was repulsed, leading to a famous victory for the Americans, and this helped Jackson on his way to becoming 7th President of the US.

'They ran so fast that the hounds couldn't catch 'em
On down the Mississippi to the Gulf of Mexico'

These two lines nicely sum up the result. You might notice that the song refers to Colonel Jackson, this appears to be a slight anomally as I believe he was promoted to Major General during the course of 1814 (the battle took place on 8 January 1815).

The song itself was a number two hit for Lonnie Donegan in the UK in 1959 and a number one hit in the States for Johnny Horton in the same year. Interestingly, it was written by a chap called James Corbitt Morris, a schoolmaster, in an attempt to make history lessons more appealing to his pupils. He went on to become a major US songwriter under the name Jimmy Driftwood, which just shows you what a bit of initiative can do.

New Orleans is named after Philippe II, Duke of Orleans, Regent of France, his title coming from the French city of Orleans. The city (New Orleans) was formed in1718 by the French Mississippi company. Under the Treaty of Paris it was ceded to the Spanish Empire and remained Spanish for 40 years before becoming American as part of the Louisiana Purchase in 1803.

The population of the city doubled between 1830 and 1840 and it became the wealthiest city in the country due to its role as a leading port. It was captured by the Union Army very early on in the American Civil War and was thus spared the destruction of many other cities, such as Atlanta.

In the early 20th Century, an engineer called A Baldwin Wood devised a pump system, which allowed occupation of low lying areas resulting in many dwellings being constructed below sea level. The city had always been subject to extensive flooding and in 1965 dozens of residents were killed by Hurricane Betsy. Another flood in 1995 demonstrated the weakness of the pumping system and because of this threat, the US Army were called in to strengthen flood defence systems through a system of levees (floodwalls). When Hurricane Katrina hit in August 2005, the levees failed below specification and 80% of the city was flooded. This infamously resulted in 1,500 deaths and much devastation, with hundreds of thousands of people being displaced. Fortunately, the French Quarter, for which New Orleans is particularly famous, was relatively untouched, but this is little consolation to all those who were made homeless, many of whom have not yet been able to return. While I was in the city I witnessed much controversy over its restoration, even though it is over two years since the hurricane and, whilst the population has returned to about two thirds of its previous 300,000, it still leaves tens of thousands in temporary locations elsewhere in the States.

Some high profile individuals are now pursuing the cause, including Brad Pitt, whose project assists with the construction of low cost, green homes (Pitt and Angelina have a town house in the French Quarter) and Harry Connick Junior, who is a native of New Orleans. Harry is involved in a project called Habitat for Humanity. These are commendable projects, but from what I saw during my visit it is clear that much more needs to be done. The role of the Federal Government has been bitterly controversial, with President Bush hardly covering himself in much glory when seeming to ignore the catastrophe by initially failing to visit the site or to grant immediate central aid.

THE FIRST PIECE OF MUSIC I ever bought was *House of the Rising Sun* by the Animals in 1964. Who can forget Eric Burdon and his gravelly voice growling those opening words 'There is a House in New Orleans...'? This record brought huge success to the Animals on both sides of the Atlantic and had a major impact on the '60s musical scene. There is a lot of debate about whether the 'House' refers to a brothel (as I'd always assumed) or alternatively 'slave pens of the plantations', or a 'Rising Sun Hall', a building used for social activity at the old New Orleans Prison for Women which apparently had its entrance decorated with a rising sun sign.

The song had been around since the 1930s and had been recorded by all manner of people, but the Animals gave it a totally different treatment, which changed the face of music. A folk singer called Dave Van Ronk, who was very influential in New York in the 1960s, claims to have worked out the arrangement used by Bob Dylan in 1962 before Van Ronk got round to recording it. This upset Van Ronk, who was unhappy when people referred to his own version as a cover of Dylan's song. Dylan was in turn miffed when his song was later referred to as a cover of the Animals' version. Whilst this all sounds quite acrimonious I am pleased to say that it appears that Van Ronk was a friend of Dylan and that Dylan loved the Animals version. Anyway I digress, for which I make no apologies as it's one of my favourite songs. I was not surprised to learn that it was voted fourth in a poll to find Britain's favourite number one of all time.

For my visit to the 'Crescent City', New Orleans' other nickname, (the name derives from the city's location on a bend in the Mississippi), I had decided to focus on *Witch Queen of New Orleans*, a song which hit number two in the UK charts in 1971 (prevented only from going top by Rod Stewart's *Maggie May*). It was a cult hit of its time and like many other people I was fascinated by the song with its references to 'gris-gris', 'zombies' and 'voodoo'.

> *'Marie, Marie, da voodoo veau, she'll put a spell on you-ou'*

Many people remember the song, but few remember who sang it. The answer is Redbone, the Native American band who were popular in the early '70s, playing a mix of tribal, rock and latin-influenced music and who performed in full Indian regalia. The band was formed by brothers Pat and Lolly Vesquas in 1968. Pat and Lolly were Yaqui/Shoshone Indians from Mexican descent and they subsequently changed their surname to Vegas to avoid the discrimination at that time against Chicano (Mexican-American) performers and population in general. The name Redbone comes from a derogatory term meaning half-breed, but Pat and Lolly clearly took that with an element of humour. They made their breakthrough with a song called Maggie in 1970 and had two other significant hit singles, *Witch Queen* in 1971 and *Come and Get Your Love* in 1974, which was a huge hit in the States and apparently is still a standard at discos today to get people on the dance floor. They had a drummer called Peter 'Last Walking Bear' Depoe, who was described as the funkiest drummer of his time.

The band were certainly well respected in their day, featuring at the Isle of Wight Festival in 1971 which had on the bill, among many others, The Doors, Chicago, Emerson Lake and Palmer, Free, The Who and the Everly Brothers. They became very controversial in the States with their 1973 recording of *(We were all) Wounded at Wounded Knee*, a reference to the Massacre of Lakota Sioux Indians by the Seventh Cavalry in 1890. *Wounded Knee* reached number one in some European countries, but was not such a success in the States where the record company at first declined to release it and where it was banned by some radio stations due to its 'controversial' content.

Witch Queen is a clear reference to Marie Laveau, the most famous Voodoo practitioner in New Orleans' history, and my mission was to find out what I could about Marie and her creole 'magic'. My first step was to embark on a cemetery tour to see what I could find out. This started at Café Beignet and was hosted by a knowledgeable lady called Gwen, who escorted us to St Louis Cemetery No. 1. As with all New Orleans' cemeteries the graves are above ground, for very practical reasons, and because of this the cemeteries are sometimes known as Cities of the Dead.

With New Orleans being below sea level, and having a very high water table, there was a nasty tendency for coffins (made of wood and full of air) to rise to the surface and burst through the ground, which must have been a pretty scary experience if you just happened to be standing alongside one when it made the breakthrough. To counteract this it became standard practice to drill holes in the coffin and put stones inside. It still didn't solve the problem and in the end it was decided to build the tombs above ground. This in truth represents a rather economical and green way to bury the departed – the tombs can be used again and again for family members as, with the hot temperatures, the tomb in effect becomes an oven and the bodies decompose. After about a year there is nothing left but ashes and bones and the area is swept through a hole in the floor, leaving the tomb available for the next lucky occupant.

The tombstone of Marie Laveau, to my surprise, was quite understated. It did, however, carry a plaque commemorating, the 'notorious voodoo queen' before adding: 'a mystic cult, voodooism, of African origin was brought to this city from Santo Domingo and flourished in the 19th Century. Marie Laveau was the most widely known practitioner of the cult.' The grave was decorated with quite a few sets of chalk triple crosses, as legend has it that this is the way to have a wish granted by Marie.

Now this is where you have to be careful, some people are clearly in need of my guidance, because I can tell them that you are supposed to mark the crosses on the ground in front of the grave and that anyone 'disrespecting' the grave can, under a Voodoo spell, expect a slow and painful death. Although the cemetery was a bit spooky everything seemed to be fairly normal, without sign of any unnerving rituals, but Gwen did say that at weekends in particular you might well come across the remains of the odd sacrificed cock, so there are still some dark goings on.

The other well-known tomb in this cemetery is the site of the infamous scene in the 1969 film *Easy Rider*, starring Jack Nicholson, where an LSD-induced psychedelic trip takes place involving drink, drugs and naked bodies cavorting around the grave. This caused outrage among Catholic audiences, although the cemetery had not given permission for filming. Understandably, film shooting in the cemetery is now banned.

There was a group of about ten of us on the tour, but I made the mistake of dwelling at the *Easy Rider* tomb to take some pictures. When I looked up I was on my own. In a normal cemetery this would not have been a problem, but, because of the high tombstones, it was like being in Hampton Court Maze, only a lot more worrying bearing in mind the many warnings not to enter New Orleans cemeteries on your own. The warnings advise that you are very likely to encounter thieves, drug dealers and other dodgy characters and I tried not to think about a chilling article I had read which had matter of factly explained that 'some careless grave-yard tourists have become permanent residents'.

Try as I might I could not find my companions. Nor could I hear them, the graves effectively acting as acoustic dampeners. All of a sudden I heard a crunch-ing noise, clearly footsteps on gravel and with my imagination working overtime, I pushed myself back into a recess in one of the larger mausoleums. The interloper passed by without seeing me, seemingly a genuine cemetery visitor, not realising what a fright he had given me. The episode served only to make me realise how much my nerves were on edge and how keen I was to get out of the predicament. I could see a way out, but it was not a gate I recognised and I was more than a little reluctant to leave by that exit and risk being disorientated on the outskirts of the city. I thought of using the mountain whistle that I had brought with me to the States for emergency, but I then remembered it was in the side pocket of my ruck-sack back at the hotel. Besides, I would have felt a prat.

Fortunately, in situations like this, it's amazing how your senses become sharper and I used my temporarily-developed aural ability to eventually track down the others, who were just about to abandon me. When I showed myself I tried to appear nonchalant and muttered something to the effect that I was just making sure I got some good photos.

Breathing a sigh of relief, I tagged on to the end of the party as we proceeded the short distance to the Voodoo temple we were scheduled to visit next. Now this was one place I was determined I would not get lost, I would hold someone's hand if necessary. From across the road I could see the building, which was a single-storey construction with pitched roof and dormer windows, decorated externally in pink, with flags of various nationalities hanging from the canopy outside.

We entered the building and found ourselves in a shop, surrounded by potions, charms and Voodoo literature, but, I am pleased to say, no snakes, which I knew were integral to the art of Voodoo. We were taken through the back into the 'temple', which consisted of two rooms full of the sort of Voodoo paraphernalia you see in films. According to the promotional leaflet this is more accurately described as a 'lavishly decorated altar room', which included, strangely and inexplicably, a picture of the Her Majesty the Queen. The inner chamber was cluttered with statues, flags, pictures of Marie Laveau and dolls. We were treated to a talk by Priestess Miriam, who is apparently a Bishop ordained within the 'Angel, Angel All Nations Spiritual Church' a 'religion which embodies many aspects of mainstream spiritualism, Roman Catholicism, Voodoo and Hoodoo.'

A lot of the stuff went over my head and the only bit I remember is Princess Miriam linking Voodoo to Catholicism in the respect that it involves the worship of higher beings responsible for different aspects of life such as love, money, happiness and so on. The practice came to America with the slave trade and after a while the slave owners forbade the practise of Voodoo, on punishment of death, and had the slaves instructed in the practice of Catholicism. The slaves got round the embargo by worshipping the Catholic saints who most closely resembled their particular areas of interest. In other words they were still worshipping their own spirits, but in the guise of Catholic saints.

On leaving the temple Gwen pointed out, across the road, the location of Storyville, the prostitution centre of New Orleans between 1895 and 1915. Some say this was the area where Jazz was really born as most establishments had a piano player or a small band. It took the nickname Storyville after Sydney Story, who had been commissioned to sort out the city's prostitution problems. After studying some European models, which sounds like an interesting assignment, he proposed settling all the prostitution in one area to keep it out of the way. He was apparently mortified when the area was named after him.

Storyville was in its heyday when Louis Armstrong was making a name for himself. He first learned to play the cornet in the nearby New Orleans Home for Coloured Waifs, where he had been sent a number of times for misdemeanours, including discharging his father's pistol. He left New Orleans and moved to Chicago in 1922 when it became the centre of the Jazz universe after the demise of Storyville.

I was interested to find out that his nickname Satchmo comes from 'Satchelmouth' because of his embouchure (the way in which a trumpeter holds the instrument to his mouth) and was amused to learn he had a thing for laxatives and had a habit of handing out packets to everyone he met, including the British

Royal Family! He was even involved in advertisements for laxative products – 'Lose weight the Satchmo way, leave it all behind ya'. I think that proves he had a sense of humour as well as being a fantastic musician and personality.

The Government closed the Storyville area during World War I under a general-al law trying to keep prostitution away from naval bases and I like the quote from the mayor of the time, Martin Behrman, who foresaw that underground brothels would spring up – "you can make it illegal, but you can't make it unpopular," he said. Clearly an astute and far-sighted man.

When I returned to the hotel I considered that I needed to know more (about Voodoo not prostitution) and decided I would go back and try to see Priestess Miriam on my own. Knowing now where the temple was situated I followed a route on my town map which would keep me safe, for most of the walk anyway. I found the temple without mishap and entered the house of Voodoo with just a little trep-idation. Priestess Miriam was busy dealing with a chap, aged about thirty, who was in the process of selecting some Mojo (charms), as far as I could gather to give him more success with the opposite sex.

When this transaction was completed I introduced myself to the Priestess who was very welcoming and offered to take me into the temple for a chat. We sat down in the eerie surroundings, surrounded by all the trinkets, ornaments statues and pictures and, after experiencing one of those 'what am I doing here?' moments, I listened while she explained in more detail the origins of Voodoo. She explained that the word 'Voudon' is a Fon word (from the African Dahomey empire in Togo) which means the 'power invisible to all people'. It is the 'infusion of traditional African beliefs with Catholicism'. She was clearly upset that Voodoo has been given a bad press by orthodox priests and writers who "publish false information which is then embellished by Hollywood producers seeking sensationalism through bloodthirsty zombies and Voodoo Priestesses" and she put forward the argument that Voodoo is a genuine religion (in fact it has just been accepted as such by the Government of Haiti). Voodoo devotees, like other religions, believe in the 'Omnipresent Creator' and in the Loa or Orisha (spirits), who act as intermediaries like the saints in Catholicism.

There are four aspects of Voodoo: the Rada, which concentrates on the posi-tive side of Voodoo only, Petro, which looks at both the negative and positive sides, Secta Rouge, the negative side and Zobop, which concentrates on the extreme negative.

Sadly, Miriam's husband, Priest Oswan, (a Belizean Voodoo practitioner) died in 1995. As he was the snake handler in the family I was somewhat relieved at not having to encounter him, although he was also good at curing snake bites apparently. The snake has a special place in Voodoo as it reflects the 'duality' of the religion's outlook in that everything that happens affects something else. In the case of the snake, its venom can poison, but that same venom is also needed to provide a cure.

Mojo (also known as Gris-Gris) is effectively a magic charm and often consists of herbs and powders contained in a red cloth bag with a drawstring. The Muddy Waters song *I've Got My Mojo Working* (but it just won't work on you) is a classic example of Mojo's relationship with romantic matters, although it is not clear how explicit the lyrics are as it depends on your interpretation.

When I asked about the darker side of things, such as sticking pins in dolls and grisly spells, Miriam told me there is a difference between Voodoo and Hoodoo, the latter being more akin to witchcraft. Whilst Voodoo is a religion, Hoodoo is the practise of magic with no religious connotations. Finally Priestess Miriam concluded that "Voodoo is a religion of the universe. The way it works is through the energies and intelligence which are directed and manifested at ourselves and our universe."

That might be the case, but I still wouldn't like to go into Cemetery No. 1 on my own after dark.

So, HAVING SURVIVED A meeting with a Voodoo Priestess I should feel more competent to unravel Marie Laveau and Redbone's story:

> 'From a shack near the swamplands, made of mudpile brick
> Marie stirred her witches brew'

This would indeed appear to be the case as, for her gatherings on the shore of Lake Pontchartrain in the early-to-mid 19th century, she did take a cauldron and boil things such as cocks, black cats, and pieces of snake before seasoning them with salt and pepper and some potions.

> 'Dime or a nickel anyone could buy-uy, voodoo of any ki-ind
> She had potions and lotions, herbs and tanna leaves
> Guaranteed to blow your mind'

This also seems fair enough. It would appear that Marie was quite entrepreneurial as, when she realised the success of her gatherings by the lake, she began charging admission. She also allegedly organised secret orgies for wealthy white men seeking black women for mistresses. This further enhanced her knowledge and power over the rich and famous, which she had accumulated through gossip overheard in her day-time profession as a hairdresser.

Despite the sinister image projected by some of her activities, it has to be said that Marie had lots of good points and she was a heroine of her day. She was a deeply religious practising Catholic and, among other things, she tended the wounded from the Battle of New Orleans and was renowned for visiting prisoners in jail and taking them food and clothes.

The song concludes:

> *'Early one mornin' into mucky swamp dew*
> *Vanished Marie with hate in her eye-eyes'*

My research fails to show up any evidence that Marie disappeared into 'swamp dew'. Records apparently show that she died in her house on St Ann Street on16 June 1881, so I think the Vegas brothers might have used a little artistic licence here. She is certainly a legend though, and apart from featuring in quite a few songs, she lives on as a superhero in Marvel comics, in which she is an enemy of Dr Strange and Dracula. Clearly a lady with a diverse range of talents.

IN THE EVENING I WAS again surprised at how quiet things were and I had to make sure I stayed on well-lit streets. My vision of semi-naked girls hanging over flower-clad balustrades had to concede to reality and left me no choice but to concentrate on more mundane things like food and perhaps some music.

I had thought of New Orleans as being a bit of a perpetual party city, but, as I discovered, carnival only runs for a few weeks and is held in February/March, although the celebrations always start on Twelfth Night, January 6th. Mardi Gras is in fact just one night – the culmination of the festivities, and this always falls on the day before Ash Wednesday (Mardi Gras being French for 'Fat Tuesday', of course).

I was exploring a menu outside a restaurant in the French Quarter when a girl who was outside having a smoke advised me it was excellent and encouraged me to go inside and join her and her boyfriend. They had come to New Orleans to attend a wedding the day before and invited me to join them for a drink as they had already eaten. The boyfriend, Dave, wasted no time in telling me one of the waiters was on cocaine and the other on heroin. "I can tell by the eyes," he declared and I couldn't help thinking he seemed something of an expert on the subject.

Discussion soon turned to all things Voodoo, which I suppose is reasonable in New Orleans and we talked about the supernatural in general. They told me they had met someone at the wedding whose Grandmother had been a notorious witch in New Orleans and suggested I might like to meet him. Apparently his Gran used to tie up her slaves with their own intestines. My observation on this would be that I would have thought they would have had to be tied up before she cut their intestines out, but there we go, I'm being pedantic again.

The girl, Kirsten, then started telling me about spooky things that have happened to her like sitting in a stationary car when it started to roll uphill and at this point I started to develop my exit strategy. I left soon afterwards armed with the name and telephone number of the great witch's Grandson, promising faithfully to ring him the next day. I did try but he was too busy to see me before my departure from town. I was fairly relieved at this as I felt I'd already had enough scary adventures in Orleans and didn't really want to find out whether he had continued the family tradition. The next time I saw Kirsten and Dave, a couple of hours later, they were helping each other along the street. I kept well out of the way.

I ended up in an authentic Cajun restaurant just past the French Market down by the river. Up until now I had been a bit confused about the difference between Creole and Cajun, not just in the food sense, but in terms of the people and culture. The food is actually very similar, usually using local produce, simple recipes and the trinity of bell pepper, onion and celery. There are subtle differences such as Cajun Jambalaya uses no tomatoes and is less elaborate, but sometimes hotter, using cayenne and paprika. I settled for Cajun Chicken, which was actually less hot than you would get if you ordered it in England and washed it down with Abita beer from a local brewery in Abita Springs 25 miles away (though I stayed clear of their speciality brew called Turbodog which sounded a bit perilous).

As I ate I spied a picture on the wall of a musician called Professor Longhair, who I had never heard of. On enquiring, I was advised he is a New Orleans icon and, though he died in 1980, his signature song *Mardi Gras in New Orleans* is still the theme song of the Mardi Gras. Apparently the Prof used to be known as the 'Bach of Rock and Roll' and the 'Picasso of keyboard funk'. He must have been quite useful as he was once flown in to play at a private party held by Paul McCartney on the Queen Mary.

Cajuns can best be described as an ethnic group, living mainly in Louisiana, who are descendants of Acadian people. Acadia was a colonial territory in north-eastern North America that included parts of Canada and New England. In the summer of 1755, after the outbreak of the French and Indian War between Britain and France the year before, there was an event which became known as the 'Great Upheaval' after the British attacked Fort Beauséjoure and burned Acadian homes. Acadians were accused of disloyalty for not having taking the oath to the British crown and were also suspected of guerrilla action. Those who refused to swear loyalty were relocated over a three year period with 6-7,000 Acadians expelled to France or the lower British colonies.

Eventually, many exiled Acadians settled in Louisiana, which was under Spanish rule, having just been transferred from France. The Spanish governor, that man Galvez again, was very accommodating and allowed the Acadians to speak their own language and generally live without interference. This resulted in them fighting, under the control of Galvez, against the British when the War of Independence came round in 1775.

The term 'Acadian' was corrupted to 'Cajun' and now the region of present day Louisiana, which is home to Cajuns, represents about one third of the State and is officially referred to as Acadiana or Cajun Country.

On my way back to the hotel I came across a number of street musicians who were really good, giving me at last the feel of New Orleans as you imagine it – jazz being played on street corners by talented, natural artists.

As I wandered the streets I was re-assured by the sight of many State Troopers, but I was amused by the difference between these and the English constabulary. I saw four troopers walking down the road smoking cigars and spitting the tobacco juice into the gutter who then, recognising some people coming in the opposite direction embarked on a big group hug. A bit of a laid back approach, but I didn't mind, I felt extremely comforted by their presence.

In my pursuit of live music I was disappointed to find that it was the wrong night for a Zydeco band at one of the nearby bars as, in reasonable doses, I find the lively sound of the accordion and washboard quite invigorating. But, to lighten my disappointment, I very soon afterwards came across the 'Jazz Emporium', which was an altogether classier place than most of the bars I had 'researched' (Bourbon

Street has unfortunately fallen victim to modern theme bars, strip clubs and T-shirt and souvenir shops).

I believe I did have to fork out to get in the Emporium, or pay a premium on the drinks, I cannot remember which, but it was more like a club, was comfortable, and it had quality music. It was quite late and the band were close to finishing, but I enjoyed a couple of beers whilst listening to excellent renditions of *Mustang Sally* (not a song I would have expected in New Orleans) and then, rather more appropriately, *Black Magic Woman* and *I Put a Spell on You*, which, bearing in mind my adventures in the world of cemeteries and Voodoo, was a fitting end to the day.

In the morning I decided to have my last stroll down Bourbon Street and, whilst indulging in one of my sad little pastimes, reading funny slogans on T-shirts in shop doorways, I was amused to read one very topical example (in view of the debate about whether compensation for Katrina was adequate): 'I stayed for Katrina and all I got was this lousy T-shirt, a new Cadillac and a Plasma.'

I hadn't been to the French Market in daylight and I decided this was where I would head for morning coffee as I had a few hours at my disposal before leaving this unique and interesting city. I came across a brass plaque on the wall of a building and being a sucker for this sort of thing went to have a look. It was entitled 'The Birthplace of Dixie' and carried the legend:

> 'On this site between 1835-1924 stood the
> Citizens State Bank, originator of the " Dixie".
> In its early days the bank issued its own $10
> note with the French word "Dix" for "ten"
> printed on the note's face. As this currency
> became widespread, people referred to its
> place of origin as " the land of the Dix"
> which was eventually shortened to "Dixieland."'

There you go, another quiz question in my pocket – it just shows what you might miss if you don't walk.

The French Market was good and there were some up-market gift shops, one specialising in pet goodies for those tourists missing their cats and dogs. The adverts in the window were enough for me: 'Because dogs are people as well' declared the sign above a picture of a couple of pooches wearing 'party collars' complete with multi-coloured ruffles. And then, below that, the same dogs in sun-glasses. I must have looked a bit funny myself standing there alone guffawing at what looked like a couple of canine World War I flying aces in goggles.

I needed to leave town at lunchtime to get up to Jackson, Mississippi, about 200 miles to the north. This would be a rare opportunity, and indeed the only one I would get, to take a train rather than the bus, as Amtrak run a service from New Orleans all the way north to Chicago.

I was conscious that I had not seen anything of the devastation caused by Katrina, but I didn't have time to spend three hours on the sight-seeing bus tour, which seemed a bit voyeuristic anyway. The train was due to leave at 1.45 pm, so I called a cab in order to get to the station early, thinking it might be like the Greyhound where you need to 'get in line' even though you have a ticket. On the way to the station the driver said I should not miss seeing the Lower 9th Ward, which was the area most affected by the floods. He advised me there was no need to get to the station early as the trains are a much more relaxed affair than the bus and that he would take a detour and give me a personal tour of the devastation for $50. It would take about three-quarters of an hour, leaving time to get my ticket and catch the train.

I felt that it was something I should see, so agreed and off we went in the direction of the Lower 9th , but only after he locked the doors on the taxi.

On the way, he pointed out a Hospital and University Medical Centre which is still closed two years on and pointed out the high water line on the side of build-ings, which I could see was getting higher all the time as we approached the area in question. When we got to the Lower 9th I was confronted by a scene worse than I could have imagined, not unlike the images you see of Hiroshima where every-thing was flattened apart from the occasional building. It was quite eerie as here we were, only a few miles from the town centre, in a deserted wasteland with just the odd person around, tinkering rather forlornly with their devastated property. During the floods, the lower 9th was at one stage under 25 feet of water, with cars, and even houses, floating down the road.

With the failure of four drainage canal levees, 200,000 homes were flooded. The Government have come up with a compensation package, but according to my taxi driver it is not enough to allow people to rebuild to the extent that would be considered reasonable (I think it was equivalent to about £70,000 per house-hold – more than enough I would have thought for a new Cadillac and plasma).

We drove on a little way and he took me to one of the few houses which are still standing reasonably intact in this particular area. This was a more elaborate building than most of the other properties had been and was obviously better constructed and stronger, which was why it was still standing. This was the house and workplace of Jazz pianist and singer Fats Domino, who had been missing and feared dead in the storm for a number of days. He had actually been rescued from his upper porch by a USA Coastguard helicopter, but due to the general confusion no-one knew that he was alive. In the meantime someone had painted on the walls of his house 'RIP Fats. You will be missed'. Fats' house has been repaired and when fully renovated he hopes to return to live in what he considers his spiritual home.

I was glad I made the visit to the district, but left feeling somewhat humbled and overpowered by the size of the task ahead for the authorities and the residents. Hopefully when everything gets sorted out some people will be in a better position than they were before the storm, but for many, particularly those who lost family or friends, or their business, they will never forget the impact of Katrina, even when it has long been forgotten by the world public. As Joe Givens, a local activist who is involved in pushing for restoration, said during a visit by President Bush the week before I arrived:

'We're on the front page today and maybe tomorrow, but then people will move on to something else. The shelf life for this catastrophe is closing.'

Also very poignant and pertinent, given the knowledge of the weaknesses of the levee system before the floods, was the message I saw painted in huge letters on the side of one of the new floodwalls, simply one word – 'Hindsight'. The taxi headed for the train station with me deep in thought about what it must have been like to have experienced such a calamity.

Witch Queen Of New Orleans

(Chorus)
Marie, Marie, da voodoo veau, she'll put a spell on you-ou
Marie, Marie, da voodoo veau, she'll put a spell on you
Marie, Marie, da voodoo veau
She's the witch queen (ahhhh) of New Orlea-ens

I'm gonna tell you a story, strange as it now see-eems
Of zombie, voodoo, gris gris, and the Witch Queen of New Orleans
She lived in a world of magic, possessed by the devils skew-ew
From a shack near the swamplands, made of mud-pile brick
Marie stirred her witches brew-ew

(Chorus)

I'm gonna tell you a story, strange as it now see-eems
Of zombie, voodoo, gris gris, and the Witch Queen of New Orleans
She lived in a world of magic, possessed by the devils skew-ew
From a shack near the swamplands, made of mud-pile brick
Marie stirred her witches brew-ew

(Chorus)

Dime or a nickel could buy-uy, voodoo of any ki-ind
She had potions and lotions, herbs and tanna leaves
Guaranteed to blow your mi-ind
Early one mornin' into mucky swamp dew
Vanished Marie with hate in her eye-eyes
Though she'll never return, all the Cajuns knew-ew
A Witch Queen never dieie—ies

(Chorus)

Words and music by Pat Vegas and Lolly Vegas

Chapter Nine

"We got married in a fever . . ."

NEW ORLEANS RAILWAY STATION was a real treat – pleasant, uncrowded and no queues to speak of. There again, as far as I could tell, there are only two trains a day that use the station.

Mine was standing at the platform; but this was not just any old train, this was the 'City of New Orleans'. The very train which is celebrated in Steve Goodman's Grammy-winning song of that name.

Good morning America how are you?
Don't you know me I'm your native son
I'm the train they call the City of New Orleans
I'll be gone five hundred miles when the day is done

The song was written by Goodman, a struggling but respected Chicago song-writer in 1970, and has been called the best train song ever written. It describes the journey from Chicago to New Orleans and is generally regarded as a plaintive commentary on the disappearing railroads. The final line sums it up in seven words:

'This train's got the disappearing railroad blues'

The song was turned into a hit by Arlo Guthrie who, prior to recording it, only agreed to listen to Goodman singing it as a demo if Goodman would buy him a beer, and even then he would listen 'only as long as it takes to drink the beer'. It went on to become a major hit for Guthrie and later Willie Nelson, as well as being recorded by other artists such as Johnny Cash and Judy Collins. Goodman, who tragically died of leukaemia in 1984, at the age of 36, won a posthumous Grammy for the Willie Nelson version, which was voted Best Country Song in 1985.

The train still travels the route today, one train per day in each direction, a distance of 926 miles and a journey time of nineteen and a half hours. Like Route 66, the journey takes its place in American history, not just because of its musical connections, but because of its place in the social development of the country, this being the method by which many of the black African-American community migrated from the Deep South in the early 20th century.

It was, and still is, a cheap way to travel, with my ticket to Jackson costing just $22, which I was more than happy with for a 200 mile trip. And this in the luxury of an upstairs seat in the double-decker 'Superliner', complete with observation car. Compared to my rail travels in the UK this was comfort indeed. But not so good if you're in a hurry. At an average speed of 47 miles per hour for the trip overall to Chicago, and not much better than that for my trip to Jackson, it can make no pretensions to being a high speed train. Indeed, the journey served to re-inforce the preference given to freight in the States, as every time a freight train was due to pass in the opposite direction my train stopped until it had thundered past.

But I did like the little touch of the conductor finding out where you were going and then putting a little yellow Post-It note on the rack above, presumably in case you fell asleep, or am I being charitable – perhaps it is to make sure you don't travel further than you have paid for?

We trundled, but trundled in comfort, through the swamplands of Louisiana, again on stilts, with me watching every tree stump sticking out of the stagnant water to see if it moved. I was actually quite happy at the slow speed of the train as I was aware that a few years earlier a train further up the line had derailed at a speed of 78 mph. This was not the sort of place you would want that to happen as it would be touch and go whether you drowned before the alligators got to you. Not to mention the Water Moccasin of course.

We arrived at Jackson at 5.30pm and I decided to employ my safety first taxi routine, except there were no taxis. I eventually found a railway employee and he arranged to call a cab which then took me to the Holiday Inn Express just out of town. Jackson was another of those towns where the city centre closes down in the evening and you need to know where to go, but, as it happens, I had a very interesting and unusual restaurant right on my doorstep, which seemed a bit odd as it was not in a residential or entertainment area. Dennery's was a strange affair as it looked totally out of place in a semi-industrial area, prominent with its Greek-style pillars at the front entrance. Inside, it was quite sumptious with an ornate fountain in the middle of the dining area and tables with nice white tablecloths and impressive cutlery. I could see that Mr Dennery is well connected as previous customers have included George Bush Snr, Ronald Reagan and Arnold Schwarzenegger, all of whom featured in the photograph gallery in the foyer.

Strangely, I hadn't got any further than accepting the menu before one of the waiting staff started to ask me about Cliveden and the Christine Keeler set. I thought this rather bizarre here in Mississippi and even more so when he went on to talk enthusiastically about Anthony Hopkins and *The Remains of the Day*. Clearly he was intrigued by the aristocratic scene in England and perhaps he fancied himself as a butler. Anyway, the meal was good and, as there was nothing else in the neighbourhood to entice me out, I sat and enjoyed an Irish Coffee and a leisurely chat with the staff who did their best to enlighten me about the history of the area.

This is real *Mississippi Burning* country, the 1988 film being about the incident which happened just up the road in Neshoba County in 1964, which isn't that long ago when you think about it. From what I was told, the killing of three civil rights workers seems to have been quite accurately portrayed in the film. I thought there may be a reluctance to talk about this sort of thing, but it would appear that the white population have purged their conscience, perhaps helped by the sentencing of Edgar Ray Killen, one of the participants, in 2005, 41 years after the event. Seven others had been convicted in 1967, but the judge, who was a well known segregationist, handed down sentences of just 3 to 10 years and later declared, 'They killed one nigger, one jew, and a white man – I gave them all what I thought they deserved.'

At least Killen got his just desserts, if somewhat belatedly, with three 20 year sentences, which at the age of 80 I suppose is a bit of a deterrent not to do that sort of thing again.

My investigations revealed another infamous case, but this time going back to the '20s when a young black man was accused of raping a white girl. This case, known as the Lynching of LQ Ivy, had an even nastier feature in that the defendant was 'encouraged' to confess while a mob dangled him by his neck from a rope whilst grinding his testicles to pulp in a lemon squeezer. He somehow declined to confess but was still burned at the stake tied to a metal post.

The Civil War is never far away when in this part of the States and Jackson is no exception. It is not far from Vicksburg, which was a pivotal location, as it was vital to the Mississippi. As Abraham Lincoln put it at the time, 'Vicksburg is the key'. Alternatively, as Confederate President Jefferson Davis put it, 'Vicksburg is the nail head that holds the South's two halves together'. Jackson, which was a strategic rail and manufacturing centre for the Confederacy was closely linked to the fortunes of Vicksburg.

On 13 May 1863, the first battle of Jackson was won by the Union and, following the victory, key facilities in the city were burned before the Union troops headed west towards Vicksburg, 40 miles away. This gave Confederate forces the chance to re-group in Jackson whilst the Union concentrated on Vicksburg.

On May 22, Union forces suffered heavy casualties in attacking Vicksburg and General Ulysses S Grant decided that siege would be the only way to take the city. Over the next six weeks the population and defenders of Vicksburg were subject to constant barrage and had to resort to living in caves dug in the hillside. With disease and starvation adding to their woes, the Confederates surrendered on July 4.

During this time the Confederates at Jackson had assembled around 30,000 troops and had built defences. The Union army set off back from Vicksburg to lay siege to Jackson. After one week, on 16 July 1863, the Confederates managed to slip out during the night and retreat across the Pearl River. With the fall of Vicksburg and Jackson, the South was effectively split and this represented a devastating blow to the Confederate cause. After this second victory at Jackson the Union completely burned the town leaving it in ruins.

In the period since the Civil War, Jackson, which was named after General Andrew Jackson to commemorate his victory at New Orleans (it was previously called Parkerville and Lefleurs Bluff) has rebuilt itself and is a thriving city with a population of around 180,000. Its nickname is the 'Crossroads of the South' re-affirming its strategic location. Unlike other major cities in the area Jackson does not stand on the Mississippi, so its growth relied on rail commerce rather than river traffic, with metal industries and agriculture being the staple means of existence until the discovery of natural gas fields in the 1930s.

THE NEXT MORNING I CHECKED out of the hotel having decided it would be best to get a bus to Memphis, Tennessee which would get me there before dark. The 5.44pm would have got me there at 10pm, which I didn't fancy, not knowing Memphis and not having any accommodation booked. I had therefore decided on the 2.45 pm bus to get me there at 7pm.

I first caught a cab down to Jackson city centre, so I could get a feel for the place before I moved on. It was very businesslike, with buildings consisting mostly of office blocks and other commercial premises. I tried to locate the tourist office, only to find this had moved from its advertised location, which wasn't exactly tourist friendly. But perhaps it was taxi driver friendly as he unwittingly (I think) took me to the old location, thus bumping up the fare nicely. I eventually met with some success in meeting a nice lady called Mara at the Chamber of Commerce. Mara explained to me that Jackson has a considerable music heritage and is known as the 'City of Soul' and is famous for soul, Jazz and blues.

She explained it as 'Rich Blues' ('a sort of soul blues'), blues having been born in the Mississippi Delta. I needed educating on this delta business as I would have thought the Mississippi Delta was at the mouth of the river, which was a long way from where I was. I discovered that the area at the mouth of the river should correctly be called the Mississippi River Delta and that the Mississippi Delta refers to an area in the North West of the State, between the Mississippi and Yazoo rivers, and which stretches from Memphis down to Vicksburg. This is the area where Delta Blues emanates from. Mara explained that musicians from the Delta tended to gravitate either north to Nashville or south to Jackson where they would record on the famous Farish Street. In case you're wondering if the Yazoo is where Alison Moyet's 1980s band got their name, this is the subject of some debate. There is a Yazoo City just north of Jackson and there is a Yazoo record label which is strongly biased towards blues. However, it is also reported that the other half of Yazoo, Vince Clarke, suggests that the name came from a corruption of the Kazoo, the mouth instrument popular in the 1970s.

Musicians from the Delta form an impressive list, including Sam Cooke, Bobbie Gentry, Ike Turner, Muddy Waters and BB King. The man who started it all, though, was Robert Johnson, described by Eric Clapton as 'the most important blues musician who ever lived'. Despite dying at the age of 27 (in dubious circumstances, involving a woman, a jealous husband and poison), he is said to have influenced, among others, Jimi Hendrix, Bob Dylan and Led Zeppelin. He might have died young, but he was voted fifth in the Rolling Stone magazine's list of 100 greatest guitarists of all time behind Jimi Hendrix, Duane Allman (Allman Brothers), BB King and Eric Clapton.

I was encouraged by Mara to go to the Blues Cafe on Congress Street that evening to see some of this Delta Blues, but I explained that unfortunately my schedule dictated that by then I would be in the even more famous blues town of Memphis. She then suggested that I should go to Hal and Mal's restaurant for some lunch before leaving, as it is something of a cult venue. This treat I allowed myself, and, unusually, I found myself having a proper hot meal during the day.

I introduced myself to the co-owner Hal, who suggested I should try the Border Burger with Jalapeno peppers, salsa, guacamole and sour cream. This after introducing me to a starter called Tamales which included chilli powder, paprika, garlic and cumin. Given the heat output of these ingredients I'm sure I can be forgiven for breaking my normal rule of 'no beer during the day' and ordered a number of cold Michelobs. Hal went on to tell me that the Mal and Hal's St Patrick's Day Parade is the fourth biggest in the States and visitors come from all over the country to take part in the world famous 'Sweet Potato Queen' competition. It was all very enjoyable and I left the restaurant with a complimentary T-shirt which might fit me one day if I keep eating like that at lunchtime.

The reason for Jackson being on my itinerary was primarily the 1967 Johnny Cash song *Jackson*, which won him and his wife June Carter Cash a Grammy in 1968. It was also a hit for Nancy Sinatra and Lee Hazlewood in the same year. The story goes that Nancy heard the Cash version, loved it, got together with Lee and recorded it in 15 minutes. Not a bad quarter of an hours work I have to say.

Well, the song is very famous, but what is it all about?

'We got married in a fever, hotter than a pepper sprout'

This is a tough one and I don't know if there is such a thing as a pepper sprout, perhaps it has just been made up by the writers Jerry Leiber and Billy Edd Wheeler.

The other references aren't so bad

'But they'll laugh at you in Jackson, and I'll be dancing on a Pony Keg'

A 'Pony Keg' is a half keg (quarter barrel), containing 29.3369415 litres if you want to be particular.

'And I'll be waiting in Jackson, behind my Jaypan Fan'

'Jaypan Fan' can safely be taken to refer to a Japanese fan, pronounced in a slow southern drawl.

I have seen various interpretations of the words and meaning of the song ranging from, 'they are going to Jackson to reconcile', to 'Jackson is a euphemism for the place he's at when he gets high' ('go ahead and wreck your health'), he's 'just going to have a bit of fun and she doesn't care', to my own interpretation — they're having an argument, with him threatening to go and 'mess around' and with her saying 'yeah, well go try it and see what happens, you moron'. Or words to that effect.

The song is most associated with Johnny Cash, whose story is well documented, most recently, of course, in the 2005 Oscar-winning film *Walk The Line* starring Reese Witherspoon and Joaquin Phoenix. I did wonder when I first saw the film if it had been a bit sanitised as I thought that he had had more brushes with the law than it suggests. I think this might be because of my own perception, as my early exposure to his music was in the Folsom Prison and San Quentin days. The truth is that he was very benevolent towards prisoners and enjoyed playing for them, indeed he also recorded an album at a prison in Sweden.

Johnny did have some minor problems with the law, but nothing serious, one of his most memorable being when he spent a night in jail after allegedly stealing a rose from private property in Starkville, Mississippi in 1965 (other reports suggest he was arrested for being drunk — perhaps it was both). This little episode led to the song Starkville City Jail on his *Live At San Quentin* album.

In his career, J R Cash, as he is properly known, (his parents couldn't decide on a first name) sold over 90 million albums. In 1980 he became the Country Music Hall of Fame's youngest living inductee at the age of forty eight, which he considered his greatest achievement, and he wrote over one thousand songs. He overcame adversity, including drug addiction and alcoholism, and left a legacy of great music behind. He also lives on in another respect — in Starkville, in 2007, there was a festival held in his honour at which he was granted a posthumous pardon for his misdemeanour. The festival may become an annual event, with the emphasis being not just on Johnny and his music, but about the spirit of redemption for those who have transgressed.

One final thought on Jackson – I don't know which version of the song you prefer, but I'm going for the ultimate combination of Johnny Cash and Miss Piggy on the *Muppet Show* in 1981, with Miss Piggy looking very sexy in her purple Stetson and cowgirl outfit, and tough guy Johnny looking as though he'd at last met his match!

City Of New Orleans

Riding on the City of New Orleans
Illinois Central Monday morning rail
Fifteen cars and fifteen reckless riders
Three conductors and twenty-five sacks of mail
All along the southbound odyssey
The train pulls out at Kankakee
Rolls along past houses, farms and fields
Passin' trains that have no names
Freight yards full of old black men
And the graveyards of the rusted automobiles.

Chorus:
Good morning America how are you?
Don't you know me I'm your native son
I'm the train they call the City of New Orleans
I'll be gone five hundred miles when the day is done

Dealin' card games with the old men in the club car
Penny a point ain't no one keeping score
Pass the paper bag that holds the bottle
Feel the wheels rumblin' 'neath the floor
And the sons of Pullman porters
And the sons of engineers
Ride their fathers' magic carpets made of steel
Mothers with their babes asleep
Are rockin' to the gentle beat
And the rhythm of the rails is all they feel.

(Chorus)

Nighttime on the City of New Orleans
Changing cars in Memphis, Tennessee
Half way home, we'll be there by morning
Through the Mississippi darkness
Rolling down to the sea.
And all the towns and people seem
To fade into a bad dream
And the steel rails still ain't heard the news
The conductor sings his song again
The passengers will please refrain
This train's got the disappearing railroad blues

(Chorus)

Words and music by Steve Goodman

Jackson

We got married in a fever, hotter than a pepper sprout
We've been talkin' 'bout Jackson, ever since the fire went out
I'm goin' to Jackson, I'm gonna mess around
Yeah, I'm goin'to Jackson
Lookout Jackson town

Well, go on down to Jackson, go ahead and wreck your health
Go play your hand you big talkin' man, make a big fool of yourself
Yeah, go to Jackson; go comb your hair
Honey, I'm gonna snowball Jackson
See if I care

When I breeze into that city, people gonna stoop and bow
All them women gonna make me, teach 'em what they don't know how
I'm goin' to Jackson, you turn loose my coat
Cos I'm goin to Jackson
'Goodbye', that's all she wrote

But they'll laugh at you in Jackson, and I'll be dancin' on a pony keg
They'll lead you round town like a scalded hound
With your tail tucked between your legs
Yeah go to Jackson, you big talking man
And I'll be waitin in Jackson , behind my Jaypan Fan

Well now, we got married in a fever, hotter than a pepper sprout
We've been talkin' bout Jackson , ever since the fire went out
I'm goin' to Jackson, and that's a fact
Yeah we're goin' to Jackson, ain't never comin' back

Well we got married in a fever, hotter than a pepper sprout
And we've been talkin' bout Jackson ever since the fire went out....

Words and music by Jerry Leiber and Billy Edd Wheeler

Chapter Ten

"Nashville Cats play clean as country water . . ."

I LEFT JACKSON, AS PLANNED, on the 2.45 pm bus, which was absolutely packed, every nook and cranny being filled with luggage, legs, or whimpering kids and we headed north up the Mississippi Highway.

I found myself sitting next to Leroy Dundee, a retired trucker, who, having done his "million miles", was now content on riding Greyhound to get to see his girlfriend. He soon established that he was not the only trucker on board and began a conversation with a hulk of man, a few seats forward, who still drives the highways and who clearly considers his cab his home. We were treated to a disquisition about his 600 gallon tank (4 x 150), his 84" King Bed and 32" plasma, not to mention his shower and microwave.

He then went on to discuss the multiple pile-ups he has seen, including one where a man had his entire sternum ripped out. He enjoyed telling the audience at large that it was through a truck breakdown that he met his wife. She, a mere 16 year-old, was nearby and asked if there was anything she could do to help. He replied, "Yes ma'am, there sure is" and that was that. It would seem he now prefers to keep his distance.

Having listened to talk of on-road disasters and mayhem, I thought it must be my imagination when I sensed the bus was not going in a straight line. The situation soon got worse and in a matter of seconds we were weaving all over the road. "Jesus, it's a blow out," exclaimed Tommy Trucker, as the driver struggled to pull over to the hard shoulder "right in the middle of friggin' nowhere," he added just for good measure, in case we weren't convinced of our plight.

Personally, I was just relieved that we had stopped safely and that my sternum was still intact.

"Thank Jesus it wasn't a steer tyre," he went on. "I've seen trucks just flip over when the steer tyre has gone. We're too heavily loaded for the tyres . . . combined with the heat . . . the tyres just couldn't take it." I don't know where he got his calculations from, and I've no idea whether there was any substance in his comments, but he succeeded nicely in dramatising the occasion even further.

This was a nightmare scenario, no-one knew how long it would take to sort the situation out or what would happen next. The driver instructed people not to get off the bus, but after about 30 minutes he was under so much pressure from irate passengers he had to amend his position on this in order to avoid a riot.

Many got out and sat on the embankment alongside the hard shoulder and one scary incident saw a little girl aged about three make a beeline for the motorway before someone managed to catch her at the last minute. We were informed that we would have to await a breakdown truck which, after about an hour, finally arrived. A delicate manoeuvre followed, which involved reversing the bus on to a plank of wood to give a few inches clearance in order to remove the offending tyre. Eventually the bus got rolling again, now running at least two hours late. To make matters worse the driver, operating on a reserve tyre, had to restrict his speed considerably, thus adding to the delay. Tommy Trucker in the meantime entertained us with a constant stream of jokes, which were memorable for their extreme and abject triteness.

The culmination of the afternoon's events was that we arrived in Memphis at 9.30pm – exactly the scenario I had tried to avoid. I walked out of the bus station with more than a little concern. It was not the most inviting situation for a newcomer to town. I had no idea where I was in relation to the city centre or whether I might be on the edge of a ghetto. I made the right decision, fortunately, and turned left rather than right, heading for the first hotel I could see. It wasn't brilliant, it was quite expensive at $140 dollars, but it was refuge, so I booked in.

I was then informed by the surly receptionist that I was lucky that they had a room and that they wouldn't be able to accommodate me the following night (Friday). This was because of an American football game on Saturday between Tennessee State and Jackson Tigers, which would involve a crowd of over 50,000 (and this for a college match). There would be no room at this inn, or any other in town, so tomorrow I was going to have to demonstrate flexibility in my logistical arrangements.

Over my unadventurous steak and chips at TGI Fridays I got my map out and ascertained that my best bet would probably be to head for Nashville, perhaps returning to Memphis at some stage in the next week or so.

ON LEAVING MEMPHIS BY BUS on Saturday morning, for the 227 mile trip to Nashville, I was impressed by some of the nice houses on the outskirts, and made comment to this effect to my seating companion, who was a young girl on her way back to college in Wisconsin. From what she said in reply, Lachunté had clearly been in some sort of trouble. She volunteered that she had been back home to try to sort herself out. "In with the wrong crowd," was her diagnosis and she had a very firm resolve, on her return, to dump her 'pals' who were leading her astray. She was actually quite a decent young person and seemed genuinely determined to turn her life around.

We spent the next hour or two doing crosswords from the book I had bought at Newcastle Airport, but hadn't as yet touched, and in the end I donated it to her as she seemed to be quite enjoying it (I suspect it was her first experience of crosswords). We also whiled away the time trying to name the 50 states in the US, which she was marginally better at, and which gradually involved a number of other passengers who couldn't resist contributing. It was bit of relief from the constant scenery of cotton fields, which are quite nice when you first see them, but which get a little repetitive after an hour or two. It also diverted me from the fact that the driver appeared to be driving with his elbows whilst fiddling with a pile of documents.

The thing that struck me most about the unending fields of the South's most important crop was the uncomfortable height at which it grows; just enough to make you stoop, but not low enough to get on your knees. What a back-breaking job that must have been in the cotton-picking days as, until the introduction of machinery in the 1950s, every single cotton ball had to be picked by hand. A good picker would apparently pick 250-270 pounds in a day, which is about 19 stone – a lot of cotton wool buds.

On arrival in Nashville at 6pm I took a taxi to the Holiday Inn Express which I had taken the trouble to book in advance in view of my problems at Memphis.

This was, as I might have expected, 4 to 5 miles out of the centre. My plan was to stay for two nights at Nashville, so I decided just to stay local this Friday evening to investigate nearby hostelries or restaurants. I asked at reception whether there were any restaurants around, apart from the usual fast food outlets. The answer was negative, which surprised me somewhat as I thought I had spotted, from the taxi, what looked like a Mexican restaurant down the hill.

It was suggested I might like to go to a local bar around the back of the hotel where they serve food and have live country music. I went round and ordered myself a beer, listened to a couple of numbers, including *House of the Rising Sun*, from a half decent singer who enlightened us on the ingredients of the "perfect Country and Western song". Apparently it should contain a combination of prison, mama, trains, and, somewhere along the line, hitting the bottle. So there you are Paula, it's not just about the dog dying.

I looked around for signs of food and saw that some people were finishing off bar meals at their tables and I caught sight of a notice for very reasonably priced Pizzas. I decided this would do and went to place the order at the bar, only to be told they had just sold the last one.

"No problem," I replied. "I'll have something else."

"Well there is a problem, sir,' came the reply. "We only sell pizzas."

Oh well, there you go, another beer would help in the meantime while I reviewed my strategy.

While I was finishing my Bud I made my mind up to go out and investigate the mirage I had seen down the hill, paid the bill and set off into the sunset. As I approached the bottom of the hill I could see the sign Marisqueria Manjar, the external décor strongly suggesting a Mexican restaurant. I walked inside and again it was one of those situations where everything stops while the locals size up the stranger. I was quite clearly the only non-Mexican in the place. I was shown by sign language to a little table and given a menu. Fortunately you don't need to be a linguist to understand tortilla, enchilada, tostada or burritos and I ended up with as much as I could eat which, together with a couple of beers, came to the princely sum of $15 including tax.

Somehow I ended up playing pool again, this time I wasn't even sure if I was playing single or doubles. It was all very confusing, with my Spanish being restricted to the contents of a Mexican menu, and someone taking his brother's turn when he went to the Gents. When the sibling came back I heard the only English I encountered in the place all night "Kick his arse, brother," but I still don't know if it was an encouragement to me from a partner or an exhortation to his real brother to give me a licking.

It was a little bit on the threatening side, but all passed off well and I had the temerity to win again before leaving while the going was good. On the way back up the hill I was feeling good about my pool exploits and wondered if the pockets are bigger in the States or whether they are just bad players, or perhaps they take pity on anyone stupid enough to wander into the lion's den and challenge the locals.

I decided to head back to the Country and Western bar to see if the music was still playing. The place had been transformed and it seemed decidedly dodgy – smoky and with some rough-looking characters around, so I had one beer and called it a night. On my way out I visited the Gents and was intrigued to see some graffiti on the wall which might go a long way to explaining why no-one felt inclined to point me in the direction of Marisqueria Manjar. 'Bring our troops back put them on the border' went the slogan. I headed back to the hotel feeling somewhat enlightened about local sensitivities.

On Saturday morning I awoke full of enthusiasm, excited at being in Nashville, 'The Music City', and not quite knowing what to expect. I took a cab into town and asked to be dropped at the Convention Centre, where I understood I would find an information desk. One of my objectives was to check out the Grand Ole Opry, the spiritual home of Country music and host to 'the radio show that has brought Country and Western to a nationwide and worldwide audience non-stop for over 80 years.'

The information desk advised me that the Opry is now located out of town, but that I could buy tickets at the old venue, the famous Ryman Auditorium, 'The Mother Church of Country Music'. I was also told that I would pass Tootsies Orchid Lounge, a renowned honky tonk bar, and that I should find the time to have a look in (as if I needed such encouragement). I set off for the Ryman, congratulating myself as I managed to walk past Tootsies without stopping – it was, after all, only just turning lunchtime.

When I walked into the Ryman building I mentally noted it on my list for a tour, if I had time the next day, as I could see it has a wonderful musical heritage. It was the home of the Opry from 1943 to 1974, and before then it had a fascinating history including performances by Enrico Caruso and Rudolph Valentino. It was also the place where Bluegrass music was born when Bill Monroe and his Bluegrass

Boys, including Lester Flatt and Earl Scruggs, performed there in the mid-1940s. More recently Coldplay have described it as 'The Greatest Theatre in the World'. Not a bad little recommendation.

After I got my ticket for the early evening performance at the Opry, I headed back to Broadway, the hub of the music scene, passing on the way Printers Alley where Jimi Hendrix used to regularly perform and Ryman Alley (connected to Tootsies by a back door), where Chet Atkins discovered the Everly Brothers. This time I did allow myself to have a peek in Tootsies. It was 12.20 pm. If I tell you that I surfaced at 4pm, and only then because I needed to eat, it will give you an indication of the contagiousness of the place. I had effectively been hijacked by the music; I saw a couple of bands in the time I was in and they were both first class. But it wasn't just that, it was the general atmosphere. The bands don't get paid a fee, they work for tips and every now and again they get one of the more attractive customers to walk around with a bucket collecting dollars here and dollars there. I should have known when I went in it was going to be lively when I saw the sign 'No dancin' on the tables with spurs on.'

I had never associated country music with raucousness and indeed the early numbers were fairly conservative. The first song I caught was appropriately *Tennessee Waltz*, followed by a couple of Roger Miller numbers and I thought to myself that you can't help admire someone who writes a song called *You Can't Rollerskate In A Buffalo Herd*. We then had some Merle Haggard (*Big City*) and Hank Williams (*I'm So Lonesome I Could Cry*, which, according to our singer, Elvis once said was the saddest song he ever recorded).

I'm not sure how it happened, but gradually a transformation took place, the tempo of the music changed, and all of a sudden people were on the bar dancing (without spurs), a Willie Nelson look-a-like was strolling around the bar posing for photographs and a drinking ritual called 'holler and swoller' was in full flow, generally when the tips bucket was in circulation I noticed. The band finished their set with a rendition of AC/DC's *Highway to Hell* – the parting shot from the front man being "just because we're Country doesn't mean we can't rock".

"Fair enough," I thought as I took another swoller.

I could easily have stayed into the evening, but I needed to eat and get to the Opry, so I turned down the opportunity of a drink offered by a couple sitting next to me, whilst I noted the singer advising that anyone who had a plane to catch in the morning would be well advised not to go to Tootsies that night.

In the evening I arrived at the Opry in good time to take advantage of the pre-show entertainment in the forecourt which consisted of fiddlers, dancers and singers creating a hoedown type atmosphere which got the country juices flowing nicely. Inside the building, the expansive auditorium, which seats 4,000, was healthily full as the first act took to the stage. This followed a warm up by a Minnie Pearl tribute act, Minnie Pearl being a famous comedienne who used to entertain the audience before the big show back in the 1940s and for decades after, becoming a famous Opry institution in the process. I felt respectably young, compared to the average age of the audience (which is perhaps not surprising bearing in mind the show has been running since 1925 and is thus popular with a lot of older fans) as the cast launched into an avalanche of sixteen different acts over the next couple of hours.

There was a selection of old-timers, as well as some up and coming, but apparently well-known, musicians. I have to confess that in my ignorance the only name that I recognised was Hank Locklin, famous for *Send Me The Pillow That You Dream On*, (which, after being a hit for Hank in 1958, went on to achieve further fame through Johnny Tillotson and Dean Martin), and *Please Help Me I'm Falling* which was a huge hit for Hank in 1960.

Hank is now 89 and amazingly still performing, and still performing amazingly, at the Opry. One of the reasons for continuing to a ripe old age at the Opry is the fact that you can only remain a member if you complete a certain number of performances each year. But more to the point, I got the impression Hank enjoyed it and, being a country legend, and the Opry's oldest living member, he is clearly determined not to relinquish his position lightly.

Although Hank was the only name which rung a bell with me, I would find out about some of the other performers the next day at the Country Music Hall of Fame. In hindsight it would have been better if I had gone to the Hall of Fame before the Opry as I would have been in considerable awe as I listened to people like Porter Wagoner and Steve Wariner. Porter Wagoner was Dolly Parton's mentor and Dolly was a regular on his TV show. Porter had hits with a number of duets with Dolly, but also had hits of his own including *Green, Green Grass of Home* in 1964 before Tom Jones recorded his version. Sadly, Porter died of cancer a few weeks after my visit.

Steve Wariner is from the generation after Porter. Now in his fifties, but looking much younger, he is a big star in the States and has had at least 10 number one country hits. He is also a renowned songwriter and co-wrote *Longneck Bottle*, which was a number one hit for Garth Brooks.

The thing that surprised me most, never having heard the show on the radio, was the adverts. At regular intervals the announcers, and sometimes the artists, would read out from a script whilst dittys were sung and logos shown for products ranging from Health Insurance (Nashville's biggest industry) to Tennessee Sausage, and the most famous sponsor, Martha White (baking products), who have sponsored the Opry since 1948. 'Use Martha's self-raising flour to get the perfect Pumpkin Streusel Muffins' . . . 'Martha White makes muffins, cornbreads, and brownies easy to bake with the down-home goodness your family is sure to love' . . . 'Martha White – a Southern Family Tradition'. This in addition to the Opry's 'presenting sponsor' – Cracker Barrel Old Country Store.

It seemed a bit perverse that one minute I was being encouraged to stuff myself full of cakes and biscuits and the next to take out a health insurance plan, but I suppose there's a connection when you think about it.

After the show I took a cab downtown to see what Broadway had to offer in the evening. I couldn't help but be drawn back to Tootsies. It was humming. By this time (11pm) people were dancing on the bar as well as the tables (still no spurs). And the music was again top notch. I thought I had better get out and about for a while and so headed off down Broadway and tested a couple more bars, including one where I had a little mishap I need to report.

I was enjoying a Corona, drinking it out of the bottle, as you must do, with the piece of lime wedged over the lip. Now, earlier on my trip, it might have been El Paso, I had seen someone put their thumb over the top of the bottle and turn it upside down while pressing the lime into the bottle. This looked cool, so I thought this must be the thing to do. I put my thumb over the neck and confidently twisted my wrist, turning the bottle upside down. So far so good. But then, as I nonchalantly took my thumb off the top of the bottle, it all went badly wrong. The scene was like the podium at the end of a Grand Prix as my precious beer fizzed all over the people standing in close proximity.

Suddenly I had a lot more space to myself than I thought would have been possible in such a crowded bar. I believe I then compounded things by trying to wipe down the young lady who'd had the biggest shower. For some reason she didn't seem impressed at all by my efforts to make her comfortable, it just goes to show some people are never grateful.

I ended up in a late fast food restaurant eating hubcaps and fries (hubcaps being mini-burgers) and was amazed to see it was a quarter to four. I should have been shattered after the day I'd had, but I could quite easily have stayed out for more as the music was still going strong. However, demonstrating rare good judgement, I decided enough was enough and went out in search of a cab.

I DID WELL TO GET UP reasonably early in the morning, packed my bag and set off downtown again; later in the day I would be taking the Greyhound to Chattanooga but my immediate objective was the Country Music Hall of Fame and Museum.

The Hall of Fame is the Mecca of country music, welcoming 400,000 visitors each year. It is housed in a state of the art building – a $37 million showpiece with classic old-style radio mast, windows designed to look like the black keys of a piano, a rotunda with roof consisting of four discs of different sizes (representing the evolution of recording technology from the '78' to the CD) and, from the air, the building is in the shape of a bass clef.

There are many places in Nashville to indulge yourself, but this one is a must, with exhibitions ranging from Marty Robbins to Ray Charles (but changing regularly) and with the history of country music laid out before you. Even if you are not a great country fan you cannot fail to be moved by the TV clips, the music, the artefacts and the history. A Johnny Cash guitar here, a Kris Kristofferson manuscript there, a Dolly Parton outfit bursting out from a protective glass case, even Elvis's 1960 gold Cadillac which he used to commute between Graceland and Nashville is on display (he actually drove it himself to the old Hall of Fame site in order to donate it to the museum).

In the rotunda the circular wall is filled with plaques outlining the lives and careers of the 101 inductees of the Hall of Fame, all under the watchful gaze of the brass letters spelling out the unofficial anthem of the museum, *Will the Circle Be Unbroken*, the title of the old Carter Family song.

I was surprised at the Ray Charles and Elvis exhibits as I would not previously have classed them as country musicians. The Ray Charles exhibition in particular gave me pause for thought, but when you look at his credentials there aren't many areas of music he hasn't had an impact on. In fact, he made an album in 1962 called *Modern Sounds in Country and Western Music*, which did wonders in extending the appeal of country to other music fans. What tickled me about his exhibition, though, was the revelation that he used to take Braille magazines on tour with him and that one of them was *Playboy*. I'll say no more on that point, but it did make me smile – perhaps almost as much as Ray!

The Marty Robbins exhibition was of considerable interest to me considering my visit to El Paso. I enjoyed it hugely and was pleased that I had come to learn more about someone I had heard of, but had not really appreciated, in the past. By all accounts he was a great guy, colourful, talented, an actor as well as a singer, and he was even a NASCAR racer, playing himself in the 1967 car racing film *Hell on Wheels*. All the while he was renowned for a great relationship with his fans for whom he always made time. His death in 1982 must have devastated huge numbers of his fans.

For an extra few dollars on the admission price you can also take in the historic Studio B (old RCA Victor studio) tour, a short courtesy bus ride away. This was phenomenal. A must if you are ever fortunate enough to visit. Try to imagine standing on the spot where Elvis recorded *Are You Lonesome Tonight?*, or Roy Orbison sang *Only the Lonely*, while the songs are played in the background. I can tell you it makes your hair stand on end and sends a shiver down your spine.

In the same studio Jim Reeves recorded *He'll Have to Go*, Dolly Parton *Jolene* and Skeeter Davis *The End of the World*, which was the only song ever to hit the top ten in all four categories of the Billboard charts – Pop/Rock, Country, Easy Listening, and Soul/R&B. It is also where Bobby Goldsboro recorded his mega-hit *Honey* which was the World's biggest song in 1968, selling a million copies in the first three weeks.

Obviously there is not much video footage available from that era, but one clip we did see shows Jim Reeves, complete in smart suit and tie, recording a song, *Blue Canadian Rockies*, using the same microphone that was on display right in front of me, and I could see he was positioned on the very spot where I would find myself standing minutes later.

Our tour guide, the genial Ron Harman, held up an album cover from one of Jim's LPs recorded just a year before his death, which eerily has him photographed standing in front of an aeroplane. Jim was flying to Nashville, on 31 July 1964, to the opening of Studio A, in the new office building next door to studio B, when his plane encountered a thunderstorm. It would appear that he became disoriented and didn't know in which direction he was travelling and that he may have been upside down without realising it. The plane plummeted to the ground and killed Jim and his manager and pianist Dean Manuel. 'Gentleman Jim' was only 40 when he died and although he had many posthumous hits the world was robbed of many years of his smooth and exceptional talents.

Patsy Cline's name cropped up and the evocative strains of *Crazy* suddenly filled my head as we were told about the similarly tragic event of her untimely death at the age of 30 a year earlier, in 1963 – again in a plane crash when headed for Nashville. Strangely, Patsy had almost forecast her own death in things she had said to friends in the weeks leading up to the crash. Another coincidence is that Jim Reeves and the pilot of Patsy's plane were trained by the same instructor.

There were many happier recollections, though, and we were treated to a fascinating tour. The studio has been kept as it was in the '50s and '60s and Ron pointed out the piece of a door that Elvis had kicked off a cabinet in frustration when he couldn't get an acetate demo to play on an ancient record player. The cabinet has never been repaired and must now be among the most revered pieces of damaged furniture you could find anywhere.

Studio B, masterminded by guitarist and producer, Chet Atkins, was open from 1957 to its closure on 17 August 1977, the day after Elvis's death. In over 16,000 separate sessions, 47,000 songs were recorded there, of which 1,000 became top ten singles. Elvis himself recorded an incredible 262 tracks in the studio and the Jordannaires became the most recorded team of all as they also regularly backed other artists recording in the studio.

RCA often rented the studio to other companies to create yet more musical history and this is where the Everlys recorded *Cathy's Clown*, *All I Have to Do is Dream*, and *When Will I Be Loved* for Warner Bros. Roy Orbison was recording here for Monument Records when engineer Bill Porter placed him behind a coat rack filled with coats and blankets to create an isolation effect which helped bring out Roy's unique voice. It's incredible to think that such beautiful recordings came out under such low tech circumstances and I am sure I will always think of that every time I hear Roy's music in the future.

Whilst recording *Are You Lonesome Tonight?*, which was amazingly done in one take, Elvis asked for the lights to be turned out (he liked recording late at night) and if you listen closely to the track you will be able to hear him bump into a microphone stand as he moved around in the darkness! The Steinway piano that Elvis used to play when warming up and which he and his session player Floyd Cramer used on recordings is still in the room and visitors are not only allowed to touch it but are actually free to play it if they wish. When standing in the studio listening to

Elvis it is quite an emotional experience and I can understand why many people say that Elvis haunts the room. You can certainly feel his presence.

Another Studio B artist and Hall of Fame inductee, Waylon Jennings, always felt guilty about giving up his seat to 'Big Bopper', J P Richardson, in 1959 for the fatal plane trip that killed the Bopper, Richie Valens and Buddy Holly. Valens was feeling unwell and Jennings didn't want him to have to travel by bus, so he gave him his seat on the plane. A kind gesture which deserved to be rewarded by more than a lifetime of guilt.

On the outside of the building, patches in the brickwork mark the spot where Dolly Parton crashed into the wall when arriving late for a recording session. The story goes that after her little accident she walked into the studio as if nothing had happened and when the car was seen embedded in the wall during a cigarette break she never admitted that it was hers. An embellishment on the story suggests that she hadn't even passed her driving test, but had simply 'charmed' a man in the Licence Bureau to get her licence. This may seem far-fetched, but the story does come from Dolly herself in her 1994 autobiography, in which she also makes the confession: 'In my rush to get to the studio that day, I forgot one basic element of driving – braking.' You can't help but love her.

ALTHOUGH I HAD ONLY BEEN in Nashville two days it felt like a lot longer and I was now quite at home. I had learnt that the town was founded in 1779 and that local legend has it that the first musical star was Davy Crockett in the early 1800s. Davy became an accomplished fiddler and buck dancer (a form of clog dancing apparently, but we won't hold that against him bearing in mind his other heroics).

Things really took off in the music sense for Nashville in 1925 when WSM radio was founded and they broadcast a show called the WSM Barndance. In 1928 it was renamed Grand Ole Opry as it followed immediately after an opera programme and the presenter, George D Hay, said, "For the past hour you have been listening to music taken largely from the Grand Opera. From now on we will present the Grand Old Opry". As the station had 'clear channel' status the programme was available to most of the country, so the name became known in households all over the States and eventually the wider world.

Another station, WLAC, was formed in 1926, but focused more on news and features. Encouraged by WSM's success they gradually diversified into music and this was particularly the case in the '50s when the station became famous for its

R&B programmes. It was really the first station to introduce black artists to its audience and the music was originally intended for Afro-American listeners in the Deep South. However, because WLAC also had clear station status, it reached a much wider audience and was later credited with being very instrumental in the development of Rock and Roll and later Reggae.

The recording industry in Nashville was born in 1944 when RCA Victor came to town to record Opry star Eddie Arnold. This was followed up in 1948 when Country star Red Foley had the first Nashville million-selling record. To cope with this demand a record pressing plant was built and the town was well and truly established in the record manufacturing business. Although Nashville had its roots in Gospel and Country, by the 1960s it had become a haven for Rock and Roll stars and all the big names of the day recorded in town including Elvis, The Everlys, Bob Dylan, Brenda Lee and the Beach Boys.

The town itself stands on the Cumberland River and is the capital of Tennessee. It was originally named Fort Nashborough after the American War hero Francis Nash. With some reluctance Tennessee had joined the secession and sided with the Confederacy for whom it was a big prize because of its river and rail transportation links. Having been the last state to secede it became, in 1862, the first to fall to Union troops. One of the bloodiest battles of the Civil War took place just south of Nashville on 30 November 1864 at the battle of Franklin. Franklin was just a small town with a population of 750 people, but after a five hour battle between Confederate and Union troops, the locals were left with over 9,000 casualties lying on the battlefield. Despite horrific Confederate losses of around 2,000 dead (including six Generals) and 4,000 seriously wounded, the rebels pursued the cause and tackled the Union again at the Battle of Nashville on December 15 and 16. The Confederate Tennessee Army was effectively wiped out at this battle and Nashville was the final action of any significance in the region.

There must be lots of songs about, or referring to Nashville, but none that I can remember being huge hits in the UK. The only one that comes to mind is *Nashville Cats* by the Lovin' Spoonful, which was a hit in 1967 on both sides of the Atlantic. The Spoonful were spawned out of an unsuccessful band called the Mugwumps, who operated between 1964 and 65. With a name like the Mugwumps I am not really surprised that they didn't succeed, but, interestingly, when the band split it formed two groups – The Lovin' Spoonful and, believe it or not, the Mamas & the Papas. John Sebastian and Zal Yanovsky formed the Spoonful and Cass Elliot and Denny Doherty formed the Mamas, with fifth Mugwump, Jim Hendricks, going on to be a successful songwriter.

Between 1965 and 1969 the Spoonful had a string of albums and single hits including *(What a Day for a) Daydream* and their only number one *Summer in the City*, which contained some memorable lines such as:

> *All around, people looking half dead*
> *Walking on the sidewalk, hotter than a matchhead*

For readers who were not around in the '60s they might recognise the song better as the music from the opening sequences of the Bruce Willis film *Die Hard: With a Vengeance* or from relevant episodes of *Only Fools and Horses* or even *The Simpsons*.

The band evidently took their name from a song called *Coffee Blues* by Mississippi John Hurt who, strangely, extols the virtue of Maxwell House in his song. But wait, is it not true that Blues artists often use metaphors in their songs and that perhaps we're not talking about coffee at all? It is up to you to decide, but bear in mind that a 'spoonful' can refer to cocaine or heroin or can alternatively have sexual connotations which I would rather not go into:

> *'I used to have a girl cookin' a good Maxwell House.*
> *She moved away*
> *I wanna see my baby 'bout a lovin' spoonful'*

Look it up and decide for yourself.

As for *Nashville Cats*, the song ('Well there's thirteen hundred and fifty two guitar pickers in Nashville') celebrates the musical heritage of the town ('and they can pick more notes than the number of ants on a Tennessee anthill').

The lines in the chorus

> *'Nashville Cats, been playin' since they's babies*
> *Nashville Cats, get work before they're two'*

are perhaps a little exaggerated, but we get the idea and it helps explain why I couldn't get out of Tootsies on a Saturday lunchtime.

The lyrics go on to make reference to 'yellow Sun records from Nashville', which is a bit odd as Sun records is famously from Memphis, as you will find out very shortly. I can only assume this was a bit of artistic licence on behalf of the Spoonful.

Whilst the band may not have achieved the same level of success as some of their contemporaries of the '60s they were very influential and were credited with bridging the gap between folk and rock by introducing electric instruments to music that had always been acoustic based. This encouraged emerging groups like the Grateful Dead to do likewise. A measure of their status is that the Spoonful were inducted into the Rock and Roll Hall of Fame in 2000.

Having drenched myself in musical nostalgia, particularly the 50s and 60s era, during my stupendous stay in Nashville, it was now time to head south and turn the clock back to the 40s in my pursuit of the enigmatic Glenn Miller. As the bus pulled out of the depot I was feeling very satisfied as I said farewell to the town, taking one last glance at the amazing BellSouth building, the tallest building in Tennessee. It is known locally as the Batman Building because of its twin spires which resemble the Caped Crusader's helmet and is meant to represent Nashville's commitment to the future. But to me it confirmed that this place is indeed the home of super-heroes and is a town that any music lover has to put on their list of places to visit. Not to be missed under any circumstances.

Nashville Cats

Refrain
Nashville Cats, play clean as country water
Nashville Cats, play wild as mountain dew
Nashville Cats, been playin' since they's babies
Nashville Cats, get work before they're two

Well, there's thirteen hundred and fifty two guitar pickers in Nashville
And they can pick more notes than the number of ants
On a Tennessee anthill

Yeah, I was just thirteen you might say I was a
Musical proverbial knee high
When I heard a couple of new-sounding tunes on the tubes
And they blasted me sky-high
And the record man said every one is a yellow Sun
Record from Nashville
And up north there ain't nobody buys them
And I said, but I will

(Refrain)

Well, there's sixteen thousand eight hundred twenty one
Mothers from Nashville
All their friends play music, and they ain't uptight
If one of the kids will
Because it's custom made for any mother's son
To be a guitar player in Nashville
And I sure am glad I got a chance to say a word about
The music and the mothers from Nashville

(Refrain)

Words and music by John Sebastian/Nashville Cats

Chapter Eleven

"Pardon me boy . . ."

I SETTLED DOWN FOR THE four hour trip to Chattanooga next to a girl in military uniform. I reckoned that if she was in the military there was less chance of her being a nutter, although that's a dangerous assumption I suppose.

At least sitting next to someone in the forces provided an opportunity for me to get to understand the way law enforcement works in the States, as I've always been unclear about the difference between Sheriffs, Police, National Guard and State troopers. Ashlie, as it turned out, was in the National Guard, more or less equivalent to our Territorial Army. As a recent recruit she was still in training, but the chances are that she will end up at some stage in one of the World's trouble hotspots as the National Guard form almost 50% of the US forces in active service. There is also a State Guard, regulated by the same National Guard Bureau as the national force, but who are under the command of the State Governor.

So where do State Troopers fit in to this equation? Well there is something called State Police, which is a police body unique to a particular state and who perform functions outside of the jurisdiction of the County Sheriff. These duties, undertaken by troopers, include highway patrol (on state roads), protection for the Governor and involvement in serious cases. The Sheriff is an elected law enforcement official who looks after law enforcement in a particular county through his force of Deputy Sheriffs. It is a little more complicated than that as the situation can vary from state to state, particularly in the North East of the country, where there is a trend towards State Police and County Police in the metropolitan areas.

Ashlie was fascinated by the UK and some of her questions served to confirm my previous experience of the peculiar views of quite a few people in the States, particularly those living outside of the cities, regarding our way of life: "Is it true that everywhere closes in England at a certain time of the day for everyone to have a cup of tea?"

"Where did you get that idea?" I asked.

"My momma told me," came the response.

"Is it true that there are no fat people in England?" she went on. "My momma told me . . . she says you have three or four things on the plate, you move your fork around, have a little bit of each and that's it, you leave the rest."

I could take all of this with a smile tonight as I was still basking in the after-glow of the Hall of Fame and the wonderful Studio B tour.

WE ARRIVED AT CHATTANOOGA around 8pm and again I got a taxi to a Holiday Inn Express as I had by now discovered that in most places they provided a low cost, but decent, standard of accommodation; the only drawback being that they were usually a few miles out of town. I ended up eating in a Taco Bell, my first ever visit to such an establishment, but it was the only eatery around and even this was about to close. The two youngsters on duty, however, were enthralled to talk to someone from England and made me feel like a star. It was a pleasure to talk to them in between reading leaflets telling me that I was sitting in the shadow of the famous Lookout Mountain which was the location of the 'Battle above the Clouds' during the Battle of Chattanooga in the Chickamauga phase of the Civil War and which was mentioned in Martin Luther King's famous 'I have a dream' speech – "Let freedom ring from Lookout Mountain of Tennessee ..."

In the morning I opened the curtains and looked out and there, sure enough, was Lookout Mountain, the bottom part of it shrouded spectacularly in mist.

I had the usual coffee and pastry and checked out – I had decided that I was too far out of town for comfort and that any savings in hotel costs were going to be eaten up by taxi fares. I had decided on a two night stay in Chattanooga in order to have the time to investigate the place and the famous Glenn Miller song bearing its name. I wasn't sure how much, if at all, *Chattanooga Choo Choo* would be cele-brated in the town but I would soon find out. I asked the taxi driver to take me into the town centre and find me a decent but reasonably priced hotel. "Why not stay at the Chattanooga Choo Choo?," he said, which answered my question at a stroke.

We drove up to the Choo Choo which can hardly be missed, bearing in mind it has a huge imitation train sitting on the roof. The building was very impressive from the outside and was clearly the old railway station, a tall red brick construction with a huge decorative arch forming the entrance. "It's the old station," the driver explained. "It's no longer in use, but it's been refurbished by Holiday Inn and is a nice hotel."

"Looks expensive," was my reply, noting it was a fully fledged Holiday Inn rather than an Express. But, it was going to be a starting point and, even if I didn't stay there, it was worth a look merely from the perspective of the song.

In the event, the nightly rate was only $100, so I booked in immediately. The reception area was brilliant, a beautifully refurbished Victorian style station hall, high ceilings with ornate plasterwork, comfortably upholstered furniture and exotic greenery. The receptionist advised me to go to the front door and there would be a buggy to take me to my accommodation. I climbed in what amounted to a golf buggy and we set off round the back of the building. As we turned the corner I was astonished to find I was in a railway complex with track, platforms, signals, Pullman cars and various other rail carriages. To add to this there was a replica engine, painted in red and green livery and complete with the type of massive funnel that you see in the cowboy films. The whole thing was effectively an outdoor museum and quite wonderful it was too. As we crossed the tracks and headed for some outbuildings I could see the site was huge, annexes to the hotel having been built in the grounds which were presumably at one time the marshalling yards.

I disembarked from the golf cart and made my way to the room thrilled at this gem of a discovery.

The town centre was about half a mile from the hotel and, despite the fact that there was a complimentary historic tram service, I decided to walk so that I could get a feel for the place. I immediately liked what I saw; the streets seemed modern but there were some historic buildings such as the Tivoli Theater, a lavishly restored survivor from the silent movie era, and the pavements were clean, being free from the curse of litter and chewing gum. There weren't many people around and it felt extremely relaxing.

I headed for the river (the Tennessee) and decided to treat myself to a trip on the Southern Belle, a three-tiered river boat. The Belle took us downriver towards Lookout Mountain and on the way I saw ample evidence of the industrial heritage of the city. In the 1930s, and beyond, Chattanooga had been known as the

'Dynamo of Dixie' and whilst this had kept the city employed it had the inevitable undesirable side effects such as pollution. I wouldn't have guessed it on this bright clear day having just walked through a beautifully clean town centre, but the air quality had been so bad in the '60s that the Federal Government declared it the worst in the nation. This, together with deteriorating infrastructure, racial tension and social problems led to investment and regeneration on an impressive scale. And it has worked. The riverfront area has been dramatically improved and is now in keeping with what I saw in the rest of the town. The only heavy industry I saw was the Alstom engineering plant with its barge-loading facility on the river. The plant manufactures boilers for coal-fired and nuclear power stations, typical of the industrial history of Chattanooga, which is famous for its association with steam power and also for steel manufacturing.

Evidence of the part the Tennessee River played, and still plays, in the economic well-being of the city is evident through the barges standing mid-river waiting to join a 'train' (that's my word – the proper term is 'integrated tow') for a trip, quite likely down to New Orleans, a six day and night journey. Barges carry coal, scrap, gravel, chemicals, wheat and soy beans, 53 million tons of it in total each year up and down the Tennessee, making it one of the nation's most important rivers.

Tug boats typically haul, or push, 15 barges in one tow, that can be as long as 1,100 feet, as wide as 135 feet and which can carry the equivalent of 900 truck loads or 225 rail cars. It's an ecologically sound way of transporting things and what's more it's safe; safer than road and safer than rail, with an accident rate of 0.01 deaths per billion ton-miles, which sounds impressive, even if I don't know what it means. The bad news is if you fall from a leisure craft in front of one of these tows then even at a distance of 1,000 metres you have less than a minute to get out of the way. So be careful if you intend to mess around on the Tennessee.

We cruised downstream towards Lookout Mountain, which was by now basking in the sunshine, not a trace of mist to be seen, and turned around at a wide bend in the river to return to explore the riverfront area of the town. This was very smart, with the regenerated riverside and Tennessee Aquarium on the south side, and Renaissance Wetland Park and Coolidge Park, complete with restored 1895 carousel, on the revitalised north bank.

We went under the 113 year-old Walnut Street Bridge, the longest pedestrian bridge in the world, and the Veterans Memorial Bridge before circumnavigating

MacLellan Island, all the while keeping our eyes peeled for the blue crested heron which populate the area. The sight of up-market housing on the north bank nicely completed the picture of a miraculous transformation from industrial workshop to attractive tourist venue and I have to say I was impressed.

As we sailed under Veterans Bridge I observed a chap in his early sixties having his photograph taken at the back of the boat under the Stars and Stripes and I asked his wife if she would like to get in the picture while I took it for them. She gratefully accepted and explained to me that her husband was a Vietnam veteran, which is why this particular bridge was of interest. After taking the picture to the best of my (limited) ability I spoke to the chap as I am always keen to ask veterans about their experiences. I asked him about his thoughts on the war and his reply was unequivocal – "I go where my leader sends me, I would never question my leader." He looked quite tough and with this sort of attitude I think he'd be a pretty good man to have in your team. When I mentioned that the most gripping book I had read about Vietnam was *Rumor of War* by Philip Caputo he was somewhat dismissive, I think his feeling was that Caputo was there too early in the war to write anything meaningful. Bearing in mind that I must have read that book almost 20 years ago, and I can still remember the impact it had on me, I'm glad I wasn't there in the later years, if at all of course.

I told him that my 86 year-old father, who is in ill health, used to be in Air Sea Rescue during the Second World War and that he still possesses a US Commando dagger given to him by an American serviceman rescued from the North Sea during Operation Market Garden in 1944. He was suitably impressed and said he would have a word with 'the man upstairs' about my Dad.

The boat's commentator advised us that Chattanooga is the home of Coca Cola bottling. Up until 1899 Coke had only been sold in fountains and when two entrepreneurs from Chattanooga went down to Atlanta to try to persuade the company to allow them to bottle the stuff they were laughed at. Eventually they got their way and bought the bottling rights for $1, which was never collected. They came back and opened the first Coke bottling plant in the world and 70 years later sold the rights back to the company for $98 million. Even taking inflation into account that sounds like a pretty sound deal.

Returning to dry land, I continued my exploration of the city, which is the fourth largest in Tennessee after Memphis, Nashville and Knoxville and has a population of around 155,000. It lies at the south-west tip of the Appalachian

Mountains and is surrounded by ridges, namely Missionary Ridge, Lookout Mountain, Raccoon Mountain and Stringers Ridge. The old industrial nature of the town has been replaced by a thriving professional community, including banking and insurance and this is reflected in the office buildings in the city centre.

Again I was in Civil War territory – it was as if I was inadvertently following a historic military trail. On September 19 and 20 1863, just three and a half miles to the north east of Chattanooga, the infamous battle of Chickamauga, took place. This turned into the bloodiest battle of the Civil War's western arena and during the two-day battle 34,000 Americans were killed or wounded.

The battle was won by the Confederates, but General Braxton Bragg failed to follow this up with an attack on Chattanooga, where 40,000 men of the Union army had retreated. The Confederates elected merely to besiege the town and Bragg's troops positioned themselves on Missionary Ridge and Lookout Mountain, both excellent positions overlooking the river. On November 24 Union troops attacked Lookout Mountain at 8am and a skirmish started around 10 am at which point fog had descended below the advancing soldiers. The battle therefore became known as the 'Battle above the Clouds'.

But in reality it was secondary to the battle of Missionary Ridge the following day. On November 25, the ridge was taken through a spontaneous charge by the Union soldiers who had been humiliated at Chickamauga and who were being taunted by other Union Divisions. Without orders, and chanting 'Chickamauga, Chickamauga', they advanced steadily under withering fire until they eventually took the Confederate position. Bragg ordered a Confederate retreat to Georgia and Chattanooga, the 'Gateway to the South', stayed safely in Union hands.

I enjoyed some lunch in the aptly named, from my point of view, Miller Park. This was opposite the equally nice and very modern Miller Plaza which has a pavilion and outdoor stage. As I ate my egg mayo submarine sandwich, I wondered whether the complex was named after Glenn or, alternatively, Miller Industries, the world's biggest manufacturers of recovery vehicles, who are based in Chattanooga and who gave the town another first when they invented the tow truck. Due to my schedule I would not be able visit the International Tow Truck Museum, although I'm sure it would have given me a nice lift!.

Arriving back at the hotel I asked if it might be possible to meet a member of the management team and ended up speaking to Julie Dodson, Director of Marketing, who was very helpful and who put at my disposal Justin, the museum manager and historic tram driver (it was the tram that was historic by the way, not Justin, who was actually quite young). Julie also kindly gave me a Glenn Miller CD, which of course contained *Chattanooga Choo Choo,* the song which had drawn me to the town.

I spent an enjoyable hour in the company of the knowledgeable and enthusiastic Justin, who took me into the carriages (rail cars as they call them in the States) which have been converted into bedrooms. He then showed me the restaurant car where on certain nights of the week you can sit and be fed in the opulence associated with the old railroad days.

He also took me to see the model railway display. This was unbelievable. It is one of the largest, if not the largest, model railway in the world, 174 feet long, 34 feet wide and boasting 120 locomotives. The display is the result of the efforts since 1973 of the Chattanooga Area Model Railroad Club and its replacement value is now over $1 million. My Triang OO set, complete with two engines and a Royal Mail set, which I still have somewhere in the loft, will never seem the same again.

Justin, complete with his classic rail uniform, was a splendid host and plied me with copious amounts of knowledge about the old railway days and about the song I had come to research. The journey in the song is from New York to Chattanooga via Baltimore ('read a magazine and then you're in Baltimore'), and Carolina ('nothing could be finer than to have your ham and eggs in Carolina'). The song originates from the 1941 film, in which Glenn Miller and his orchestra featured, called *Sun Valley Serenade* starring Sonja Henie (Olympic Ice Skating champion) and John Payne. The plot sounds sensational, sensationally dreadful that is; the band decide to adopt a foreign refugee for good publicity, but then discover the refugee is actually not a child but an attractive young woman . . . need I go on? Probably not, but at least some good music came out of it with one scene featuring the *Chattanooga Choo Choo* song and dance routine performed on a railway station set. The film also features probably Glenn Miller's best-known tune *In the Mood.* This became, in February 1942, the first record to be awarded a gold disc and is still often heard today (and, interestingly, if you listen to the Beatles song *All You Need Is Love* you will hear snippets from it just after the three minute mark).

The lyrics of choo choo do not refer to any specific train and certainly not one that runs the route described, as Justin told me that it would have been necessary, heading south from New York Pennsylvania Station, to change at Washington in order to get a Cincinatti Southern Railroad (CSR) service to Chattanooga. The inspiration for the name 'choo choo' comes from a small wood-burning steam locomotive which operated on the CSR in 1880. When it first arrived in town from Cincinatti a member of the public asked a press reporter which train it was. The reporter, rather sarcastically, it seems, replied, "It's the Chattanooga Choo Choo of course," and the name stuck.

The station, when it opened in 1909, featured that imposing external brick arch and, inside the entrance hall, sported the largest free-standing dome of its time, complete with extravagant chandeliers. It was designed by Don Barber from New York, who whilst at architectural school had won a competition for the design of a railway station. Five years later, when Southern Railway announced a competition to design the new Chattanooga Terminal Station, he dusted off his plans and was selected as the winner. The hotel restoration has carefully restored the original features and is a monument to the glory days of rail travel – not to be missed if you're passing by Chattanooga!

Glenn Miller unfortunately died at the age of 40, another plane crash victim. This time with a difference, being due not to bad weather but to a freak accident and plain bad fortune.

Having established himself as a top artist before the Second World War, Glenn volunteered to serve in the forces, but was turned down by the Navy in 1942. Eventually he persuaded the army to take him on and he went on to form the Army Airforce Band. This was not without controversy as he met with considerable resistance from some traditionalists when he introduced an element of blues and jazz into traditional marching music. The troops liked it, however, and he became immensely popular, performing over 800 times with his band of 30 musicians.

On 15 December 1944 he took off from RAF Twinwood in Bedfordshire to fly to Paris to play a concert for the troops who had liberated the city. But he never arrived and no trace was ever found of him or his light aircraft. Many theories abound, but the generally accepted version is that he was hit by a bomb being jettisoned by an RAF bomber which was lightening its load over the sea on return from an abortive mission to Germany. That really is bad luck, and very tragic.

Glenn had some critics in the music industry, many considering that he was too commercial and did not encourage improvisation in his music. He was also regarded as a not very warm person. I think the popularity of his music and the recorded sales speak for themselves in the music sense and he obviously gave people what they wanted. As for the personality issue, I think the fact that he volunteered for the forces, when he could have had a safe war, and then performed morale-boosting concerts for a reputed one million servicemen, is enough to convince me he was a pretty decent guy. Another sad loss.

As I was making my way back to the room I got into a lift with two other people and passed the time of day with them in the short journey from Ground to Second Floor. As I walked along the corridor, just about to open the door to my room, I heard footsteps behind me, obviously someone hurrying in my direction. When I turned round it was the big chap from the lift, whose name turned out to be Dan.

"What are you doing tonight?" he said. An hour later I was sitting in Murphy's Irish Bar, a short drive away, with Dan and his wife Tabitha, who were joined by a work colleague, Rodney, and a friend, David, who lived locally. Dan explained he is a Park Ranger, and his wife a biologist, and that they were attending a wildlife conference at the hotel. So, I was able to find out why I had seen a number of fish floating on top of the water during my Southern Belle cruise. Apparently it was due to low oxygen levels and the exceptionally hot summer, coupled with low water levels in the river. We made sure we didn't suffer from low liquid levels, immediately ordering some refreshments. Dan and at least one of the others were drinking Newcastle Brown Ale, just to make me feel at home I'm sure. Dan and Tabitha, realising I was on my own, had asked me to join them for the evening, which I thought was a tremendously nice thing to do when I had only known them for about thirty seconds. But what's more they insisted on paying for me, which was even more hospitable.

They told me that as well as their professional occupations they run a 500-acre family ranch some distance away, but live more locally in Tennessee, on Old Hickory Lake where Johnny Cash used to live. The Cash house, where he lived with June Carter Cash for 35 years, tragically burnt down in 2007 after being bought by Barry Gibb, who had intended to maintain its historic status. It was being renovated when it caught fire and Dan told me the heat was so intense it melted the scaffolding, so I don't suppose much survived.

One of the stories emanating from the Cash mansion is that Kris Kristofferson used to send so many demo tapes to Cash that Johnny used them as Frisbees and threw them into the lake. Until, that is, the day when Kristofferson, who was at one time an army helicopter pilot, landed on the front lawn with demo tapes, including *Sunday Morning Coming Down*. Cash agreed to see him and ended up recording *Sunday Morning*, which won him the Country Music Association song of the year in 1970.

Although they live in deepest Tennessee, Dan and Tabitha have a son called Calum, who they named after the young vet in *All Creatures Great and Small*, which just shows the extent of TV power (aren't there any fat people in that programme or doesn't Ashlie's momma watch this?).

David, who lives not too far away in Knoxville, filled me full of encouragement about the next day's Greyhound journey by talking about the incident in the summer of 2000 when, on the same route, the Interstate 24 going north through Manchester, a deranged passenger slashed the driver's throat. I actually remember reading about this and David told me that, although the driver survived, despite two five inch long cuts in his neck, six people died and all the other passengers were injured when the bus overturned. I understand why there is now a perspex canopy at the front of the aisle preventing access to the driver, not that it would stop a loony or a terrorist, or a combination of both.

We had an excellent meal including lots of ribs and 'things' and David went on to state his view that Tennessee is usually only remembered for two things – Jack Daniel's (the distillery is just north of Chattanooga) and Davy Crockett, the famous frontiersman. To prove the point we ordered a shot of whiskey each and rounded off the night, to the bemusement of fellow customers, with a rousing rendition of Davy, Davy Crockett, King of the Wild Frontier.

Next stop Clarksville to see if I could make a monkee of myself.

Chattanooga Choo Choo

Hey there Tex, what you say?
Step aside partner, it's my day
Lend an ear and listen to my version
(Of a really solid, Tennessee excursion)
Pardon me boy, is that the Chattanooga Choo Choo?
(YesYes) Track 29!
Boy you can give me a shine
(Can you afford to board, the Chattanooga Choo Choo?)
I've got my fare
And just a trifle to spare
You leave the Pennsylvania station 'bout a quarter to four
Read a magazine and then you're in Baltimore
Dinner in the diner, nothin' could be finer
(than to have your ham and eggs in Carolina)
When you hear the whistle blowin' eight to the bar
Then you know that Tennessee is not very far
Shovel all the coal in
Gotta keep it rollin'
(Whoo Whoo Chattanooga there you are)
There's gonna be, a certain party at the station
Satin and Lace
I used to call funny face
She's gonna cry
Until I tell her that I'll never roam
(So Chattanooga Choo Choo)
Won't you choo choo me home.
Get aboard . . .

Words and music by Mack Gordon and Harry Warren

Chapter Twelve

"Don't be slow, oh no no . . ."

I WAS AT THE CHATTANOOGA Greyhound station a good hour and a half before the bus was due to leave. This was Tuesday morning and I needed to ensure that I could get a seat on the bus as I had a mission – one that would be thwarted, for the moment at least, if I didn't make it to Clarksville by noon.

There are many Clarksvilles, and just as many Clarkesvilles, in the States. So knowing which one might be the subject of the famous Monkees' song was something of a challenge. I had discovered some ambiguity about whether *Last Train to Clarksville* should have the second e or not, but I had decided to my reasonable satisfaction that it was without. I then had to decide which Clarksville it was and had come to the conclusion that, on the balance of probability, it was going to be the one in Tennessee. Besides, it was more or less on my route.

Over the previous few days I had done some digging in this respect and had discovered there is an old disused L&N (Louisville and Nashville) railway station in Clarksville which is now a museum. But only part time, open 9am-1pm Tuesday, Thursday and Saturday. I couldn't afford to wait until Thursday as I planned to be in Memphis midweek, so I really needed to crack this one today.

I grabbed a coffee at the bus station, which, by recent standards, was actually a quite civilised and fairly pleasant terminus, very small but clean and tidy. It had a TV screen and there was a soccer match on – the FIFA Women's World Cup as it happened. And it just turned out to be England v Japan! This was great and I found myself I found myself embroiled in the match as I watching the match as I waited for the bus. Unfortunately, I did bring unwelcome attention to myself when I leapt to my feet shouting, 'Never, ref!' when we had an offside given against us. This caused some interest among the other waiting passengers as nobody else had the remotest idea what was happening. After that little aberration I tried to keep my head down as I didn't want to start explaining to any of my travelling companions how the offside law works. When the bus came I was quite frustrated at having to leave the game behind. It was a few days before I found out the result (a 2-2 draw). Not that it made a lot of difference as, taking a leaf out of the men's book, our ladies were headed for an ignominious exit, losing 3-0 to USA.

As usual, as the time for departure got nearer, my subconscious vetting of the other passengers began; I decided I particularly didn't want to sit next to the fat and greasy character wearing the 'I'm famous in Europe' T-shirt. He looked quite a slob and I had a feeling he could smell a bit. On boarding the bus I took a seat next to a pleasant-looking young chap aged about 20. As I sat down he shook my hand and introduced himself, a most unusual (and perhaps worrying) occurrence. He was called Ray and was on his way to college up north in Kentucky. It was the first time he had been away from home and I was pleased to be able to keep him company. He asked me what I was doing so I told him about my quest and the book which I intended to write, which interested him as he was also writing a book. When I asked him what it was about he said it was called the *Four Minds of a Murderer*, which really put me at ease. He went on to say that it was about a young student, aged 20, who was very confused and wasn't sure whether or not he was the person who had committed a recent string of murders. I shuffled a bit nearer to the aisle as Ray went on to say that his friends think he is a bit strange, with me sensibly replying that I couldn't imagine why.

My ticket indicated that the journey would take an hour and a half, but everything was not as it seemed, as I hadn't realised there was a time zone issue, and the journey time would actually be two and a half hours. Thankfully, in terms of arrival time I would still be OK as the bus tickets show local time, so it would not interfere with my visit to the L&N station.

The bus briefly dipped into Georgia, one of the eight States which border Tennessee, before coming back across the state line where I noticed a large sign saying 'Tennessee, the Volunteer State'. It is called this because of the high number of residents who took part in the War of 1812, particularly the Battle of New Orleans. I have also seen references linking it to the Mexican War and World

War I. I think if we just say they have a reputation for volunteering we won't be far wrong.

We headed north towards Nashville, safely passing through Manchester, before reaching Clarksville, which is located in the far north of the state, almost on the Kentucky border. The bus was going on to Chicago, another 12 hours to the north, but I abandoned ship wishing Ray luck with his book (this was getting to be something of a habit) and breathing a sigh of relief that I hadn't inadvertently provided more material for it.

Time was tight for getting to the railway station before 1pm, and it was actually the one hour time difference which saved the day. I got a taxi to the station and arrived about 12.30, being dropped off at a small, wooden, single-storey building with pitched roof and a chimney stack. Alongside the building was a single platform with one set of rails. It did appear to be a working track, for freight as it turned out. The platform was sheltered by an old fashioned canopy supported by cast iron pillars and there was an old diesel engine standing at the far end of the site. The place looked deserted and I had an uncomfortable feeling as I approached the door to the station building. I tried the handle and happily the door opened, revealing a small room with a polished wooden floor, some attractive old display cabinets and a wooden desk with a classic 1930s style typewriter.

Sitting at the desk was a lady who immediately got up to greet me as if I was the only visitor she had seen all day. This was Rachel, the part-time museum curator, and I was as pleased to see her as she evidently was to see me. By the time I explained who I was and what I was doing it was almost closing time, but Rachel was so enthusiastic about my visit that she said she would stay open especially for me. When I enquired about the Monkees I wasn't sure if I would be greeted with a blank stare but no, Rachel's eyes lit up and she took me along the corridor to a framed display on the wall. I was really excited to see in the frame an old vinyl 45 record, together with a record sleeve carrying a picture of the Monkees and the title *The Monkees – Last Train to Clarksville/Take a Giant Step*. This was a huge boost for me and served to confirm my view that I was in the right place. Rachel told me that the disc had been donated in the '60s, but by whom it was not clear.

My previous enquiries had failed to find any definitive statement about what and where the song was about. The sentiments behind the lyrics are still a matter of some debate in the States, with many people believing it is an anti-war song, subtly disguised by its writers Tommy Boyce and Bobby Hart because scripts for the Monkees Show had to be strictly non-political. As the Vietnam war was in full flow at the time of the record's release it has been suggested that the lyrics might refer to someone being drafted to Vietnam:

'Cause I'm leavin' in the morning
And I must see you again
We'll have one more night together
'Til the morning brings my train
And I must go, oh, no, no, no
Oh, no, no, no
And I don't know if I'm ever coming home

Given this interpretation, the lyrics assume a rather haunting dimension and this theory would fit well with Clarksville, which is the town serving the huge army base at nearby Fort Campbell, home of the 101st Airborne Division, the 'Screaming Eagles' (motto 'Rendezvous with Destiny').

This had to be the right place, particularly as the residents of Clarksville clearly believe this to be the case, and I was in a very happy, and almost generous, mood as I dropped a contribution into the voluntary donation box, which was the least I could do as the admission fee to the museum was only $1.

Rachel continued to display a very enthusiastic approach to my project and after showing me around the museum, with all its old railway paraphernalia, she asked if there was any possibility of me being guest speaker at the following Monday's Montgomery County Historical Society. I was flattered by the invitation, but I had to reluctantly decline as I would be long gone by then. I left, thanking Rachel for her valuable assistance, promised to keep in touch and gratefully accepted on the way out a copy of the latest Historical Society newsletter. It made interesting reading over a cup of coffee and I was sorry to have missed the previous month's speaker Billy 'Rocket Man' Copeland, who had just entered the *Guinness Book of Records* for attaining 98.5 mph aboard his rocket-fired street luge. I was even more sorry to have missed the July speaker who was a survivor from the USS Indianapolis during World War II when hundreds of sailors were left floating in the Pacific for more than three days, subject to dehydration and attacks by sharks. I'm not sure that I could have lived up to such exalted speakers but, as I say, I was honoured to be invited.

The Monkees, as most people know, were a 'manufactured group' in the 1960s, coming together as a result of answering an advertisement for 'Rock and Roll musicians to act as four insane boys'. They were, however, quite talented and had considerable musical ability with two of them, Mickie Dolenz and British born Davy Jones, having quite a bit of acting experience.

The musical aspirations of the four led to friction between the group and one of the producers, Don Kirshner, who didn't want them to play their own instruments or to get involved artistically. In fact, for *Last Train to Clarksville* the only part the band played was the voiceover on the track. The friction allegedly came to a head when Kirshner released *A Little Bit Me A Little Bit You* (written by Neil Diamond incidentally) without the band's consent. Mike Nesmith apparently punched a hole in the wall with his fist, looked at Kirshner and said 'That could have been your face 'mother ******'. Stirring stuff indeed.

The boys gradually won the power struggle and became much more involved in the musical production, writing and playing their own compositions. Kirshner was eventually sacked and went on to make The Archies, which, being animated, didn't give him problems with people having their own ideas.

The Monkees became hugely successful, having a string of top-selling singles and albums before they disbanded in 1971. In 1967 they were so popular that they outsold the Beatles and Elvis combined and they also had one of the biggest selling hits of the entire '60s with *I'm A Believer*, again written by Neil Diamond.

Surprisingly, Jimi Hendrix, during his ascent to fame, was for a short while a supporting act for the band. This didn't last long, though, as he quit after a few shows as the Monkees audience wasn't interested in Jimi's music and he didn't take kindly to them chanting for the Monkees as he strutted his stuff. This is coincidental as I found out a little more about Jimi in connection with my visit to Clarksville as I shall explain shortly.

I FOUND A REALLY GOOD hotel not far from the Cumberland River called, appropriately, Riverview Inn. This again proved my theory that in the less well-known towns quality accommodation could be had for around $100. It was very, very nice and even had novelty phones in the room, unless I just dialled a wrong number that is, as when I was trying to make an external call, a sultry female voice came on the line seductively whispering, "Oh baby you're so sexy," at which point, being a prude, I hung up.

It was early afternoon so I had plenty of time to go out and explore and I walked into the town. Clarksville has a population of around 120,000 and was founded in 1875 and named after General George Rogers Clark, a frontier fighter and Revolutionary War hero. The tourist literature tells you that Clarksville is the town 'Where rivers roll, spires rise and eagles soar' which is a bit rhapsodic, but I can see what they're getting at. I'm not sure if the eagles reference is to wildlife or to the 101st Airborne I mentioned earlier, but I can see where the reference to spires comes from. The architecture of the town is very different, unique even, involving lots of 'pointy bits'. I apologise if that's not a proper architectural term, but if you ever have the pleasure to visit Clarksville you'll see what I mean. There are five churches, built between 1867 and 1882, all with distinctive spires and all on the National Register of Historic Places. The building of the churches in that period reflects the wealth of Clarksville during the mid-1800s when it was one of the major tobacco centres in the States. With its 'type 22' it boasted the strongest tobacco in the world.

The rest of the architecture was also very eye-catching and I particularly enjoyed the old Customs House, which had even more pointy bits. I couldn't do better than quote the official description: 'The unique architecture consists of Italianate ornamentation, Far East-influenced slate roof, Romanesque arches, and Gothic copper eagles perched at the four corners.' A bit like I described the Palace Theater in El Paso actually – but different. And I did notice yet another reference to eagles.

It's not often I would feel inclined to follow a tourist map walk through town, but in this case I was quite happy to make an exception. I came across the Roxy Theater, another art deco throwback to the movie picture house days. It features a classic exterior, with red brick walls and two profiled, neon 'Roxy' signs at the front, one horizontal, one vertical, together with a canopy above the entrance which carries the title of whatever show is being featured at the time (in this case *Grease*). The building is so stylish that it has featured in many TV adverts and music videos including that for Sheryl Crow's 1993 hit *All I Wanna Do*.

The city has had its share of disasters in its history including the Great Fire in 1878 which, apart from burning down half the downtown area, also burned down the two fire stations, which I don't suppose was very helpful. More recently there was a major tornado in 1999, with winds of 200 mph causing extensive damage. The good news is that if I hadn't read about it I wouldn't have known, so full marks to the restoration committee.

Suddenly realising that I hadn't eaten all day, I went into a coffee shop at 3pm and, as I was the only customer, struck up a conversation with the two young girls behind the counter. As they were intrigued by what I was doing I decided to share with them something I had learned about their town that no-one I had so far met seemed to know.

"Did you know that Jimi Hendrix once lived in Clarksville ... and even started a band here before he went on to greater things?" I offered.

"You gotta be kiddin'," was the immediate response as I went on to explain that Jimi apparently had a couple of fall-outs with the law (involving riding in stolen cars) and was given the option of two years in jail or joining the military. He chose the latter and ended up at Fort Campbell just down the road.

"That's awesome!" exclaimed the girls in perfect unison. They were even more taken aback when I told them that there was a suggestion that he left the military early, according to some, for homosexual tendencies. I did go on to explain that other reports say he pretended to have such tendencies in order to get discharged. Other stories say he was just not a good soldier, whilst Jimi himself said that he was discharged after breaking his ankle during a parachute jump.

After his discharge Jimi started a band called The King Kasuals who played locally around Clarksville at small, low-paid venues, before he took the plunge and moved to Nashville. Having suitably impressed the girls with my encylopaedic knowledge of their local affairs I shut up and focused on my very nice blueberry muffin and cup of coffee.

As I mentioned earlier, Clarksville sits on the Cumberland River and this was very instrumental in its rise as a tobacco town, as the vast quantities of tobacco produced could be transported by river to the Ohio where they could be taken north to Pittsburgh or south to New Orleans. The river was next on my agenda and I headed off to continue my stroll (rather more than a stroll actually as I had already covered about three miles).

When I reached the riverfront I was intrigued to see a statue of a black woman, obviously an athlete, on the embankment alongside the very pleasant riverside walk. I investigated and found it was a memorial to Wilma Rudolph. The name seemed familiar, but I couldn't quite remember why. It turns out that Wilma was the first woman to win three gold medals at a single Olympics, winning the 100 metre and 200 metre events and being part of the winning 400 metre relay team in the 1960 games in Rome. Her achievements take on even greater proportions when you consider that she had polio as a child and had to walk with a leg brace. After her success in Rome she declined the usual segregated homecoming and insisted on an integrated event, the first mixed event in Clarksville and she went on to play a key role in ending segregation in the city. Regrettably Wilma died of a brain tumour in 1994, aged 54.

In the evening, I managed to find a pub, The Blackhorse, which had its own brewery in the glazed entrance foyer, and which looked a good bet for decent food. For some reason the waitress decided I should have a complimentary starter of a huge bowl of Nachos, with accompaniments, which in itself would have satisfied me. I could hardly not order a main course after this hospitality, so I ended up slumped in my chair struggling to finish my pint of Coalminer's Stout, 'Brewed in the tradition of the great stouts of England and Ireland'.

Back at the hotel I finished the evening by reading the local paper and caught an article about the impending execution, scheduled for the next day, of Daryl Holton. As he had committed his offence before 1999 he had a choice between lethal injection, or the old method, the electric chair. He chose the latter. The paper reported on the debate about whether 1750 volts was sufficient or whether 2000 might be more comfortable. I tried not to think about it.

Last Train To Clarksville

Take the last train to Clarksville
And I'll meet you at the station
You can be there by four thirty
'Cause I made your reservation
Don't be slow, oh no no!
Oh no no no!

'Cause I'm leavin' in the morning
And I must see you again
We'll have one more night together
'Til the morning brings my train
And I must go, oh no no no!
Oh, no no no!
And I don't know if I'm ever coming home

Take the last train to Clarksville
Now I must hang up the phone
I can't hear you in this noisy
Railroad station all alone
I'm feelin' low. Oh no no no!
Oh no no no!
And I don't know if I'm ever coming home

Take the last train to Clarksville
Take the last train to Clarksville

Words and music Tommy Boyce and Bobby Hart

Chapter Thirteen

.

"She could not leave her number . . ."

IT WAS NOW WEDNESDAY and time to try Memphis again. I went for the 12.25pm bus, conscious that I would have to change at Nashville and endure what is called a 'layover' — in this case three and a half hours. The journey from Clarksville to Nashville would be one hour and then from Nashville to Memphis four hours. But, add the three and a half hour layover, and suddenly it's a painful eight and a half hour slog. It turned out for the good though as I rang Ron Harman at the Hall of Fame and we ended up getting together for a while in the late afternoon in Nashville, which was a pleasant diversion.

The layover also meant I would arrive at Memphis in the dark again, but I wasn't worried this time as I knew my way around a little. I rang the Benchmark Hotel where I had stayed the previous week and booked a couple of nights to avoid any accommodation problems this time around. On arrival at Memphis I headed in the direction of the hotel, but decided that I would pop into TGI Fridays again as it was just across the street and I hadn't had a meal all day. As I approached the restaurant a figure came out of nowhere and moved menacingly across my path. He then moved towards the restaurant door and pulled it open gesturing for me to enter. "That's nice," I thought and I chastised myself for judging people by first appearances. As I tried to enter, however, he suddenly blocked my path and advised me I owed him a dollar.

I said I had no change, which was true, and this is when he started to get nasty. As there was no-one else on the street I thought the best bet would be to get myself inside and I don't know who was more surprised, him or me, when I suddenly barged him out of the way using the considerable weight of my rucksack to good advantage. I got through the door as quickly as possible and just as quickly decided that I had earned a beer, so that was my first task sorted out.

Over my meal I had a look at the local newspaper, the *Memphis Commercial Appeal* and caught the story about the execution of Daryl Holton. No late appeals or reprieves, the grim procedure had gone ahead, by electric chair as requested by the prisoner. Holton reportedly suffered burns on his head and legs, so perhaps it was as well the power wasn't increased to 2,000 volts after all. The State Medical Examiner won my prize for the most unnecessary statement of the week, 'The cause of death was high voltage electrocution'; well I suppose he had to say something.

The following day I got up bright and early, determined to make the most of two days in Memphis. I headed for the Visitor Bureau, which I knew was down towards the river as I had paid a brief visit the previous week before abandoning town. On that occasion I had met a lady called Jackie who had offered me complimentary tickets to some of the places I might want to visit. Unfortunately she was now off sick and no-one else had access to the safe, so my luck was out. I satisfied myself with a town map and left feeling somewhat disappointed as a couple of freebies would definitely have got the day off to a good start.

Desperate for a coffee I called in a little café, the Front Street Deli, just around the corner. It was a deserted, authentic-looking place not much larger than a snooker table, a large snooker table perhaps. Requesting a coffee, I was advised to help myself from the flask on the shelf on the back wall and I noticed just above it a signed picture of Tom Cruise. I spoke to the chap behind the counter who turned out to be the owner, Lee Clarke Busby, who told me that scenes from the film *The Firm*, featuring Tom Cruise and Holly Hunter, were shot here in 1993 and that his shop is mentioned in the dialogue when Tammy Hemphill (Hunter) says to Mitch McDeere (Cruise) "Did anyone order a fried egg sandwich from the Front Street Deli?". What else could I do but order a fried egg sandwich, so I did, and, while I was waiting, proceeded to study the other pictures and framed newspaper cuttings on the wall, not all about *The Firm*, I might add.

I was quite pleased that I was the only customer as, when I stretched to read one of the articles, my coffee, which was precariously perched on the shelf in its cardboard cup, went flying through the air and onto the floor. But it was nothing that a dozen sheets of kitchen roll couldn't sort out and after replacing my refreshment I asked Lee about the article featuring the person who started the deli. It was referring to Lee's father Buzz Busby and the article was an obituary from a local newspaper. This described him as quite a character – entrepreneur and charity fundraiser among other things. The bit of the article which particularly caught my attention was that referring to Elvis.

In 1956 Buzz lived across the street from Elvis on Audubon Drive and Elvis was outside his house one day signing autographs when Buzz asked him to come across.

"We're happy for all your success son, but the crowds out here are almost intolerable for us as your neighbours," Buzz explained

"Mr Busby, you must be reading my mind. I just bought a house in Whitehaven (Graceland) and at the end of the year I'll be moving down there," responded Elvis with utmost courtesy. Lee was only three at the time, but vaguely remembers Elvis and recalls him as a very polite young man.

I said goodbye to Lee, wrongly asking him if he was a Memphibian, which on reflection sounds like something that usually resides in a pond; the correct term as I learned later is 'Memphian'. Turning left out of the deli brings you down to the banks of the Mississippi and it was time to say hello to Old Muddy again and find my way to today's destination, the National Civil Rights Museum. It was a pleasant morning and I took in the views of the river and its bridges, including the Hernando de Soto Bridge, named after the 16th century Spanish explorer who was the first European to set eyes on the Mississippi from Memphis. The bridge has gained fame in the *Guinness Book of Records* as the largest free standing letter of the alphabet in the world, as the two metal arches form a curved letter M across the width of the river. It is known locally as the Dolly Parton Bridge, for reasons I can't quite imagine!

The bridge also spans Mud Island, home of Mud Island River Park which also featured in *The Firm*, as the location for a cable car chase. The park boasts a marina, as well as the Mississippi River Museum which includes a working model of 1,000 miles of the lower Mississippi. I wasn't in museum mode at this early stage of the day, however, and I was more concerned about getting some fresh air and exercise. I had, after all, to maintain my level of fitness if I wanted the comfort of thinking I could run away if I got into any bother on my travels.

There is an expansive riverfront walk heading south from Mud Island and I wandered along it, passing the 'River Queen' riverboat berth, and then the Tom

Lee memorial which commemorates a river rescue in 1925. 'A very worthy negro' reads the inscription on the stone obelisk, before it goes on to explain that Tom, with his boat 'Zev', saved 32 lives when the steamer US Norman sank, twenty miles downstream from Memphis. Now I don't wish to be contentious, but, given the segregation and racial attitudes of the day, I wonder if any of the survivors might have hesitated about having their lives saved by a negro? Somehow, I think not.

I reckoned that if I was reading my little map correctly I would be able to find my way via the river to the Lorraine Motel, the site where Martin Luther King was assassinated and where the Civil Rights Museum is located. After about two miles I turned left off the river walk and into what appeared to be attractive riverfront housing, but very soon I found myself in a run-down, disused commercial area with ramshackle buildings and rubbish strewn across the streets. I didn't feel comfortable here. The presence of some workers who were busy throwing building material into a skip provided some re-assurance, but I walked briskly, ever ready to demonstrate how quickly I could move in my trainers and shorts.

My concerns were short lived as very soon I surfaced in a more populated area and when I checked my bearings I was impressed with my orienteering as I had ended up not far away from Mulberry Street, the home of the Civil Rights Museum. The museum has been constructed alongside the Motel where King was shot from the building across the street, on 4 April 1968. He had been in town lending support to the striking sanitation workers and had made a keynote speech the day before.

I bought a ticket for the museum and spent the next couple of hours learning about the struggle for human rights since the introduction of the first Africans into America in 1619. It was purely slavery at that point, of course, and it took almost 170 years to even give the Africans some form of recognition as humans. In 1787 the constitution was changed so that blacks could be considered equal to three fifths of a white man in terms of representation in Government. Very generous I'm sure. Then, another 75 years on, Abraham Lincoln 'freed' the slaves in 1862. But this was not as straightforward as might be imagined as action was still required by individual states to make anything happen, and, as we know, particularly in the South, injustice carried on regardless. In 1954 a landmark ruling was made in the Brown v Board of Education case which ruled that segregation in schools was unconstitutional. This led to the confrontation at Little Rock, which I would coincidentally learn about later in the trip as I travelled through Arkansas on the way west to Oklahoma and beyond.

Seeing the reality of what took place in relatively recent history is an enlightening experience and it brings home the bravery of the people involved in the stand against racism. In the early '60s some progress had been made and segregation on buses was supposed to have been abolished, but, in reality, it was still continuing unabated in many places.

The Boynton v Virginia case in 1960 had overturned the conviction of a black law student for trespassing by being in a bus station restaurant area which was designated as 'Whites Only'. This was a key decision, but one which needed testing in practice. So, in 1961 a group of people, black and white, put their lives at risk by volunteering to ride buses across state lines. Predictably, as the buses got further south, riders were arrested for unlawful assembly, violating state laws and any other pretence that could be aimed at them. Worse than that they were frequently beaten and even firebombed by white mobs, often aided and abetted by local police, particularly in states like Alabama. Never wanting to miss a party, the Ku Klux Klan were never far from the action and all in all it was a desperately risky venture unless you had a desire to be beaten with lead pipes and metal chains. These protesters became known as the 'Freedom Riders' and went down in the annals of racial equality, at great personal cost.

'Yes we are the freedom riders
And we ride a long greyhound
White or black we know no difference
Lord, for we are glory bound'

At one point the riders decided to adopt the policy of filling the county jail with numerous arrests, which wasn't hard to achieve given the determination of their aggressors, and on one occasion, because the protesters kept singing freedom songs in jail, the sheriff bussed them all to the state line and dropped them off saying he just couldn't stand their singing! But if you were to visit the museum you would not want to trivialise the confrontation as it was clearly quite horrendous and white sympathisers, 'nigger lovers', were singled out for particularly brutal beatings. White ambulance crews even refused to take the injured to hospital.

The turning point came when the Attorney General, Robert Kennedy, sent one of his staff John Seigenthaler to observe what was happening and he too was badly beaten and left in the street, presumably mistaken for a sympathiser. This forced Kennedy to take further legislative action. More than that, though, the demonstrations inspired many more blacks, and indeed whites, to take strong stances against segregation and to gradually break down the barriers in the South.

The most moving part of the museum experience is definitely seeing the room where King was staying when he was shot. It was his regular room for his visits to Memphis, room 306. It has been preserved as it was on that fatal night when he ventured out onto the balcony and was shot from a rooming house across the street. (It was 6pm by the way, and not in the morning as suggested in U2's *Pride (In The Name of Love)*. Two months later James Earl Ray was arrested at Heathrow airport and charged with the shooting. He was subsequently jailed for 99 years after first admitting, and later denying, he was the killer. He died in jail aged 70 in 1998 after serving 30 years.

As always, conspiracy theories abound: was the assassination carried out on the orders of J Edgar Hoover, Director of the FBI, who was an arch- enemy of Dr King? Or by the Johnson administration who resented King's opposition to the Vietnam war? Or was it just a white extremist operating on his own? The chances are we'll never know.

What I do know is that Martin Luther King is one of the greatest orators who ever lived. If you have not read or heard in full the 'I Have a Dream' speech (Washington, August 1963) I would recommend you to do so, if just because of the amazing way it is put together. And the power of his words is immense:

> 'America has given the Negro people a bad check,
> a check which has come back marked "insufficient funds"'

Ironically the night before his assassination he delivered another famous oration, the 'I've Been to the Mountaintop' speech in which he prophetically declares:

> 'I've been to the mountaintop
> And I've seen the promised land ...
> I may not get there with you'

Sadly he was right.

The Lorraine Motel went into decline in the years following the assassination and by 1982 was out of business. This was all a multiple tragedy for the owner Walter Lane Bailey as his wife Loree, for whom the motel was named, died of a brain haemorrhage two hours after King was shot. It was a tragedy also for race relations and the power of the music industry in bridging the gap between black and white; the Lorraine was where many of the Stax record label artists of the time would stay when visiting the city and many songs were written there by people such as Eddie Floyd and Steve Cropper (Booker T and the MGs), who stopped by Wilson Pickett's room and wrote *In The Midnight Hour*. It is also where Eddie Floyd wrote *Knock On Wood*. Fried chicken would be provided by Walter and Loree to keep them going and it was a refuge of racial harmony, like Stax itself, as I will come to later.

After I left the museum I turned the corner and on seeing a hairdresser's salon decided it was time to tidy myself up. I went in to have my hair cut by an attractive girl called Shelly who employed an unusual technique of cutting one side of my hair, then asking if I liked it, before cutting the other. What she could have done to repair the bit already cut I'm not sure, but she was very nice so I didn't lose any sleep over it. She mentioned that not so long back President Bush had visited the museum and that for the duration of the visit the girls were not allowed out of the salon. She was quite happy about this, however, as the 'cute white boys in their smart suits' (the FBI Agents) were winking at her and her colleagues through the window.

Never trust an FBI agent," I advised her in a sub-conscious fit of jealousy. "For starters they'll always know where you are and what you're doing."

Suitably shorn I made my way back to the hotel to have a little breather before seeing what Memphis had to offer at night.

Beale Street is the place. That's what I'd been told. 'Home of the Blues' and 'Birthplace of Rock and Roll'. A view ably supported by Marc Cohn in his hit *Walking In Memphis.*

'Put on my blue suede shoes
And I boarded the plane
Touched down in the land of the Delta Blues
In the middle of the pouring rain
WC Handy – won't you look down over me . . .'

I wondered who WC Handy was and resolved to unearth his story during my visit.

'Then I'm walking in Memphis
Walking with my feet ten feet off of Beale . . .'

Not too confident of walking the streets of Memphis in the dark, I had chosen a route to Beale Street, only a couple of blocks away, which would take me past the famous Peabody Hotel. I had a look in the foyer/shop area in the hotel and it was worth it, this is a hotel described as the 'Savoy of the South' and one of the interior shops is the business home of Elvis's tailor Bernard Lansky. Lansky started clothing Elvis from high school prom days and through the early days of Elvis's career when he couldn't pay. He was given credit however and once said to Lansky, "When I get rich I'll buy you out." Lansky replied, "Do me a favor. Don't buy me out just buy from me." And he did, right to the end – Elvis was buried in a Lansky suit.

Now get ready for this; if you think the duck racing at Deming was bizarre you will love this. The Peabody, which is a really plush hotel, has a duck parade twice a day. Believe it or not, they have a 'Duck Palace' on the roof, with five ducks kept in prime condition and specially trained for their walk through the hotel. They are led down the elevator by their 'Duckmaster', who teaches them the 'Peabody Duck March' and when they reach the Ground Floor a red carpet is rolled out for the ducks to walk past the admiring (and I would imagine somewhat stunned) guests to the strains of Sousa's King Cotton March.

This takes place at 11am each day and the ritual is reversed at 5pm. Where they go in the meantime I am not sure, but let's hope they stay away from the kitchen. The tradition apparently began in 1932 and was to do with a couple of residents going off on a hunting trip and having rather a lot of Tennessee whiskey on their return. They had with them three English calling ducks which were used as live decoys and they put them in the hotel fountain while they had a nightcap or two. The hotel guests were impressed and one thing led to another. 75 years on, The Peabody rightly now calls itself the only five duck hotel in Tennessee – and a lot of other states besides I would think.

I left the Peabody, turned the corner and heard live music which was clearly coming from outdoors. I tracked it down to a park across the street, which turned out to be WC Handy Park. Up until this point I had no idea who W C Handy was but, as there was a statue of him in the park entrance, I soon educated myself and found out that he is the 'Father of the Blues'. Handy discovered blues music in 1903 while he was waiting for a train in Mississippi and heard a young black guitarist playing his guitar with a penknife using the 'slide' technique. Handy was an educated musician and became a music teacher before touring with his band and then establishing himself on Beale Street in 1912. His *Memphis Blues* in that year is regarded by some as the first blues song and he followed this up with *Beale Street Blues*, mentioned in F Scott Fitzgerald's novel *The Great Gatsby*, and *St Louis Blues*. He had a major impact on jazz when artists started picking up his numbers and he was played by Nat King Cole in a film of his life, *St Louis Blues*, in 1958 the year he died.

The music was coming from inside the park and I went over to find a blues band featuring a singer with those rasping black vocals and a really impressive supporting outfit – and this was a free concert. Again a bucket for tips, of course, but it was well worth a dollar for a couple of numbers before giving in to my stomach and transporting myself into the Rum Boogie bar and restaurant (slogan Eat, Drink, Boogie, Repeat).

This place was very popular, and quite famous it transpires, so I was quite fortunate to get a seat after ten minutes or so. I soon found out why it was so popular when a singer called James Govan belted out *Knock On Wood*, with his Boogie Blues Band providing tremendous sax and trumpet support. Next we had *High Heel Sneakers* (Put on your red dress baby . . .), wonderful stuff from a first class band and I really enjoyed it.

After finishing my meal I moved on up the street to BB King's, probably the most famous club in Memphis, something reflected by the fact that there was an admission charge, although it was minimal. BB gets his name, incidentally, from his nickname when he was a Memphis disc jockey – 'Beale Street Blues Boy'.

I caught the back end of a lady singer, let me rephrase that, I came in just as a lady singer was finishing her number, *I Will Survive*, to rapturous applause. What little I heard of her let me know she had a fabulous voice. But my timing was poor as it was break time for the band so I sat with a pint, taking in the surroundings and atmosphere, until the band came back. Unfortunately they were minus the lady, who I assumed must have gone off to perform somewhere else. I decided to go elsewhere to see if I could catch her in another bar, although I noticed it was getting quite late by this time so she may well have been finished for the night. But it was a good excuse to have another drink and try another bar so I crossed the road and went through the doors of the Blues City Café.

It was 1am and the place was in full flow with a three-piece band setting the room alight. There was a drummer belting out his stuff, a guitarist on his knees running an empty beer bottle up and down the frets of his guitar, which was flat on the floor and producing great sounds, and a double bass player/singer who appeared to be making mad, passionate love to his instrument. It was amazing stuff and I loved it. Unfortunately, I only caught their last three numbers and I regretted not having been in sooner; on the other hand I was pleased that I had caught them at all.

When the applause died down and the band left the stage I collared the singer/bass player who readily accepted my offer of a beer at the bar – he certainly would have been ready for it. When I asked him how he would describe his music he replied simply "Rockabilly" and went on to introduce himself as Joe Fick, who, with his colleagues Brad Birkedahl and Ron Perrone, make up The Dempseys. (Joe was being modest in his conversation with me as I have since seen his band described rightly as 'High Octane Rockabilly' and 'The most entertaining Rockabilly band on the planet'). He advised me that they are the band who played as Johnny Cash's backing band in the film *Walk The Line*, which impressed me immensely. The Dempsey's are regulars at the Blues Café and I could see why. Another indication of the high regard in which they are held is the fact that they have received the keys to the city of Tupelo, Elvis's birthplace, for their contribution to his memory. Quite an accolade.

I read somewhere that Beale Street was named after an unknown military hero in 1841, but that seems like a contradiction in terms, or is it just me? But never mind, it served as General Grant's headquarters during the Civil War and gained fame, or perhaps infamy, in the 1920s when it thrived on gambling, drinking, prostitution, murder and voodoo. Definitely the place to be. One club, the Monarch, was known as 'The Castle of Missing Men' as its gunshot victims and dead gamblers could be easily disposed of at the undertaker's parlour that shared the back alley. Machine Gun Kelly was a regular on the street, selling whiskey from a clothes basket on his way to the big time. By comparison I felt relatively safe as I walked back to the Benchmark.

THE SUN SHINING THROUGH the curtains woke me up at 8am and I set about the routine of packing my bag once more, something of an increasingly tedious task, but it didn't bother me as I was in a good frame of mind after the previous evening and also the fact that I had another day in Memphis.

Memphis — the word just conjures up pictures, sounds, feelings. Elvis, Otis Redding, Johnny Cash, Aretha Franklin, Jerry Lee Lewis . . . the list goes on. Even Justin Timberlake was born in Memphis. With a musical heritage like this I was going to have a busy time and the first stop today had to be Sun Studios, a two mile walk from the hotel (I was told it was a lot closer, hence the election to walk). To be fair, the porter had said "just down the road," which it was, he just didn't say how long the road was.

I got to Sun in good time for the 10am tour and while I was waiting I took some photographs of the outside of the building which is an unmissable photo opportunity as it has a huge guitar suspended above the sidewalk at second floor level. For such an acclaimed place in musical history this is a tiny concern, a small, odd triangular shaped, two-storey brick building situated on a busy road junction on the outskirts of town.

Although Elvis figured prominently during my visit to Nashville it was here where he started his journey to fame. In 1950 Sam Phillips set up the Memphis Recording Service 'We Record Anything, Anywhere, Anytime' (they even recorded funerals) and anyone could go in and record a tune for $3. Sam followed this up a couple of years later by founding the associated Sun Record Company.

In 1951 BB King arrived, as did Chester Burnett (better known as Howlin' Wolf), not to mention a 17 year-old Ike Turner. It was Ike who was behind what is considered to be the first Rock and Roll record ever produced — *Rocket 88*. This was accredited to Jackie Brenston and his Delta Cats. There was no such band, Jackie was one of Ike's band members and it is thought that for 'financial reasons' the song was attributed to him rather than to Ike who wrote the song. *Rocket 88* by the way is a tribute to the classic Oldsmobile 88 car introduced in 1949.

The first big hit for Phillips was in 1953 with Rufus Thomas's *Bear Cat*, recorded on a single-track recorder. This led to problems, however, as it was an 'answer song' to *Hound Dog* recorded by Big Mama Thornton and was almost identical. Sam was sued for $25,000 for copyright infringement and this almost bankrupt him.

That same year Elvis walked in and invested his $3, recording *My Happiness* and presented it to Sam Phillips who wasn't impressed. Elvis left a copy with Marion Keisker, the revered office manager and receptionist, who in due course reminded Sam about Elvis when he was looking for a singer for a song called *Without Love*. Although that didn't work out, Elvis came to the studio and hung around playing some sessions with Scotty Moore and Bill Black and during these Sam heard Elvis 'messing around' with *That's All Right (Mama)* and everything took off from there.

Sam signed Elvis for three years but, partly due to the financial situation caused by the Bear Cat legal action, he agreed to sell Elvis's contract to RCA for $35,000 after 17 months, in November 1955. It was also helpful for Elvis to go to a bigger studio and it didn't take him long to make his breakthrough with *Heartbreak Hotel* a couple of months later.

Sun was a breeding ground for up-and-coming young talent such as Roy Orbison, Jerry Lee Lewis and Carl Perkins, who provided the first gold record for Sun with *Blue Suede Shoes*. Johnny Cash, in his Sun days, recorded *Cry Cry Cry*, his first hit, and *Walk The Line*, which he played with a dollar bill stuffed behind the strings to create a drum effect as drums were not used in country music at the time. In 1957 Jerry Lee Lewis gave Sun one of its biggest hits with *Great Balls Of Fire*, which took 48 takes to record, but was surely worth the effort.

The recording studio itself is just about 30 feet x 18 feet and, like studio B at Nashville, is as it was in the glory days. Sam effectively built the studio, completing the renovations with the help of one carpenter, and he re-arranged the ceiling tiles into pyramid formation to get the acoustics he wanted. It became known as the 'House that Sam Built' and apparently even today the sound is unique. When you stand there and listen to *Balls Of Fire* it is another spine-tingling experience not to be missed.

In 1960 the lease on the premises ran out and Sam moved two blocks to what became the Phillips Recording Studio. The original studio stood empty for a long time until it was rescued and restored in 1987 and, apart from being a tourist attraction and National Historic Landmark, it is a live studio with artists such as U2 (*Rattle and Hum*), Ringo Starr and Justin Timberlake taking advantage of its unique facilities.

One of the most iconic pictures in pop history hangs on the wall in the studio, showing Johnny Cash, Jerry Lee Lewis and Carl Perkins crowded round Elvis, who is sitting at a piano. This meeting came about by chance around a year after Elvis left Sun and he had come back on a social visit. The foursome started a jam session playing about 40 songs or part-songs and the ever cute Sam switched on a tape to record the session for posterity. He also called the local press who ran an article the next day, complete with the famous photograph, heralding the 'Million Dollar Quartet', a name which has stuck ever since.

I left Sun Studios at lunchtime feeling invigorated once again and I knew there was yet more to come later in the day. I grabbed a quick sandwich and went looking for a taxi to take me to the Stax Museum of American Soul Music, which is situated a few miles out of town. The museum is located in a neighbourhood called Soulsville, where Aretha Franklin was born, and is housed in a purpose built building, the original having been pulled down after the unfortunate demise of the Stax label in 1975.

When I walked in I was greeted by the sound of Otis Redding singing *Try A Little Tenderness,* which reminded me how much I had enjoyed his music, and soul music generally, back in the '60s. Stax was one of the key labels of the Soul movement featuring such stars as Otis, Sam and Dave ('leased' from Atlantic), Isaac Hayes, Eddie Floyd, Rufus Thomas and his daughter Carla, and Booker T and the MGs, who for much of the time were the house band and who played on many of the Stax hits. The Stax sound was more raw edged, and 'southern', than the smoother Motown sound from Detroit, which tended to be more melodic but less adventurous. I liked them both.

The label was started, as Satellite Records, in 1957 by Jim Stewart and his sister Estelle Axton. When Stewart realised there was another label called Satellite, he changed the name of the company to Stax, a combination of the first two letters of his and his sister's surnames. The Stax recording studio was unusual as it was housed in an old movie theatre and the floor sloped, giving an inimitable sound to its recordings. Although Stewart and Axton were white they quickly moved from Country music to Rhythm and Blues, which brought them a wider black audience. They were at the forefront of racial integration in the music business with Booker T and the MGs being one of the first integrated bands in the country. Unfortunately, much of this good work was undone with the 1968 assassination of Martin Luther King as the atmosphere at Stax was never the same again.

In the late '60s the company got into difficulty as they had entered into agreements with Atlantic Records and this eventually led to contractual problems after Atlantic were taken over by Warner Brothers. This, coupled with the tragic death in 1967 of its top star, 26 year-old Otis Redding (together with members of his backing band in yet another plane crash), led to the decline of the company and it eventually went into forced bankruptcy in 1975.

But, there is a happy ending; in 1998 the Stax site was an empty waste ground and the area around it was rundown and crime-ridden. A group of Memphians, however, had a vision to restore the neighbourhood using Stax as the catalyst. After involving civic authorities, private donors, housing authorities and Federal Government they have succeeded in turning the empty lot into the multi-million dollar museum and, adjacent to it, have constructed the Stax Music Academy. The museum and the academy are the cornerstone of a $100 million dollar neighbourhood revitalisation scheme and with the improvements and facilities so far introduced the area is buoyant and crime has dropped by 90% compared to levels of 10 years ago. A fitting legacy from an admirable label.

From the Stax museum I got a taxi to Graceland, which is located six miles south of town. I had no accommodation booked, so I tried to check in at the Heartbreak Hotel, part of the Graceland complex, just across the road from the mansion. Unfortunately, I had just missed the last room, as was the case at the nearby Days Inn. So, I slung my pack on my back and started the slog down Elvis Presley Boulevard, a long and wide main road fronting Graceland, and arrived 20 minutes later at the Scottish Inn Suites. This was a motel-type establishment, but was quite cheap and had an outdoor pool. As this was only 5pm I was able to enjoy the late afternoon sun and a rare hour's relaxation by the pool (my original plan had been to have occasional rest days, but somehow they never seemed to materialise!).

Graceland, Elvis's mansion, is behind locked gates on one side of the road and on the other side is the shopping and attraction precinct, along with Heartbreak Hotel. The precinct/hotel side of things is a bit on the shabby side now and plans have been proposed for a major redevelopment of the complex. If given the go-ahead this will provide facilities which will accommodate twice the number of visitors, which already stand at 600,000 per annum, second only in terms of visitor numbers in the States to the White House.

As the Scottish Inn don't do evening meals I tramped back up to the precinct and was surprised to find that most of the facilities close down in the evening. There were a few fast food restaurants in the vicinity but fortunately I spotted a neon sign and, on investigation, found that the Rock and Roll Café does remain open most nights. This was clearly a good bet, if only because it was licensed, so in I went, to be greeted by a young waitress who made my night by wasting no time in getting me a suitable refreshment. She asked me whether, for a four dollar charge, I would like to go into the room at the back where there would be a live act. This had me thinking for a moment, but, remembering where I was, I realised it would be all perfectly decent and legal so I thought, "why not?"

The entertainer turned out to be Joe Kent, an Elvis tribute act. Well, it was an interesting evening, he wasn't bad and it kept me entertained for an hour or so while I had a meal and a few more beers. For his finale Joe really had the audience of 60 -70 people going, all singing along passionately to 'An American Trilogy' (the musical medley with extracts from *Dixie*, *All My Trials* and *Battle Hymn Of The Republic*), with much waving of the arms and people getting to their feet. Well worth four dollars.

Before he left the stage Joe announced that there was a relative of Elvis in the audience and introduced an elderly lady, Louise Smith, who received a very generous round of applause. Louise, he went on to explain is a cousin-in-law of Elvis, having married his cousin Gene, who was very close to Elvis when they were in their late teens. I took the opportunity to introduce myself to Louise at the end of the show and she was quite happy to give me a few moments of her time. She was actually with some other, younger, members of the family and a friend of hers who used to hang around with her and Elvis in the early days. Louise, who is now a widow, told me the story about how she was working in a store in downtown Memphis as a 17 year-old when in walked Elvis and his cousin. They apparently both tried to impress Louise and asked if they could take her to a coffee shop at 5pm when she finished work. She agreed, and they turned up as promised. What happened then was that they both continued to chat her up, obviously vying for her attention. Elvis did himself no favours as Louise was a bit put off by his flashy clothes and the way he kept singing to her, not to mention wiggling his hips as they walked down the street. She went for the more conservative of the pair and ended up marrying Gene.

Most people, when I relate this story say 'whoops', but to be honest she may have done the right thing as she ended up having a normal life rather than being part of a surreal and outlandish existence. She and Gene remained close to Elvis, even living in Graceland for five years, and she had nothing but praise for him, describing him as "One of the greatest guys I've ever met." When I spoke to

Louise's friend she said pretty much the same and added that whenever Elvis was speaking to you he made you feel like the most important person in the world, always looking after other people before himself.

'ELVIS FANS PARKING AREA – violators will be all shook up' read the sign in the car park as I made my way to the ticket office. A fitting start to my Graceland visit I thought, quite appealing to my sense of humour this Saturday morning. The box office is situated in the shopping/attraction complex and when tickets are obtained visitors are shown to a queue to await the shuttle transfer into the grounds of Graceland, professional photographers taking pictures just before you board the bus. All very Disney-like.

I hadn't been keen on joining this tourist circus, but on the other hand I didn't want to come to Memphis and not visit Graceland. It is something that has to be done. I saw a few chaps in the queue who were wearing 'Vietnam Veterans Reunion' T-shirts and I ended up sitting next to one of them who introduced himself as Burton Haugen. We got involved in a fascinating chat which continued as we waited in the queue to enter the mansion. Burton told me he is mentioned by name in a book called *Unfortunate Sons*, by Larry James, about an ambush just north of Saigon in 1968 following the Vietnamese 'Tet offensive'. We didn't have much time to chat as we were soon ushered inside the front door and he rejoined his pals from the Fighting 9th 'Manchu' regiment. I have since researched the incident and it turns out this was one of America's biggest disasters of the whole Vietnam conflict. 92 American soldiers were sent out on a mission expected to last all day, but they were soon ambushed and within eight minutes 49 of them were dead or dying, with another 28 wounded. I found some information about Burton and discovered that he is the recipient of two purple hearts (which are awarded for being wounded or killed – obviously not the latter in this case) and two bronze stars (awarded for heroism or outstanding achievement /meritorious service). A true hero and I hope he enjoyed his day, he certainly deserved to.

Graceland is an imposing 32-room mansion, a double fronted colonial style house with four two-storey high pillars supporting the triangular roof over the front entrance. It was built in 1939 by the Moore family, Ruth Moore having inherited the land from her uncle, S E Toof, publisher of a Memphis newspaper. The grounds were named after Toof's daughter Grace and the mansion was likewise given the Graceland name.

The tour of the house was well worthwhile and I was surprised at how much I enjoyed it. I could go on forever, but the highlights for me were the corridor decorated floor to ceiling with gold discs, many for songs I'd never even heard of, the costumes, and the famous Jungle Room, which is a monument to bad taste; quite apart from the hideous Polynesian style furniture and effects, the ceiling is covered in the same green thick pile carpet as the floor. I could just imagine being in there for after a few drinks – it would be hard to know which way up you were.

On a more sombre note the graveside where Elvis is buried with his parents Vernon and Gladys is very poignant and I think the whole thing can be summed up by the first words on his gravestone:

> 'He was a precious gift from God
> Much loved and cherished ...'

I was pleased I had made the visit and I have to say that it showed Elvis in a different light and made me more aware of the person he was before he became the bloated King of Vegas. I was particularly impressed that he was a keen sportsman and had achieved black belts in two different kinds of Karate (his instructor referred to him as 'Tiger') and that he liked horse-riding and racquetball, even having his own racquets court at Graceland. He was a model soldier when he was in the army, and he was a polite, churchgoing, caring person in his youth. I was also surprised at how well read he was and I was impressed when I saw the books on his desk – one was a book about the life of Winston Churchill and the other *The Warren Report* investigating the death of John F Kennedy.

My next stop was Elvis's Automobile Museum, which was excellent, and then his two private jet airplanes which were equally impressive. I particularly liked the interior of his larger plane, the 'Lisa Marie', which was incredibly furnished inside and had a large, luxurious, bed in a private room. Tommy Trucker would have been impressed.

Having become totally absorbed in the Elvis experience I couldn't leave without a peanut butter sandwich and there was no time like the present. Rockabilly's Diner was the place and, with some misgivings, I placed my order and also ordered a Dr Pepper, which I understand Elvis was partial to. It was a culinary experience – I hadn't realised the sandwich would be grilled. If you can imagine peanut butter mushed up with banana, heated and served inside grilled bread, I still don't think you would be prepared for the gooeyness that is generated by the process. It sticks to the roof of the mouth like nothing I have ever experienced and the taste stayed with me all day, which wasn't necessarily a particularly pleasing consequence. But at least I had tried it.

AS I SUGGESTED EARLIER, the name Memphis just rolls off the tongue and conjures up musical thoughts, none more so than *Memphis Tennessee*, the Chuck Berry classic from 1959.

> *'Long distance information, give me Memphis Tennessee*
> *Help me find the party trying to get in touch with me'*

The song is a bit of a tease as in the first three verses we could be deceived into thinking that the female being referred to is an estranged wife or girlfriend; then, later

> *'Help me information, more than that I cannot add*
> *Only that I miss her and all the fun we had'*

but all is revealed in the penultimate line of the final verse:

> *'Last time I saw Marie she's waving me goodbye*
> *With hurry home drops on her cheek that trickled from her eye*
> *Marie is only six years old, information please*
> *Try to put me through to her in Memphis Tennessee'*

and we sadly discover that he is trying desperately to get in touch with his young daughter and the words 'because her mom did not agree' refer to his problems with the girl's mother. Cleverly written and typical of a man who wrote some great lyrics. Take *Roll Over Beethoven* for instance:

> *'My heart's beatin' rhythm*
> *And my soul keeps on singing the blues*
> *Roll over Beethoven*

And tell Tchaikovsky the news'

Or outstandingly for me, the first verse of *Brown-Eyed Handsome Man*:

'Arrested on charges of unemployment
He was sitting in the witness stand
The judge's wife called up the district attorney
Said you free that brown eyed man
You want your job you better free that brown-eyed man'

All great songs and supplemented in his repertoire by a host of others such as *Sweet Little Sixteen*, *Johnny B Goode*, *Come On*, and *No Particular Place To Go*.

He is also a great performer with his distinctive strutting around the stage while playing his guitar, including the famous 'duck walk' where he skips across the stage on one leg with his other leg outstretched in front of him. His music has been so influential that one of his songs *Johnny B Goode* was sent into space as part of the Voyager 1 collection of earthly artefacts and is now circulating in the outer solar system, 15.49 Terameters (9.6 billion miles) away. I hope the aliens eventually find it and let us know what they think. I am a little concerned, however, at the message President Carter put alongside it "We hope some day, having solved the problems we face, to join a community of Galactic Civilisations." Given our experience of 'European Community Civilisation' I shudder to think what a Galactic Community would bring.

Chuck Berry's prolific hit making is illustrated by the fact that in 1964 he had five chart hits, including *No Particular Place To Go*, *Nadine* and *You Never Can Tell*. It is ironic that after all the great music he wrote and performed, he only had one number one hit and that was with the novelty song *My Ding-A-Ling*, which many people, not surprisingly, thought was somewhat smutty, including anti-smut campaigner Mary Whitehouse, who tried to have it banned. On a more musical note Chuck was voted 6th on the *Rolling Stone* list of 100 greatest guitarists of all time just behind Robert Johnson.

Chuck has had some ups and downs in his interesting life, but is still managing to do the athletic duck walk in his eighties! He has survived three jail terms, one as a victim of the draconian Mann Act whereby transporting a female across a state border for immoral purposes was declared illegal, so, if you wanted to take your girlfriend for a fruity weekend in a different state you could actually be arrested. In Berry's case while he was playing in El Paso he invited a 14 year-old Apache waitress from Juárez to work at his nightclub in St Louis. After she was sacked by Berry she was arrested for prostitution and because he had brought her into the state he received a three-year jail sentence.

In earlier days, as an 18 year-old, he hijacked a car at gunpoint after his own car broke down, again resulting in three years inside. He was jailed again in the '70s for tax evasion, this time getting a four-month sentence. More was to come when in 1990 he was reportedly forced to reach a settlement with 59 women after a number of them had sued him for installing a videotape in the women's restroom in one of his restaurants. But let's not underestimate his contribution to Rock and Roll. He is one of the founding members of the club and has had a huge influence on many famous performers like John Lennon, Keith Richards and Angus Young of AC/DC who has even copied his duck walk, as has Jimmy Page of Led Zeppelin. Despite his indiscretions Chuck will always be remembered for his music.

BEFORE LEAVING MEMPHIS I needed to understand more about its history and I discovered that it was founded in the early 1820s by three entrepreneurs, including General (later President) Andrew Jackson. It was named after the ancient capital of Egypt because of its strategic position at the head of the Mississippi Delta, similar to its namesake in Africa, which was at the head of the Nile Delta. As the Mississippi is sometimes called the 'American Nile' I guess it makes sense.

The town was based on the cotton trade and relied on slave labour before the Civil War and was also an important timber town. During the Civil War it briefly became a Confederate stronghold, but was captured by the Union in 1862 at the Battle of Memphis, which was a river battle, with relatively few casualties for once – it was all over in 90 minutes.

Like Chuck Berry, Memphis has had its ups and downs, suffering from recurring yellow fever epidemics in the 1870s, which devastated the city to the point where it lost its charter. Towards the end of that century, however, it made a recovery and nowadays is a thriving city of over 600,000 people. Because of its location it is a major centre for distribution, boasting the world's busiest cargo airport and is the headquarters of many large corporations such as FedEx – hence the FedEx Forum, off Beale Street, which is the home of NBA Basketball team

Memphis Grizzlies. Also just off Beale Street, there is the world famous Gibson Guitar factory, which is a significant tourist attraction, as is the Victorian Village, on the east side of downtown, which consists of mansions built in the mid-1800s by wealthy Memphians.

The town centre is pleasant, the streets are wide and airy and a streetcar service rambles through the Downtown area, presenting a relaxing opportunity to tour the city. Prior to the 1990s Memphis was in some disrepair, as epitomised in the cult film *Mystery Train*, featuring Joe Strummer (as Johnny aka Elvis), but since then it has enjoyed a renaissance and I am happy to declare that it appears to be in excellent health.

Memphis Tennessee

Long distance information, give me Memphis Tennessee
Help me find the party trying to get in touch with me
She could not leave her number, but I know who placed the call
'Cause my uncle took the message and he wrote it on the wall

Help me information, get in touch with my Marie
She's the only one who'd phone me here from Memphis Tennessee
Her home is on the south side, high up on the ridge
Just a half a mile from the Mississippi Bridge

Help me information, more than that I cannot add
Only that I miss her and all the fun we had
But we were pulled apart because her mom did not agree
And tore apart our happy home in Memphis Tennessee

Last time I saw Marie she's waving me good-bye
With hurry home drops on her cheek that trickled from her eye
Marie is only six years old, information please
Try to put me through to her in Memphis Tennessee

Words and music by Chuck Berry

Chapter Fourteen

"I got some news this mornin' from Choctaw Ridge ..."

HAVING RESISTED THE TEMPTATION to buy an Elvis costume at Graceland – there is a wide selection available, ranging from $1,700 to $3,700, I thought the least I could do was to visit Tupelo, his birthplace.

It would have been possible to have made it by Greyhound, but I would then have had no way of getting to the next destination, Nutbush. So I had little alternative but to hire a car for a few days, much as I was not enthusiastic about driving in Tennessee, or anywhere else in the States for that matter. From Graceland I got a taxi to Memphis airport, which wasn't far away and I ended up hiring a nice little Chevrolet Coba, which was stylish, comfortable and easy to drive – not bad for the equivalent of £10 per day! The insurance more than doubled that unfortunately. Filling the tank was a pleasure though, as the cost of gas was the equivalent of £1.25 a gallon, about a quarter of what I was used to. And still lots of people I talked to in the States complained about the price; mind you they do have a few more miles to travel. I suppose if you hiked the price up to even half the level we pay in the UK you would wreck the whole economy.

I set off down Interstate 78 on the 100 mile trip to Tupelo which would take me back into Mississippi. This might sound like bad planning but it hadn't been en-route as I came north the previous week and this was the best solution I could find. In the event, once I got clear of the manic highways around the airport, it was quite a pleasant Saturday afternoon drive along a quiet highway, the only settlement of any consequence along the way being Oxford, Mississippi the home of the famous

'Ole Miss' university. This was the place that Bob Dylan sang about in his song *Oxford Town* on his *Freewheelin'* album in 1963:

> 'Me and my gal, my gal's son
> We got met with a tear gas bomb'

referring to the 1962 riots when James Meredith attempted to become the first black student at the University of Mississippi. Two people, one of them a French journalist, were killed in the commotion, which was also mentioned in Billy Joel's *We Didn't Start The Fire*:

> *'Lawrence of Arabia, British Beatlemania*
> *Ole Miss, John Glenn, Liston beats Patterson'*

A little Mississippi town unexpectedly becoming a piece of history because of racial attitudes, but the incident became a watershed in the civil rights cause and James Meredith eventually got his degree.

Switching on the radio I settled down to listen to one of the many Country Music channels, in truth there wasn't much alternative. Having eulogised Chuck Berry in the last chapter for his (generally) impressive lyrics I now need to examine the other end of the spectrum. One of the first songs to come on the radio was by a singer called Joe Nichols and the song in question was entitled *Tequila Makes Her Clothes Fall Off*, which gave me a fair indication that this wasn't going to be a run of the mill sentimental Country ballad. The lyrics were interesting and certainly attention-catching; in mid-song I was serenaded by the unforgettable and elegantly composed line:

> *'Them panty-hose ain't gonna last too long*
> *If the DJ puts BonJovi on.'*

I wondered, somewhat mischievously, if Joe would go down well at The Opry, but thinking about it I suppose his songs would provide possibilities for widening the scope of the advertising strategy – I guess Tequila would provide rather more exciting marketing opportunities than Tennessee Sausage or Martha White's Pumpkin Streudels!

It only took a couple of hours to reach Tupelo and I rolled into town at around 3pm. The first thing I noticed was the city badge which boasts the logo 'Tupelo, we let our hospitality show.' Unfortunately this didn't extend to opening the Tourist Office at a weekend. Ironically it was more or less the first building I came to, whereas finding the bureau in previous locations had usually involved some detective work and often a long walk or taxi ride. As it happened, there was a Hilton Hotel next door and I went in to enquire about the cost. My theory on good hotels in quieter towns held good again and I checked in for a room rate of $100, which was exceptional for what was clearly a classy hotel. The day was going well – I had visited Graceland, sorted out a car, driven 100 miles, found a hotel and it was still only three o'clock. I decided to take advantage of this as I knew I needed to push on the next day and was conscious that I would have a longer drive up to Nutbush, on the other side of Memphis. So, as I was advised that Elvis's birthplace museum was not too far away, I thought I might as well capitalise and get straight up there.

I didn't need a Sat Nav to find Elvis Presley Drive (previously Old Saltillo Road) and arrived at number 306 in pretty short order. The site contains a small museum, memorial chapel, Walk of Life and Story Wall as well as the house in which Elvis was born on 8 January 1935. The house is the main attraction, of course, and I am pleased to say that this was not a mass tourism experience like Graceland. There were very few people around at the time of my visit, which is just as well considering the size, or lack of it, of the building, which emphasised Elvis's humble beginnings. Consisting of a white-painted, wooden building about the size of a static holiday home it has been carefully restored in recent years. Four wooden steps at the front took me up to an outside porch on which peacefully swayed a five foot long wooden seat, suspended from the roof by metal chains; the same swing Elton John talks about in *Porch Swing in Tupelo* on his *Peachtree Road* album:

> 'And this place don't change
> Some places move slow
> I'm just rocking myself on this porch swing in Tupelo'

It was not hard to imagine a young Elvis sitting swinging gently, perhaps singing to himself or to anyone who cared to listen.

I went inside the building and was greeted by a lady who was very keen to tell me all about Elvis and the family, especially as I was the only visitor. Strangely, the first room as you step in is the bedroom, but then again it is only a two-room house. This type of building is known locally as a 'shotgun house', the reason being that if you opened the front door and the backdoor at the same time you would be able to fire a gun straight through without impediment. Not recommended I'm sure, but that's how they describe it.

It was a strange feeling standing in the room where Elvis was born and where his twin brother Jesse Garon died at birth; made more poignant in the knowledge that Elvis grew up as an only child and often talked about his lost brother, blaming himself that he survived and Jesse did not. On the wall, I spotted a picture of Elvis as a small boy with his Mum and Dad. I was somewhat mesmerised by this as he was only about three years old at the time and I could clearly see his distinctive curled lip which became one of his trademarks. I didn't know it at the time, but I now understand this photo was taken in prison when Elvis and his mother, Gladys, went to visit Vernon, Elvis's dad, in Parchman Farm, the Mississippi State Penitentiary.

The back room was furnished with a couple of easy chairs and a small kitchen table which was decorated in a green checked tablecloth and was set for a meal for three. If I describe the set up as cosy it would be charitable and it certainly provided a sobering contrast to Graceland.

The museum, on the other side of the garden, chronicles the hard times in the area in the '30s and the circumstances in which Elvis and his family lived. When Elvis was three, Vernon was sent to jail for three years, along with two associates, for altering a $4 cheque to $8 (he served eight months). The consequent financial hardships meant they had to give up the family home, moving in with Vernon's parents. This was particularly tragic as Vernon, with help from his father Jessie and his brother Vester, had built the house himself with a $180 loan borrowed from his employer.

The family continued to live in Tupelo, usually on the 'wrong side of the tracks' (literally, as the area Elvis was born in and subsequently lived in was in East Tupelo, a deprived area separated from the more refined part of Tupelo by a railway track). On this East side, Elvis took to listening outside churches in the nearby black community of Shakerag, which gave him his liking for gospel music. He was also influenced, particularly in Country and Bluegrass, by a local musician called Mississippi Slim whose real name was Lee Carvel Ausborn. Lee's brother James was a childhood friend of Elvis and this gave Elvis access to the real world of music and radio with the pair of them sometimes visiting the WELO radio station in Tupelo where Slim would show Elvis how to play a few chords on the guitar.

Elvis made his first public appearance at a talent show at the age of ten at Tupelo Fairgrounds, singing Old Shep. For this he won a prize of $5 and free admission to all the rides, which I would imagine was a big thrill for him at the time (in later years he used to hire entire fairgrounds late at night for himself and friends). In 1948 when Elvis was thirteen the family moved from the area, to Memphis, as Vernon struggled to find a better way of life for the family (and also, according to some, to get away from problems of 'running moonshine'). Vernon can't have imagined what this move would lead to, although Elvis had by this time become something of a showman having given an informal concert at school on his leaving day. As Elvis put it when commenting on the move to Memphis, 'We were broke man, things just had to be better'. They would be.

In the evening I had a walk around Tupelo which was very quiet. There was a night club on the main street, however, and they must have been expecting some action as there were five heavies on the door. The band had obviously arrived, as their van was outside, and I noticed they went by the glorious name of the 'Spunk Monkeys'. I have to confess that I was not familiar with the term, so I looked it up in something called the Urban Dictionary. It would appear that there are many interpretations of spunk monkey, but I will refrain from sharing these with you for reasons you can probably imagine.

Tupelo is a long straight town and I couldn't see much in the way of restaurants. It was one of those occasions when you say to yourself "I'll just walk one more block . . ." So, many blocks on, I came to a road junction and all that was required was a death-defying crossing of the intersection and I would be rewarded by yet another Mexican restaurant. I decided to take my chances crossing the road to take the tortilla trail again and was rewarded by being served by a rather aggressive young Mexican girl whose brace on her teeth seemed just right for her scary demeanour.

There was an American Football game on TV and, like the basketball game in Phoenix, which now seemed like a very long time ago, I found myself being drawn into the action. The match was between Alabama Crimson Tide and Arkansas Razorbacks, played at the Bryant-Denny Stadium in Tuscaloosa. The fans were going nuts and I guess I must be a sucker for anything where the atmosphere is good – I couldn't believe the crowd was 92,138 and that this is actually the attendance for almost every home game. The crowd got their reward with an amazing comeback in the last eight seconds for the home team to win 41-38. It was entertaining stuff, though I still can't claim to understand what was going on. Still, it was sport and as it was a Saturday night it made up for not being able to watch *Match Of The Day*.

On the long haul back to the hotel I resisted the temptation to go and see the Spunk Monkeys, put off partly by the need for their fellow simians on the door. I instead followed my instincts down a back lane and ended up in Stables Bar where I struck up a conversation with a couple called Valerie and Darryll. This somehow turned into a geography lesson with me explaining through drawings on beer mats where in the world England is. I enjoyed a very nice couple of drinks at what I remember was a very reasonable $1.50 for Bud Light; on reflection at that price I wish I'd been able to drink more, but I think I was full of beans. Perhaps that constraint wasn't a bad thing considering I'd be driving in the morning and I'd already had a few beers to calm my nerves while watching the football and being served by Maria the Mexican.

IN THE MORNING, I had a proper breakfast, a luxury I wasn't used to, given the type of place I'd been staying in a lot of the time. Although I wanted to get moving and on my way to Nutbush I had time to go out and have a look at Tupelo's main street in daylight and to stretch my legs before the drive.

One of the first stores I came to was the Tupelo Hardware Co., a double-fronted building with a window display consisting of theodolites, measuring wheels and high visibility jackets. But, alongside these, stood somewhat incongruously an acoustic guitar. It was this store which received a visit in 1946 from Elvis and his mother when they went initially to buy a bicycle. Elvis, however, got his eye on an air rifle. Gladys was not prepared to let him have the gun so, after a few tears from the young boy, they compromised on a guitar after the assistant Forrest L. Bobo took it out of the display cabinet and let Elvis have a little strum to calm him down. After paying $8, Gladys handed the instrument to Elvis saying, 'You just take that home with you and learn to play it. You might be famous some day'.

There is a plaque outside the store, provided by the Convention and Visitors Bureau to commemorate this famous event. To get them back for not being open when I arrived I have pleasure in now advising them that they have spelt Forrest's name incorrectly on the inscription!

Next time you are feeling unlucky, perhaps having just missed out on the £10 lottery prize, consider this: a chap called Bill Williams in Florida has (or had) what is thought to be that same guitar and in 2002 he decided to auction it. There is a credible history accompanying the instrument, but nothing to definitively confirm its provenance, so it didn't sell. As it had a reserve price of $350,000 I call that unfortunate.

I wandered across the road towards what I could see was a very attractive grassed area, complete with fountain, in front of a nicely designed modern building. This turned out to be the new City Hall and I spotted a statue which I went to investigate. It was of Chief Piomingo ('Mountain Leader') born in 1750, died 1798. Piomingo was Chickasaw war chief of Longtown (South Tupelo) and was designated 'America's most influential Chickasaw ally'. He was awarded the Washington Peace Medal in 1792 and actually had an audience with George Washington in Philadelphia In 1794.

"Could I once see the day whites and reds were all friends it would be like getting new eyesight," reads Piomingo's quote on the plinth of the statue. It's as well he wasn't around over the following 50 years as he would have been mightily disappointed, to say the least, as his people were swindled out of their land and eventually relocated to Oklahoma.

The Chickasaws have always been a proud nation, known in historic times as the 'Spartans of the Lower Mississippi' ('Unconquered and Unconquerable') and in 1540 they saw off Hernando de Soto, of Dolly Parton Bridge fame. In that episode the Chickasaws pushed the Spanish explorers west and onward to the Mississippi, towards the discovery that made de Soto famous. So, really, he has quite a lot to thank them for.

In the early 18th century the Chickasaws, armed by the British, drove back the French and their Indian allies, the Choctaws, at the battle of Ackia, a victory that helped Britain strengthen their foothold in North America at a time when the French were intent on pushing north from the Gulf to extend their influence over the Mississippi valley. In more recent times the tribe fought on the Confederate side in the Civil War, forming part of the respected Choctaw/Chickasaw mounted regiment and were actually the last Confederate community to surrender.

The Chickasaw nation still maintains a proud tradition and, as well as having a modest presence in Mississippi, have their base in Ada, Oklahoma. They number among their famous, Hulk Hogan, wrestling superstar, and even an astronaut, John

Herrington, the first Native American in space. During his space mission in 2002 Herrington took a Chickasaw Nation flag into space. Piomingo would have been proud.

Flying over the City Hall building was, on one side, the Stars and Stripes and on the other the Mississippi State Flag. The State Flag was interesting as it has, incorporated in its top left hand corner, the Confederate Battle Flag. The topic of flags has been the source of much controversy in the southern states in recent years as the continued appearance of the Confederate design is seen by some as a defiant statement. In Georgia for instance, the General Assembly were forced, after much political wrangling, to adopt a compromise design in 2003. In Mississippi a referendum on this issue was held in 2001 as some Mississippians were offended by the present flag. The vote concluded that most of the electorate valued the historic symbolism of the existing flag, with its rebel connotations, by a ratio of 2:1. On checking the demographics of the state I couldn't help noticing that this ratio also applies to the split of the population white v black, which probably speaks for itself.

The park area was deserted except for one person – a lady practising yoga in front of the fountain located in the middle of the paved walkway. This turned out to be Catherine Crews who is an artist and who is the proprietor of 'True Colors 'art studio on the main street. Catherine was just finishing her yoga session in the mid-morning sunshine and as she rolled up her mat she said, "Good morning," like any good Tupellian would (I have no idea if that's the right term but it sounds good). She asked me what I was up to and, when I explained, Catherine told me that her husband is a journalist on the local newspaper and asked if I might be available for an interview the next day. Much as this would have been nice I had to decline as I wanted to return the car to Memphis by Monday lunchtime and get on my way west to Arkansas, although I promised to get in touch once the book was finished.

Catherine mentioned that Reeds department store just opposite the hardware store had a book shop and that she would be able to arrange book signing sessions. As this is one of multi-million-selling author John Grisham's favourite signing places I felt very honoured. She also offered to introduce me to the owner of the hardware store, whose father was in charge when Elvis and his mum visited. As the store was closed, with it being a Sunday, I had to put this one on the shelf also. It was a very pleasant way to start the day though and after thanking

Catherine for her help and kindness went back to the hotel to have a cup of coffee in the palatial surroundings before moving on. I had a feeling that my immediate future would not involve such niceties.

TUPELO IS SITUATED AT THE south west of the Cumberland Plateau and the Appalachian Mountains, near the junction of the Tennessee, Alabama and Mississippi borders.

It lies on the 'Natchez Trace', a 440-mile historic route constructed to facilitate trade between settlers in Northern Tennessee, and the Natchez Indians to the south, near the Louisiana border. It followed the migratory route of the bison and, before the development of river cities such as Memphis, provided a means of access to the Gulf and New Orleans.

The town was originally named Gum Pond due to the high number of Tupelo trees, known locally as blackgum. It was renamed after the Civil War in recognition of the small scale – if you call 20,000 participants small scale – Battle of Tupelo, which took its name from the tree. At this battle, sometimes known as Harrisburg, the Confederates, under the leadership of war hero Major General Nathan Bedford Forrest (whose name crops all over the place in the South), attacked the Union forces of General Sherman, who were trying to protect the supply route for the advance to Atlanta and the 'March to the Sea'. The Union forces retreated to Memphis, whilst claiming victory, as they had inflicted heavy casualties on Forrest and had succeeded in their aim of diverting him from attacking the supply route in middle Tennessee.

After the Civil War the town developed through its railway links and manufacturing power and it was the first city to be lit with electric power through the Tennessee Valley Authority initiative in 1934. Nowadays it is a thriving town of 35,000 people with one of its main industries being manufacture of furniture. It has rid itself of its colourful reputation of the thirties as a 'shakedown' spot for southern gangsters hiding from the law, including infamous duo Bonnie and Clyde who hid 'east of the tracks' while trying to evade federal and local authorities. The Citizens State Bank of Tupelo lays claim to fame (or infamy) as it was the site of 'Machine Gun' Kelly's last robbery, on 30 November 1932. Kelly outraged the establishment a year later with the kidnap of two wealthy residents of Oklahoma City and was subsequently captured by the FBI, spending the rest of his life in jail.

Tupelo's main claim to fame is, of course, as Elvis's birthplace and this is something that will always be an attraction as it is hard to see the Elvis phenomenon dissipating. At some stage, though, I would imagine that people will begin to believe he is dead. In advance of a documentary film released in August 2007, called *The Truth About Elvis*, a digitally aged photo was shown on a billboard in Tupelo and a website set up. The producers got bookmakers William Hill to put up a reward of $3 million for the first confirmed live sighting of Elvis and the response was so huge that the website exceeded its bandwidth. I don't think it was one of William Hill's biggest gambles!

On the song front I had fully expected that I would be reporting on Van Morrison's *Tupelo Honey*, the title track from his 1971 album:

'You can take all the tea in China
Put it in a big brown bag for me
Sail right round the seven oceans
Drop it straight into the deep blue sea
She's as sweet as Tupelo honey
She's an angel of the first degree . . .

But . . .there is a sting in the tail! My enquiries suggest there is no connection with Tupelo the town. Tupelo Honey is in fact produced in Florida in the swamps of the Ogeechee, Apalachicola and Chattahoochee river basins, along the Gulf Coast. The Tupelo Beekeepers' Association, based in Panama City, Florida will keep you right, but don't let them persuade you to engage in one of their favourite hobbies of wearing bee beards (involving thousands of live bees) at public displays!

So, no Van Morrison, but, instead, cast your mind back to 1967 if you were around. If the names Tallahatchie and Choctaw Ridge sound familiar you'll no doubt be thinking at this moment of poor Billie Joe McAllister and Bobbie Gentry.

'I got some news this mornin' from Choctaw Ridge
Today Billy Joe McAllister jumped off the Tallahatchie Bridge . . .'

Bobbie (real name Roberta Lee Streeter) was born in Chickasaw County just down the road from Tupelo. Although she only inhabited the pop world for around 10 years she made a major impact, particularly through *Ode to Billie Joe. Billie Joe* was originally the B side to *Mississippi Delta*, but radio stations took to the intrigue of its lyrics and it became a huge hit, selling 750,000 copies in its first week and knocking the Beatles' *All You Need Is Love* from the US number one spot in August 1967.

It must be one of the most evocative songs ever written and one of the most discussed. It was obviously the narrator who the preacher had seen up on Choctaw Ridge with Billie Joe. Was Billie Joe's suicide the result of his girlfriend's unwanted pregnancy, was it an aborted or stillborn child that the preacher saw them throw over the bridge? Or was it that Billie Joe was black and thus a forbidden love of Gentry's character? Or was it a ring they threw over; the heartbreak of the failed romance causing Billie Joe to go the same way later on? Or perhaps it was, as suggested in a subsequent book and film of the same name, that he jumped off the bridge because he was gay?

All of this Is actually irrelevant, despite the fact that it has kept people speculating for nearly forty years. The song is really about the matter of fact way the family talk about the incident, 'well Billie Joe never had a lick of sense, pass the biscuits please', unaware that the narrator is all churned up inside and is clearly the girlfriend of the deceased, 'I'll have another piece of apple pie, you know it don't seem right . . .'. It is hard to listen to the words and not cringe at the unintended cruelty of it all, a very perceptive and thought provoking song.

Bobbie Gentry herself has never revealed what was in her mind, but she won four Grammy awards whilst keeping everyone guessing. In some ways her career was unfulfilled, but probably only in the minds of her fans as to me it appears she was something of a reluctant star. She did have other successes though, including a number one hit in the UK in 1969 with the Burt Bacharach and Hal David number *I'll Never Fall In Love Again* for which she won a Grammy for Best Song of the Year. Bobbie retired from show business in 1978 at the ripe old age of 34 keeping her little secret about Choctaw Ridge to herself.

Ode To Billie Joe

It was the third of June, another sleepy, dusty Delta day,
I was out choppin' cotton and my brother was balin' hay
And at dinner time we stopped and walked back to the house to eat
And Mama hollered out the back door 'y'all remember to wipe your feet'
And then she said 'I got some news this mornin' from Choctaw Ridge'
'Today Billie Joe McAllister jumped off the Tallahatchie Bridge'

And Papa said to Mama as he passed around the blackeyed peas
'Well, Billie Joe never had a lick of sense, pass the biscuits please'
'There's five more acres in the lower forty I've got to plow'
And Mama said it was a shame about Billie Joe anyhow
Seems like nothin' ever comes to no good up on Choctaw Ridge
And now Billie Joe McAllister's jumped off the Tallahatchie Bridge

And Brother said he recollected when he and Tom and Billie Joe
Put a frog down my back at the Carroll County picture show
And wasn't I talkin' to him after church last Sunday night?
'I'll have another piece of apple pie, you know it don't seem right'
'I saw him at the sawmill yesterday on Choctaw Ridge'
'And now you tell me Billie Joe's jumped off the Tallahatchie Bridge'

And Mama said to me 'Child what's happened to your appetite?'
'I've been cookin' all morning and you haven't touched a single bite'
'That nice young preacher, Brother Taylor, dropped by today'
'Said he'd be pleased to have dinner on Sunday, oh, by the way'
'He said he saw a girl that looked a lot like you up on Choctaw Ridge'
'And she and Billie Joe was throwing somethin' off the Tallatchie Bridge'

A year has come 'n' gone since we heard the news 'bout Billie Joe
And brother married Becky Thompson, they bought a store in Tupelo
There was a virus going 'round, Papa caught it and he died last Spring
And now Mama doesn't seem to wanna do much of anything
And me, I spend a lot of time pickin' flowers up on Choctaw Ridge

And drop them into the muddy water off the Tallahatchie Bridge

Words and music by Bobbie Gentry

Chapter Fifteen

"Nutbush, oh Nutbush . . ."

I SAW A SIGN FOR BOONEVILLE. The very name suggested it would be worth a visit, conjuring up images of the true Wild West and I thought it would be worth a little detour. I had been driving for an hour or two on my way north to Nutbush and was becoming mesmerised by the mile after mile, acre after acre, of bright white cotton fields shimmering by the side of Highway US45. A quick decision and I took the slip road which would take me the two or three miles into Booneville and hopefully a coffee and, who knows, a piece of pumpkin pie.

US45 is full of references to childhood heroes; I was on a section of the David Crockett Highway, the map showed a Casey Jones railroad museum and Daniel Boone's name came up regularly as this was the territory of the famous frontiersman and settler of Kentucky, which lies just to the north.

I made the wrong choice – the place was deserted and dead. In defence of the town I had to remind myself it was a Sunday, but then I thought, "Wouldn't that actually be a good day to attract tourists?" Perhaps I should stop thinking. More to the point, perhaps I should respectfully remind myself that small town America tends to be deeply religious and not to expect too much on the Sabbath.

I followed the signs for the Rails and Trails Museum, but when I found it the place was deserted and all I could see was a red caboose from the Gulf, Mobile and Ohio railway and a sign on the museum door declaring 'Open Thursday – Saturday'. I did manage to get an ice cream at the adjacent shop, so at least I got refreshment. Despite appearing virtually uninhabited I could see that the town was very pleasant and also very tranquil, as you might expect, as it declares itself a 'Certified Retirement Town'. With an average household population of 2.4 you are hardly going to be bothered by screaming kids and come to think of it you're not likely to come across much aggro, either with a crime rate for the previous year reading: murders 0, rapes 0, robberies 4, auto theft 1. Perhaps the residents are too old to bother with those sorts of things.

Back on to the main road and more miles of cotton fields. Resisting the temptation to branch off to stoke Casey Jones' engines, or put my feet up in Davy Crockett's cabin, I turned onto the I40, heading west towards Memphis. I had to be on my toes now knowing I had to take a turn off for a place called Brownsville if I was going to find Nutbush, which wasn't even on my map. I had established in advance that Nutbush was somewhere between Brownsville and a small town called Ripley, but that was the best I could do.

After about half an hour I saw the Brownsville turnoff and turned north-west, away from Memphis. Suddenly I was in a remote area with little to keep me company apart from the unrelenting white fluff, before signs told me I was approaching Brownsville. 'Brownsville – a great place to live', read the first sign, quickly followed on subsequent lamp posts by 'Brownsville – Certified fluorided water', 'Passive alcohol sensors in use', (these 'sniff' alcohol at 'Sobriety Checkpoints' apparently), 'No driveway connections without permit', 'To report crime or suspicious incidents call . . .', 'Brownsville – home of champions' (followed by a list of local heroes)', 'No soliciting', 'Brownsville – awards won . . .' and so on. In view of the distractions I wouldn't have been at all surprised to see one saying 'Brownsville – beware 50 traffic accidents per week.'

I drove through the town square (and it was a square, not one of the common linear main streets I had become used to) and picked up the signs for Ripley on Highway 19. Now I became excited.

> *'A church house gin house,*
> *a school house outhouse,*
> *on highway number nineteen . . .'*

Tina's lyrics came flooding back to me.

> *'the people keep the city clean. Nutbush, oh Nutbush . . .'*

I was even more excited when I saw the green and white sign 'Tina Turner Highway', which the road has now been officially named. I had the road to myself and it seemed quite weird. Here I was on an early Sunday evening, on my own in a remote part of Tennessee on the road named after one of my all time heroes. It was great. If somewhat lonely.

Ahead of me was a road sign and I just had to pull up for a photograph. The sign read:

NUTBUSH
UNINCORPORATED

I was indeed at Nutbush City Limits – except there is no city, it is an unIncorporated town. Now, don't ask me to explain local government in the States. It's on a perplexity scale exceeding even our own in the UK and clearly Tina was using a little artistic licence in this respect. But who cares – as far as I was concerned I was at the 'city limits' and feeling rather smug I have to confess.

Climbing back into the car I drove on for another mile and saw one or two buildings, mostly churches, by the wayside and then suddenly I was in Ripley. Hang on, what happened to Nutbush?! It was gone – there and gone in a flash.

I turned around at Ripley, itself a small town, with the annual highlight apparently being the County Tomato Festival, and re-approached Nutbush from the west. I came across another city limits sign and for some reason felt inclined to get out and take another photo, a different perspective, I thought, looking east.

As I now knew where both the boundary signs were I managed to work out where the town centre was. The truth is there isn't one. There was one general store (closed), a cotton processing plant and a small gin factory. There was no-one about and it was obviously not going to be possible to find accommodation this Sunday evening in Nutbush. At least I knew I was in the right place as the store had a notice above it 'Welcome to Nutbush, Tennessee, Birthplace of Tina Turner'. I would come back tomorrow and have a mooch around and see what I could uncover, if anything.

I headed back to Brownsville a little concerned that I might not be able to find anywhere to stay as this was not the sort of area you find the usual big chain hotels or motels.

There were quite a lot of imposing antebellum (i.e. built before the Civil War) houses on the outskirts of Brownsville and many of these had plaques on the lawn telling of the history of the property, usually to do with wealthy cotton plantation owners. One of these houses had a Bed and Breakfast sign, so I drove up, parked the car and approached the building from the front, along a wooden porch. This place had a real spooky feel to it. The house looked just like the Addams Family mansion and I was relieved when no-one answered the door. I slunk away, trying not to make loud footsteps on the wooden porch, hoping nobody would suddenly grab me as I passed the side entrance. I drove the remaining distance to the town centre and I spotted a single-storey motel building just before the main part of town.

I went into the reception and was somewhat overpowered by the strong aroma of curry powder in the small office. However, the chap who came to assist was helpful enough and very quickly had me installed in a room for $34, which was quite handy as I was getting a bit concerned about the budget situation. I'm afraid that even at the equivalent of £17 it was overpriced; I had what looked like a 1950s television, the furniture could have been picked up at a house clearance and the wardrobe consisted of a coat rack screwed to the wall. Add to this the frustration of a fly which I couldn't catch, and which took great delight in dive-bombing me for the duration, and you get a feel for my misery.

I gained some relief by venturing out into Brownsville in search of food and in the small main square I saw a lady, in her 30s I would guess, unloading stuff from her car into her house which fronted on to the square. I decided to go across and have a word with her about the dining opportunities, which looked quite sparse, and she turned out to be very friendly and helpful. We got talking and she introduced herself as Bevelin Jones and, as usual, I was asked what brought me to town. Bevelin was quite excited by what I was doing and told me that her mother had been a childhood friend of Tina Turner and had actually taught Tina how to play the guitar when they were in their early teens. She went on to tell me that her mother was called Daisy Mann and she gave me her phone number.

"She'd love to talk to you," said Bev. So, armed with this information and feeling quite delighted, I dined in yet another Mexican restaurant for yet more flour, beans and rice. This time the waitress was very pleasant, unlike the previous evening, and she couldn't tell me enough about her plans for going travelling to Europe.

"I'm gonna go to France, and Switzerland, and London and England," she exclaimed with commendable excitement, if not geographical talent.

Walking back to the motel I couldn't help notice a convoluted tangle of tall, metal structures, in fact it was impossible to miss. It was as if someone had dropped ICI Teesside, in its prime, into their back yard. I found out the next morning from a lady selling fruit from a barrow that this was the 'Mindfield', the work of Billy Tripp, a local 'outsider artist' and heir to the Tripp Country Ham family fortune. This installation was quite bizarre and, apart from consisting of dozens of metal contraptions up to 125 feet high, the centre point was a round water tower which the artist had transported in pieces from a factory in Kentucky and had assembled personally, with the help of his pet crane which sits in his yard. The tower, having been outlandishly painted, now looks like a psychedelic, globular penny lolly, dominating the surrounding skyline. It carries in huge letters the wording 'Mindfield Cemetery . . . In Honor of Mom and Dad'.

The site, which has been under construction for nearly twenty years, is still a 'work in progress' and will apparently continue to develop until Billy dies, at which point he will be interred on the site. I am not sure what the locals make of it, but as planning laws in the States would appear to be somewhat relaxed, if they exist at all, they are stuck with it.

In the morning I said goodbye to my friend the fly, at which point I realised I was becoming like Tom Hanks in *Castaway* when he loses his friend Wilson the volleyball. I set off to have a closer look at Nutbush, hoping to lift my spirits. If the general store was open there might be a good chance of talking to someone who might know something about Tina, where she used to live etc. I parked right outside, went to the front door and tried the handle, but to no avail. I tried again and still nothing. It soon became clear that the store, the only shop in town, was no more.

This was a disheartening state of affairs. I was desperate to find out more about one of my heroes.

"What else might I do?" I asked myself. This was the only building on this side of the highway and on the other side there was only the cotton processing plant and the small gin factory. As there wasn't another soul around I decided to be cheeky and to walk into the gin factory. I was greeted by a chap who appeared to be the manager and he introduced himself as Tim Turner. The question was obvious, but the answer negative. No, he was not related to Tina. But he knew someone who was – "Ring Joe. He's Tina's cousin, but be aware he's a bit old and he's got a scratchy voice."

Tim was good enough to give me Joe's telephone number and when I got back to the car I decided to give Joe a ring, only to find that Nutbush doesn't have any mobile phone reception, which, all things considered, I can't say surprised me. As I had a two o'clock deadline to get the car back to Memphis I had to decide whether to try to fit in a visit to both Joe and to Daisy Mann, Beverlin's mum. As I left Nutbush I realised that Tina's childhood home is no more. As I crossed the 'city limits' Tina's voice was ringing in my ears.

'Little old town in Tennessee,
that's called a quiet little old community,
a one horse town that you have to watch . . .'

Unfortunately, I couldn't even find the horse.

As soon as I could pick up a reception I rang first Joe and then Daisy. Tim was right about Joe's scratchy voice. He seemed very amenable, but the only thing I could make out was that he wouldn't be available that morning. Daisy was, but didn't want to see me unless her daughter could be there. This was tricky as Bevelin was at work and probably couldn't get free until after I needed to be on my way. In the end I decided to locate Daisy's house in the hope that Bevelin might get there in time.

It was really tough finding the address and I went round in big circles a number of times, conscious all the time that I was racing against the clock. I finally parked outside the house and rang Daisy, telling her where I was and in the end a compromise was reached, she agreed to meet me on her porch and I bought her a bunch of flowers. I think it is fair to say that she regarded me with a great deal of suspicion, which I suppose is quite understandable. She eventually opened up a little and told me she used to stay on the "white man's farm" (owned by an Irvine Miller, I believe) at weekends when she was fifteen and Tina was nine (Tina was living with her Grandmother, having been deserted by her parents). She related how Tina used to sing and dance while she (Daisy) played the guitar, and how she would show Tina a few chords and generally give her a chance to broaden her musical talents outside of the church choir. Apart from this they spent all their time talking, 'fooling around' and eating ice cream. Daisy said she could see that Tina had talent, but they parted when Tina went to live with her mother in St Louis at the age of 16.

Although I didn't actually learn a lot new from Daisy I really enjoyed sitting talking to someone who had known Tina closely and who clearly liked and respected her. I couldn't help thinking as I sat talking to Daisy how incredible Tina's story is; from such a difficult early life, to making it big with Ike then walking penniless away nearly 18 years later. She fought her way back against the odds, when most people thought she would sink into oblivion without him, going on to sell millions upon millions of records and setting all kinds of records, including selling out a concert in Brazil with an audience of 184,000, and selling more concert tickets for a solo act than anyone in history. A superhero in my opinion, particularly with those legs.

Of Ike, it is a shame that we remember him most as the person who abused Tina, particularly if you have seen the film *What's Love Got To Do With It*. He always protested at the way he was portrayed in the film saying it wasn't like that, but he has also apparently gone on record as saying, "Sure there have been times when I punched her to the ground without thinking. But I never beat her." Oh, well that's OK then. If it's true then he can't blame anyone but himself for his demonisation. In Tina's autobiography she states that he broke her nose. I don't think she would lie.

Nevertheless, let's be charitable to the deceased and credit Ike with creating Tina in the first place, converting her from Anna Mae Bullock, and introducing her to the world. Also let's acknowledge the contribution he made to music and Rock and Roll in particular (remember *Rocket 88*, that 'first' Rock and Roll record). Ike was a talented musician and a pioneer in pop history and it's sad that because of his drug abuse and violence he has gone to the grave leaving us with a memory of an ogre rather than an icon.

SURPRISINGLY FOR SUCH A celebrated song *City Limits* never hit the top in either the UK or the States. Indeed, I was taken by surprise at the number of people in the States who, although they knew of Tina, didn't know this particular song. They were invariably taken aback when I told them it is now a standard at parties and discos in the UK. It actually did better in the UK, reaching number four in the singles chart in 1973, whilst in the States it reached only number 22.

I hate to do this to Tina, who wrote the song, but on examination of the lyrics I have to say they are not the most perspicuous I have come across:

> *'twenty five for speed limit*
> *motorcycle not allowed in it'*

(can this be true, apart from being not very tuneful?)

'you go to the fields on weekdays
and have a picnic on labor day'
'you go to town on Saturday
and go to Church every Sunday'

And that's apart from Nutbush not even being a city. Well, let's look at it another way – if you had seen the lyrics before you heard the song would you honestly have given it a chance? I think only Tina could have gotten away with it.

Now this is fascinating; at least I think so. I was surprised at the number of gin factories in Tennessee, as I thought it was a whiskey-manufacturing state. I also kept coming across the term 'cotton gin' and was intrigued as to the connection. Well, I can now tell you that it's nothing to do with making gin from cotton plants. Cotton Gin refers to an invention by Eli Whitney in 1793, which mechanised the production of fibre from cotton ('gin' is short for engine). Unlike its coastal counterpart (long-staple cotton), inland cotton has sticky green seeds, which are hard to pick out of the fluffy cotton bolls. Before Whitney's invention it was very time-consuming to pick out these seeds, slowing down the process considerably.

This might not seem an earth-shattering invention, but it was to have a profound effect on America and has even been cited as one of the causes of the Civil War. The idea behind the gin was that it would take less labour and thus less slaves to process the cotton, but it was so successful that it had the reverse effect. With the new invention the yield of raw cotton doubled each decade after 1800 and by 1850 America was producing three quarters of the world supply. This led to an unexpected growth in slavery in order to grow and pick the cotton. Southern planters saw their profits soar and slaves were an essential part of the industry. By 1860 approximately one in three of the population in the South were slaves. So, this made the issue of abolition an even bigger affair than before and Abraham Lincoln is quoted as saying, 'How could such a simple invention alter American history in such a king-size way?'

Ironically, Eli Whitney is also indirectly accredited with ending the war as he became the 'Father of Mass Production' in the North and the prolific output of muskets, using his techniques, gave the North the edge. Eli had quite a dramatic and topsy-turvy career. He didn't make much money from inventing the gin because of wrangling over patent rights, but he did become rich from manufacturing muskets which ended the war he was instrumental in starting!

Nutbush City Limits

A church house gin house
A school house outhouse
On highway number nineteen
The people keep the street clean
They call it Nutbush, oh Nutbush
They call it Nutbush city limits

Twenty-five for speed limit
Motorcycle not allowed in it
You go to store on Friday
You go to church on Sunday
They call it Nutbush, oh Nutbush. They call it Nutbush city limits

You go to the fields on weekdays
And have a picnic on labor day
You go to town on Saturday
And go to church every Sunday
They call it Nutbush, oh Nutbush. They call it Nutbush city limits

No whiskey for sale
If you get drunk no bail
Salt pork and molasses
Is all you get in jail
They call it Nutbush, oh Nutbush. They call it Nutbush city limits

A little old town in Tennessee
A quiet little community
A one-horse town
You have to watch what you're putting down
In old Nutbush, oh Nutbush

Words and music by Tina Turner

Chapter Sixteen

"We are now in occupied territory . . ."

THE NEXT LEG OF MY journey was going to be a logistical nightmare. Having returned the car to Memphis, I needed to get to Tulsa. Whilst sitting at home with a map a few months earlier it hadn't looked too much of a problem. I'm afraid a scale of 1:5,000,000 really does takes some getting used to, though, and now I was getting a reality check on the distances involved.

The journey from Memphis to Tulsa is 428 miles and scanning the Greyhound schedules was not a happy experience. I had the choice of leaving Memphis at 5am and arriving twelve hours later at 5pm or leaving at 2.50pm, arriving in Tulsa at 4.50am. Neither of these options had me falling over with enthusiasm and I decided that I would be better off breaking the journey somewhere.

Looking at the map, the best option seemed to be a stopover at Little Rock in Arkansas, which was about a third of the way to Tulsa. So I opted for this and, rather than get the 10pm bus which would deliver me to Little Rock in the early hours, I decided I would be better off waiting till morning and getting the 8.15am service. I therefore had the luxury of another night in Memphis. However, as my budget was getting tight and I didn't want to pay the high rates downtown (and that's assuming I could get a room), I thought it would be best to stay near Graceland, which is a cheaper area. This was quite handy as it was down the road from the airport where I had just, by five minutes, succeeded in returning the car without incurring another day's rental.

I booked back into the Scottish Inn Suites, killed an hour or two by the poolside, and then decided to try the Heartbreak Hotel which I was sure would serve non-residents with a meal. They did, but I was a bit disappointed at the 'restaurant', which served only basic bar meals. This was probably a reflection on the needs of the clientele because they were, as you would imagine, all Elvis enthusiasts and their evening meal routine consisted of sitting in a big food court type area with a massive screen showing footage of Elvis performing. It was somewhat unusual, looking around and seeing everyone sitting in semi-circles at their tables, all facing the same way so they could see the screen while they scoffed their dinner. One section of the Elvis 'concert' finished and another came on, with Elvis singing a gospel number. At this point everyone in the room put down their knives and forks and started snapping their fingers in time to the music, which was a bit off-putting while I tried to enjoy the 'burning hunks of chicken' I had selected from the Elvis-themed menu.

As I made my way back down EP Boulevard I reflected that this was the end of the Mississippi/Tennessee part of my adventure and that after four weeks of constant travelling I would now be on the way west towards what would, in a week or so, be the final phase of my mission.

ON THE BUS TO LITTLE ROCK I was sitting next to a chap from Michigan who had a few days off from his job as a hospital cleaner and was on his way to Dallas to see an ex-army pal for a few days. As his journey time was 28 hours to cover the 1,254 miles, I made a resolution not to complain about any of my bus adventures. In my case it was only a couple of hours to Little Rock and I arrived in late morning, under sunny Arkansas skies.

There are actually two cities, Little Rock and North Little Rock, the two communities being separated by the Arkansas River. The Greyhound station is on the north side and a helpful employee at the bus station gave me a contact at a nice-looking hotel across the street. I made my way there, but unfortunately I was out of luck. They were full. But the manager was very helpful and, as I didn't know the city, he kindly fixed me up, booking me in at the Comfort Inn, which was a mile or so out of town on the south side.

North Little Rock is the junior partner in the twin town set up, with a population of around 60,000, compared to the 180,000 on the south side. The name Little Rock refers to an outcrop of rock protruding into the river, and was named in the

1720s by a French explorer, Jean-Baptiste Bénard de la Harpe (Bernard to his friends), who called it 'La Petite Roche', which doesn't take a lot of translating. There are actually two outcrops, La Petite Roche and La Grande Roche (a slightly bigger outcrop, you won't be surprised to hear), but he based the town at La Petite as there was already an Indian settlement there.

Before then our friend Hernando de Soto had his finger in the pie again when he travelled through the area in 1541, no doubt causing the usual mayhem as he introduced himself and his mates. But he was to get his come-uppance the following year when he succumbed to fever, in May 1542, in lower Arkansas. His comrades laid him to rest in the Mississippi River, so that the Indians couldn't dig him up and prove he wasn't a God, as he had encouraged them to believe. The remainder of his party took to the river and, despite pursuit from not very happy locals, most made it to the Gulf and then back to Mexico City.

Out of the original 600 men in de Soto's expedition, 311 survived the three year adventure. Bearing in mind the task was to conquer North America in four years you can't say it was a great success, but they did enhance the European knowledge of America considerably whilst traversing the South-Eastern states. At a cost to the indigenous population, however, as it is estimated that the diseases they left behind killed at least 10,000.

The expedition also gave the natives a taste of things to come over the next few hundred years. It might have been better for all concerned if Hernando had rested on his laurels from his previous big expedition when he helped Francisco Pizarro to conquer the Incas in 1531 and 1532, becoming a rich man in the process. As it was, he couldn't resist the temptation of seeking a sea passage to China in order to trade the Spanish New World gold, plundered from the South, which was another of his objectives for the American excursion.

Little Rock, which is the capital of the state of Arkansas, was incorporated as a city in 1831. It flourished as a river port through agriculture, lumber and bauxite (aluminium ore). It now has a strong white collar feel about it, one of its largest employers being the University of Arkansas for Medical Sciences, which has nearly 9,000 employees.

The state fought on the side of the Confederacy in the Civil War, but the town was occupied by the Union in September 1863 after the Battle of Little Rock. An interesting feature of this particular conflict was the fact that two Confederate Generals, John S Marmaduke and Lucius M Walker had a big fall out and challenged one another to a duel. With the Union forces approaching they settled their differences by the Arkansas River with pistols at ten paces. They both missed with their first shots, but then Marmaduke hit Walker with a second, fatally wounding him. Before he died Walker forgave Marmaduke when the latter offered his assistance. All a bit pointless really, and not exactly a morale booster for the lads as 14,000 Union troops came charging over the horizon.

After checking in at the Comfort Inn I wandered across the street to the Holiday Inn where I had been advised I could get a reasonable lunch, the recommendation being the Clinton Club Sandwich. Incidentally, here's a good quiz question – by what name is Little Rock's most famous son William Jefferson Blythe better known? Well you've just had a pretty generous clue and you've probably guessed that it's former US President Bill Clinton, whose father was killed in a car crash before Bill was born. Four years later, Bill's mother married Roger Clinton and Bill took his step-father's name.

Little Rock is steeped in the political adventures of 'Slick Willie', not least by the presence of the William J Clinton Presidential Center, which houses a library and museum, with archives covering the eight years Clinton was in office as President, as well as containing a replica of the Oval Office and cabinet rooms of the White House. Such a library is the reward every town gets for donating one of its sons to be Top Cat, the practice starting when Franklin D Roosevelt raised private funds in 1940 to create a library in his home town of Hyde Park, New York. Provision is now made under the Presidential Libraries Act passed in 1955 and in the case of the Clinton Center $165million was appropriated for the facility.

Apart from Bill Clinton, Little Rock is famous for an event that took place in 1957 and which shook the nation, causing a constitutional crisis. It was centred on Little Rock Central High School and revolved around its refusal to admit nine black students.

I took a cab up to Central High, a couple of miles out of the town centre, with my plan being to walk back to see the State Capitol building and then head down to the Arkansas river to walk along the River Trail. Not for the first time this turned out to be a bit further than I thought.

The school is huge and is an impressive building, part art deco, part gothic, but very attractive to look at. Across the road it has a museum, located in a wonderful little red and white restored Magnolia Petrol Company filling station, which actually looks like a perfect Matchbox model. I went into the museum and enlightened myself on the background to the 1957 episode.

There was, at the time, massive resistance in the South to school desegregation and Little Rock was the first test of the 1954 Supreme Court ruling (Brown v Board of Education) that 'separate educational facilities are inherently unequal'. The State Governor, Orval E Faubus, spurred on by other southern politicians and many constituents, invoked what he claimed to be 'State Rights' and instructed National Guardsmen to keep out the black students, who became known as the 'Little Rock Nine'.

President Eisenhower was determined that the Federal Constitution would be upheld and on September 24, three weeks after the crisis started, he ordered 1,200 soldiers from the 101st Airborne Unit to Little Rock. He also federalised the entire 10,000 strong State National Guard taking them out of the hands of Faubus. After this intervention Faubus appeared on television telling the residents of Arkansas, "We are now in occupied territory." The troops, who stayed until November, got the students into school where they endured a year of abuse and intimidation before Faubus played his next card.

After the first graduation of a black student, Ernest Green, in May 1958, Faubus ordered all three public high schools in Little Rock to be closed. They remained closed for the 1958-59 academic year and students had to go to other districts or enrol in all-white private schools. During 1959 a federal court ruled the closures unconstitutional and the schools re-opened in August with black students finally being admitted.

The confrontation split the community and brought the nation to crisis. I don't know if I'm exaggerating but it seems to me there was the potential for another civil war when you consider the similarities between this and the causes of the 1860s catastrophe.

During my visit, extensive preparations were in place for a visit the following week by Bill Clinton and the world's press to celebrate the 50th anniversary of the incident. With workmen all around me erecting an outdoor stage, and gardeners sprucing up the grounds, I took a few photos, half wishing I was going to be around to say hello to Willie, who I can't help liking for some reason.

Leaving the High School, which I had found inspirational, I set off in the direction of the State Capitol a mile and a bit away. This was another impressive building and I suddenly thought I was in Washington – it is virtually identical to the

Capitol building in Washington DC, complete with dome and cupola and Romanesque pillars. In the smart grounds I had a stroll around the memorial garden for recipients of the Medal of Honor, which included General Douglas McArthur, the supreme Commander of Allied Forces in the Pacific in World War II, who was born in Little Rock.

On my way down to the river I came across a bust of Count Casimir Pulaski 'Polish Patriot and Revolutionary War Hero'. The name seemed familiar but I couldn't think why, until that is, I realised that Little Rock is situated in Pulaski County. I was intrigued as to how a Polish Count in the 1700s could become an American war hero. It would seem that the Count was a bit miffed at not being able to repulse the Russians from his home territory and went to live in Paris in 1777. There he met Benjamin Franklin, who at that time was American Ambassador to France. When Franklin invited him to join the Americans in their fight for independence from the British he was only too pleased to volunteer as he remembered that a few years earlier the British had recommended the partition of Poland. Pulaski came to the States, organised a cavalry unit and immediately made an impression at the Battle of Brandywine in September 1777. This earned him a commission as Brigadier General of the entire American cavalry. In 1779 he took part in the attempt to recapture Savannah and was wounded in the leg, a wound which turned out to be fatal. He is an enduring hero in the States and it transpires that many counties and towns across the country are named after him.

I decided to point myself in the direction of Little Rock's little sister North Little Rock across the river. I crossed the Broadway Bridge and enjoyed the view downriver while on my right, on the far bank, I admired the new Dickey-Stephens Ballpark, home of the Arkansas Travellers baseball team, situated right on the river bank. Once across the bridge I turned right, following the river walk and, alongside the footpath, I came across some display plaques. These plaques commemorate an historic episode called the 'Trail of Tears', which I had not heard of previously. It seems Arkansas was a focal point of 'Indian Removal' in the 1830s, a policy designed and enforced by the Federal Government removing the 'Five Civilised Tribes' (so called because they had converted to 'European ways') to newly-designated Indian Territory in what was later turned into the state of Oklahoma. One of the staging posts for this enforced journey was Little Rock.

The five tribes were the Chickasaw, Muscogee (Creek), Seminole, Choctaw and Cherokee nations. The removal came about as a result of the migration of white settlers into the ancestral tribal lands, fuelled in part by the search for gold. Supporters of the policy said the removal of the Indians was "For the benevolent good of the tribes east of the Mississippi to stop them being overwhelmed and lost in the onslaught of an expanding American population". In reality it freed up millions of acres of land for the settlers. Theoretically, the Indians were being given compensatory land in Oklahoma, but this turned out in many cases to be inhospitable and infertile. The removal turned into a real tragedy with many of the tens of thousands of Indians dying of disease, starvation or cold. This is now recognised as one of the less glorious events in American history and The Trail of Tears National Historic Trail, stretching 2,200 miles across nine states, was opened in 1987 to make sure it doesn't disappear from the nation's consciousness. One of the many heart-rending statements of the time sums up the despair of those being forcibly relocated:

'Last evening I saw the sun set for the last time, its light shine upon the treetops, the land and water that I am never to look upon again. No other evening will come, bringing to Menawa's eyes the rays of the setting sun upon the home he has left forever.'

Muscogee Chief Menawa 1836

Moving on, I approached Main Street Bridge by which I would make my way back to Little Rock and the hotel. Before clambering on to the bridge I had a look at an old submarine, the USS Razorback, which is a decorated veteran of World War II, Vietnam and the Cold War. It was one of the 12 submarines to take part in the surrender of Japan in Tokyo Harbour in 1945 and is now a Little Rock tourist attraction, along with a tugboat, the USS Hoga, which saw action at Pearl Harbour.

The nickname Razorback applies to all the male sports teams of the University of Arkansas (like the football team I had watched on TV a few nights earlier), whilst the female teams go by the more demure title of 'The Lady Backs'. The term Razorback comes from the proliferation in the south eastern states of the Razorback pig which is a wild boar-type animal introduced to the country by none other than our friend Mr de Soto. As well as having inflatable pigs as mascots for sports events the University have a live mascot – a 400 pound hog called Tusk, which attends all home matches!

I found out that the submarine was not named because of any Arkansas connection, but after the Razorback whale, commonly found in the Pacific. Obviously, because of its name, it has an affinity with the town and this would no doubt have been one of the reasons for it being purchased in 2004 when it ended its active service after previously being sold to the Turkish Navy.

In the evening I decided to take the hotel courtesy bus, a rare way to save taxi fares, downtown to River Market, a revitalised area with bars and restaurants. I got talking to another hotel guest on the bus who was clearly more familiar with the area than myself and he gave me a few pointers on where to eat. In the end we decided we would go for a pint together and we ended up having a meal, eating in one of his favourite bars, which served very nice food.

I discovered my friend's name was 'Hoppy', which I thought was a bit unusual and after a couple of beers I felt brave enough to ask him about it. He explained that his real name is Howard Boyd Williams, but, as Hopalong Cassidy was very popular at the time he was born, and was played by William Boyd, one of the nurses in the hospital called him Hoppy which stuck from then on!

Hoppy lives in Austin, Texas and is Vice President of a dry cleaning business. We had an interesting chat ranging from shootings in Greyhound bus stations to Vietnam to Ku Klux Klan and the music scene in Austin. I was intrigued by the Klan discussion and Hoppy told me that the Klan is still prevalent in Arkansas. As my later enquiries discovered, he is quite right. Arkansas apparently has the most active Klan chapter in the USA with a core membership estimated at 500.

Across the country there are 150 Klan chapters with an estimated 8,000 members. The organisation was formed at the end of the Civil War, in 1865, in Pulaski, Tennessee, (named after the same Casimir Pulaski I mentioned earlier) and was the result of half a dozen bored ex-Confederate soldiers who set up the 'secret' organisation as a prank and who thought it was a wheeze riding about at night draped in white sheets. Other people then got on board and directed the 'club' in a far more sinister direction.

They took the name from the word 'Kyklos', which is Greek for circle and 'Clan' (brotherhood) and rather neatly named their ritual book the 'Kloran'. They thought up outrageous titles such as 'Grand Imperial Wizard' (overall leader of all 'dens' across the country), 'Grand Dragon of the Realm' (presiding over a state), 'Grand Titan of the Dominion' (with responsibility for several counties) and so on. The 'Grand Cyclops' ran an individual den and was assisted by two

'Nighthawks', and all members were called 'Ghouls', which I would suggest is remarkably appropriate.

I suppose the end of the Civil War was an ideal time for the Klan to be formed as there would have been lots of disillusioned people who had been fighting on the losing Confederate side whose attitude to slavery and other such issues was not going to change overnight. Indeed, the war hero I mentioned earlier, Nathan Bedford Forrest, is reputed to have been the organisation's first Grand Wizard. When approached to join the Klan he is reported to have said something along the lines of "Great, we can use that to keep the niggers in their place."

The first incarnation of the Klan petered out after a few years, during 1869, some say at the instigation of Bedford Forrest who was alarmed at the escalating violence, while others suggest it was because by that time white supremacy in the South had been restored.

But there was a second incarnation, in the early 1900s, arising partly as a response to mass immigration, and by 1924 the Klan had millions of members – estimates range from 3 million to 6 million, so it wasn't an organisation to be trifled with. It has been reported that Warren G Harding, President of the United States between 1921 and 1923, was inducted into the Klan, although it should be noted he was also a freemason and many people linked the masons to the Klan. During the depression in the late 1920s and the 1930s, membership dropped dramatically and in-fighting and financial difficulties also weakened the organisation. There was a resurgence in the 1960s because of the Civil Rights movement, but the organisation never attained its previous strength or notoriety.

As Hoppy says, the Klan are still active in Arkansas, which is the headquarters for the Knights of the Ku Klux Klan, who are based in Harrison in the north of the state. In some parts of the country, faced with dwindling interest, the present Klan leadership are trying to tone down their message, at least publicly, in order to attract more members. They are even getting involved with such initiatives as 'Adopt-a-Highway' clean up programmes. In Missouri, the State tried to prevent the Klan from adopting a road, but were overruled by the US Supreme Court and notices were therefore allowed declaring 'Adopt-a-Highway. Next mile adopted by Knights of the Ku Klux Klan, Realm of Missouri'!

In an area where many black children are bussed to school this must be fairly galling and it is hardly surprising that the state has been plagued with the tearing down of the signs, which then have to be re-erected.

After an excellent evening I said goodbye to Hoppy and thanked him for his company and the fact that, like Dan and Tabitha in Chattanooga, he had insisted on paying for my meal. It simply confirmed everything I had experienced about Southern hospitality and I felt very humble to be the recipient of such generosity. I may not have uncovered any musical connections on this stopover, but it had opened my eyes to what an integral role Little Rock has played in American history.

Chapter Seventeen

"I hate to do this to you, but I love somebody new . . ."

AS I STOOD IN LINE, as they say in the States, at Little Rock Greyhound station, I had to chuckle at the article on the national TV news which we were all watching while waiting for the bus to Tulsa. It featured the debacle in Seattle, Washington State, caused by the colloquial name being given to the new trolley system in town. Unfortunately, it seems the new service was provisionally designated as the 'Salt Lake Union Trolley', so it didn't take too long for someone to come up with a suitable acronym. I would suggest that the slogan 'For a good time call the S.L.U.T.' is not really the sort of headline you would want to generate if you are a civic official.

Apparently oblivious to such possibilities, the contracting company Vulcan (owned by Paul Allen, the ex-Microsoft billionaire) and Seattle City Council proceeded to introduce the $50million system, unaware of the hilarity and embarrassment the abbreviated name would cause.

Frenetic efforts are now being made to call it a Streetcar rather than a Trolley, and the authorities now dispute the original title, but too late, the name has caught on. But it's an ill wind and, whilst there are no doubt some red faces, there are some enterprising people who are taking advantage of the opportunity to make a few dollars and have a bit of a laugh. T-shirts are now being displayed all around the city with slogans such as 'Ride the SLUT' and 'Love the Seattle SLUT' and I am sure Mr Allen would admire the business acumen of the entrepreneurs who sold hundreds of garments within days of the launch.

But I digress, I'm supposed to be taking you to Oklahoma, and Tulsa in particular.

I boarded the bus and was pleased to see that it was a Jefferson Lines coach. There is something about the Jefferson trips that seem to be more civilised, perhaps because they are on the less-frequented routes and tend to be less crowded. And this was to be the case on the journey to Tulsa. We even had a very nice driver, a lady called Cindy, who went to great lengths in her announcement to include a request to "be nice to your neighbour". She couldn't do much, however, about the guy behind me who was snoring like a Razorback.

After about three hours on the I40, travelling in the direction of Oklahoma City, we drove through the depressing approaches to Fort Smith, which looked decidedly industrial and messy. We stopped for a 45 minute layover before changing direction and heading north towards Missouri and Kansas. Now it was a different story, the industrial wastelands turned into beautiful countryside and we started gaining height, which was a novelty as I don't think I'd been on anything other than a flat road since Arizona, and I worked out we were now in the Boston Mountains, part of the Ozark Mountain region. It was quite spectacular and, as the bus climbed, we went across some viaducts, taking us across deep valleys. It was not for the acrophobic, but it made a nice change from the endless cotton fields I had been subjected to over the last week. Looking out to the mountains, forests and hillsides I found it quite difficult to imagine that there wasn't enough land in the days of the settlers to accommodate everyone without ejecting innocent people from their homelands, but that's history.

We stopped at Fayetteville, apparently not a place in which to take liberties or stroll too far away from Foodruckers burger shop. It was outside here, while I was littering the pavement with crumbs from my cinnamon pastry, that one of my fellow travellers told me that his ancestors are from Scotland and that there is a family castle somewhere in the Highlands where he will always be welcome. This wasn't the first time I had heard this line from travelling companions. It had become apparent to me that these Scottish castles won't get too crowded with guests as no-one I spoke to had ever been across the Atlantic to check out the theory!

In mid-afternoon we arrived at Joplin, Missouri, an old lead and zinc mining town on Route 66, where we were scheduled to a have a one-hour layover and change of bus. Unfortunately, this turned into a three-hour ordeal in one of the most depressing bus stations you can imagine. A three-hour delay would have been enough in itself, but this was the worst station I had ever been in and it was staffed by a rude and unhelpful employee who seemed to take delight in not letting us know what was happening. All he would offer is "the bus's running late" and he made it pretty clear he didn't give a toss.

The station had no café and not even a TV set, which was unusual – just a vending machine and a noisy amusement machine. I went outside to get a bit of fresh air and saw that the surrounding area was awful. All around, the buildings seemed to be derelict and there was nothing anywhere of assistance to a hungry or thirsty traveller. There were two guys from the bus sitting on the pavement with their backs against the wall and I joined them for a while. One of them had been on the bus since Sunday (this was Wednesday) and when I asked him what he was doing on such a long trip he said he was going to get his nephew out of jail (I assumed he was going to bail him but didn't press for details). Whatever the means of release, that's what I call a dedicated uncle. I hope the youngster appreciated it.

The other chap was a cabinetmaker and he had been stranded in a place called Rogers for the last six weeks having been let down by a 'pal' who had promised him a job if he went there. He had apparently stayed the last two weeks with complete strangers while he tried to save the money to get back home. In view of the circumstances of these two I suddenly felt less put out about having to hang around for three hours.

The delay meant I didn't get to Tulsa till 8pm and I settled very quickly for a budget hotel. My room smelt like a urinal, presumably due to a plumbing problem, but as it was the only room available I didn't have much choice but to get used to it. Not a scintillating day I have to say, but at least I had made it to Tulsa and I could have the next day looking around. I could also look forward to the next evening in town as I wouldn't be moving on till Friday.

I found a restaurant called Ruby Tuesday, feeling as if I just wanted to keep myself to myself after the day I had endured. Of course I ended up with an over the top waitress who wanted to talk all the time. Irritatingly, she kept calling me "sunshine", and replied "awesome" to everything I said. After she guessed that I was first Australian and then Swedish I thought I would give her a clue and suggested "just below Scotland".

"Netherlands," she answered with undisguised glee. I can't even remember if I put her right.

After a decent night's sleep in the urinal I packed my bag again and vacated the hotel as there was no way I was going to stay there for a second night. The very helpful staff in the Tourist Bureau pointed me in the direction of a recommended hotel and off I went, humping my heavy pack in the bright sunshine.

Unfortunately, the hotel had recently undergone a change of name as well as ownership and it was hardly a surprise that I couldn't find the Great Western, as it is now called the Downtown Plaza. But it was worth finding as it was very nice for the price and I was just a bit unlucky that the restaurant had closed down the previous day for refurbishment and that on the next day, when I had planned to do my laundry, I would find all the pipes on that floor were being dismantled. I was not downhearted, however, as I had liked what I had seen so far in Tulsa and I had been given lots of useful information by the helpful ladies in the Tourist Bureau.

Tulsa is a city on the up. Like Little Rock it is situated on the Arkansas River, which, incidentally, flows 1,500 miles from the Colorado Rockies down to Napoleon, in south-east Arkansas where it joins the Mississippi. The town has become well known over the last century as the Oil Capital of the World, but it went through hard times in the early eighties when a recession hit oil prices.

It is now completing the regeneration process and there is a spectactular showpiece arena, 'The BOK (Bank of Oklahoma) Center', under construction, which has been designed by César Pelli, the man who built the amazing Petronas Towers in Malaysia. When this is finished Tulsa will be a wonderful town to visit from the architectural point of view as it also boasts some superb art deco skyscraper buildings dotted around the town. It is a real treat to walk around the town with a map of fifty historic buildings, all within close proximity, where you can admire the 'Zigzag' and 'Streamline' styles of the '20s and '30s on buildings constructed from the wealth of the early oil barons.

Tulsa is not a shy city. It sports the largest free-standing statue in the world – the 'Golden Driller', six miles out of town at the Expo center. This is a 76 foot tall figure of an oil worker leaning on a real oil derrick recovered from a disused oil field. Even this statue, which is 10 feet higher than the Angel of the North, is to be surpassed, in style, very shortly by 'The American', a 217 foot bronze statue of a Native American with a bald eagle on his shoulder. The statue will be 60 feet taller than the Statue of Liberty and the eagle itself will have a wingspan of 82 feet. As I say, not a shy city, but certainly an architecturally interesting one.

The town has its origins in the Trail of Tears, having been founded in the 1830s by Creek Indians relocated from Alabama. They called it Tallasi (old town) and by the late nineteenth century, as the town grew, it became known as Tulsey Town. At this point in its development it was known as 'a cow town on the prairie'. Incorporation as a city followed, in 1898, and then the world changed for Tulsey when oil was discovered in 1905. The 'black gold' transformed the area and the population grew rapidly, bringing the construction of hotels, schools and even an opera house. By 1912 it had established itself as the World's leading oil centre.

A tough time, socially, followed in the early twenties when, in 1921, the biggest race riot ever to hit the States took place after the arrest of a young black man, who was accused of molesting a white girl in an elevator. As a lynching party descended on the jail, the black community took up arms and went to the jail to offer assistance to the Sheriff in protecting the accused, who by most accounts had only stumbled into the girl. This, of course, occurred at a time when the Klan were strong and it has been reported that the Sheriff's Office and the local newspaper (which actively fuelled the incident) were well represented by Klan members. The incident got out of hand and when a gun went off accidentally all hell broke loose. At one point thousands of whites, mostly armed, were driving around town shooting at any black person they saw.

The National Guard were called in to quell the riot and at the end of it the Greenwood area of the city (known as the Black Wall Street because it had been so prosperous) was in ruins, having been set ablaze by the rioters. Unofficial estimates put the death toll at around 300, though some say it may have been thousands. 10,000 people were left homeless and many businesses were destroyed. To make matters worse insurers would not pay out and no whites were ever called to account for their actions. It took the area ten years to get back on its feet – some say it has never really recovered – but it is now an integral part of the revitalised city, housing the Greenwood Cultural Centre which has a memorial outside dedicated to those who lost their lives in the riot.

Greenwood is flanked by the Brady Arts District and the Blue Dome District, both of which provide a wide selection of bars, restaurants and music venues. I was surprised to find such a wide range of culture in this prairie town and, for those who are that way inclined there is a Tulsa Symphony Orchestra, Tulsa Opera, Tulsa Theatre and the "renowned" Tulsa Ballet (I hope I'm not being facetious when I say *Billy Elliot* sprang immediately to mind – ballet and a tough old oil town somehow don't seem to roll off the tongue together). Seriously, I was impressed and I haven't even mentioned the Oklahoma Jazz Hall of Fame yet.

Tulsa also has immense 'Mother Road' credentials as it was local business-man Cyrus Avery, known as the 'Father of Route 66', who began the successful campaign in 1927 for a road linking Chicago and California. The town was a key rest stop for the route in its heyday and is still an attraction for Route 66 enthusiasts.

I ONCE HEARD JAZZ DESCRIBED, somewhat derogatorily, as a "collection of notes played in no particular order". Well, I thought it was derogatory, but I might need to reconsider that viewpoint if I consider Louis Armstrong's similar but different view, if you know what I mean, that "Jazz is music that's never played the same way once".

The truth is that it's impossible to define Jazz. There are an infinite number of varieties and styles and I think what Satchmo was saying is that more than any other form of music it provides endless scope for improvisation by the performer. Whilst it has never been my favourite form of music I am always prepared to keep an open mind (well, sometimes) and so I decided I would pay a visit to the Jazz Hall of Fame in its new location in the historic Union Depot, one of Tulsa's 'Art Deco Jewels', up towards the Brady and Blue Dome districts.

The Union Depot was Tulsa's passenger railway station until 1967 when the trains stopped running due to lack of demand. It was opened in 1931 amidst a tremendous hoo-ha with 60,000 people thronging the surrounding streets. Among the celebrations, which went on into the night, were 'Singing and dancing to Jimmy Wilson's Catfish Band', 'Indians performing stomp dances on the tracks' and 'train loads of revellers rolling in from Dawson and Broken Arrow'. For those who couldn't make it the proceedings were broadcast on the radio!

So quite a start in life for the depot ('Union' depot or station, by the way, means a jointly-owned facility serving a number of railway companies, in this case the Frisco, Santa Fe and 'Katy' [Missouri, Kansas and Texas] railroad companies). The depot is indeed a gem and it has now been impressively restored to become a wonderful new home for the Jazz Hall of Fame.

The Hall had only been open two months when I visited and finishing touches were still being put to parts of it. David Webber, one of the key officials, willingly gave me some of his time in an attempt to enlighten me on a form of music to which I hadn't really had much exposure in the past. He explained that whilst New Orleans was the birthplace of Jazz, lots of black musicians had stopped at Tulsa on their migration to bigger venues in Chicago and New York and that they were received more hospitably in Tulsa than in many other 'non black' towns.

In 1928 Count Basie, while staying in Greenwood, heard from his bedroom window a band marching down the street. They were called the (Oklahoma) Blue Devils and were among the kings of the Battles of the Bands events, which used to take place at that time. These battles would be advertised on posters pretty much like a boxing match these days 'George Lee and his Novelty Singing Orchestra (Have never been beaten)' v 'Walter Page and his famous Blue Devils (Have never run from a contest).' Basie ended up joining the Devils for a short while and then he left to join Bennie Moten's Kansas City Band. When Bennie Moten died Basie reformed the band, bringing in some of his ex-Blue Devils colleagues and they eventually became the Count Basie Orchestra, who went on to become Undisputed Champions of the World.

All around the museum were pictures on the wall of musicians and bands, with text underneath outlining their place and role in the development of jazz. One of these prompts me to issue a word of advice for any aspiring trumpet player – don't get into street fights and get your teeth knocked out. This is what happened to one of Oklahoma's most famous jazz musicians Chet Baker, although some stories say his teeth just rotted through heroin and cocaine abuse. Whatever the truth about how he lost his teeth, in 1966, when he was 37, he made a comeback after a couple of years, changing his style to accommodate his dentures and admirably resurrecting his career despite continuing drug use. He even collaborated with Elvis Costello to play a solo on Elvis's anti war song *Shipbuilding* on the 1983 album *Punch The Clock.*

Baker eventually fell from grace, literally, when he was found on the pavement outside a hotel in Amsterdam after falling from a second floor window. It was never established whether it was murder, suicide or, as is most likely, an accident while he was under the influence of drugs. Another tragic shame, and unnecessary death of a fine musician, but at least there is some consolation in that he survived to the age of 59, which some people would say was surprising considering the way Chet lived his life.

While I was talking to David I could hear in the background some music I recognised and I soon realised it was Norah Jones singing *Lonestar* (where are you out tonight?) from her album *Come Away With Me*. Now that is an album I like very much, so perhaps I am a jazz fan after all!

I left the museum and, rather than head back to town, I turned towards the Brady Arts District (Brady Village) as I wanted to have a look at Cain's Ballroom, the 'Cradle of Swing'. It's not hard to find as you can see the distinctive red and white sign 'Cain's Ballroom Dancing' from a distance; this is a sign you are likely to see in any advertising literature about Tulsa as it is one of the birthplaces of modern pop music. Converted from a garage in the late 1920s, it had become, by 1934, famous as a music venue, with Bob Wills and the Texan Playboys holding court to audiences sometimes counted in the thousands. Mixing all sorts of tunes from ragtime, jazz, blues and country, the band varied their approach according to the demands of the audience on the night. Their daily shows were broadcast coast to coast and a new type of music developed called 'Western Swing'. The common factor in all of this was that it was adapted for people to dance to, whatever the basic theme of the music.

It is generally considered that this was the pre-cursor to Rock and Roll. Bill Haley, for instance, when he was coming onto the scene in the late 1940s, named his band Bill Haley and the Four Aces of Western Swing. Chuck Berry's first Rock and Roll success, *Maybellene*, was inspired by a Bob Wills hit in 1938 called *Ida Red*.

It is hard to imagine Cains as a venue which hosted thousands as it is just like a medium-sized barn and I would have thought a couple of hundred people would have made it cosy. Perhaps this is one of the reasons why it got a bad reputation, with lots of fights (while the band nonchalantly played on), and in 1947 the State Prosecutor declared the ballroom "a menace". The place closed down in the 1960s and stood empty for a number of years until it was re-opened in the '70s, eventually coming under the ownership of Promoter Larry Shaeffer, an enthusiast of the old Bob Wills days. Larry refurbished the hall and brought in contemporary bands like the Sex Pistols, The Police, Huey Lewis and the News and Van Halen. Ironically, the early appearance of the disrespectful Sex Pistols gave Cains respectability as a concert venue!

Just to prove the point, as I wandered about the hall, the Stoney LaRue band were setting up for their performance that evening of their 'ornery Red Dirt rocking' featuring their 'cathartic barroom brand of spirituality, where venues are complimented for good bar feng shui and where time and dimension can be traversed via emotive lyrics and melodic riffs'. All this under the watchful gaze of

Bob Wills, Tex Ritter, Roy Rogers, Hank Williams and Eddy Arnold, whose photographs were prominently displayed around the room. I'm sure they would have approved.

Back at the hotel I just happened to pick up the newspaper which I had acquired earlier, the *Urban Tulsa Weekly*. I was more than a little alarmed to see a section on page twelve headed 'BODYCOUNT', which carried a sub-title 'City's Weekly Casualty Report'. This carried an outline sketch of a gun at the top followed by the report: 'It's been particularly deadly since our last report, with four murders in the space of seven days . . . the homicide count for 2007 is 50 – nearing the all-time record of 56 – with more than three months to go'. It was almost like a challenge – go on lads you can do it, get the quota in before the accounting period ends. I'm sure this wasn't the case, but I was a bit surprised by the casual nature of the article tucked away in the bottom corner of the page. It certainly wasn't what I wanted to read before I ventured out on my own in the dark.

The evening passed peacefully and I survived intact, having settled for a trip to the upmarket Cherry Street area just out of town. I had gone into a restaurant, attracted by one of the many 'Duelling piano' acts that I had seen advertised in the paper. As the name suggests this was two chaps sitting at pianos, but their main concern seemed to be extorting money from the audience in return for playing requests. It would have been more tuneful if they had stuck to playing the piano rather than trying to sing, which they were not very good at. I think I'd been spoilt by too much musical class in the last few weeks in Nashville and Memphis. Anyway, I got back to the hotel without incident so I was quite happy.

Late Friday morning, and having spent a couple of hours finding somewhere to get my laundry done, I was on my way to the river to see what I could uncover. I don't feel you've ever seen a town until you've been to the river. As I made my random way in the direction of the Arkansas I was walking through a residential area and I saw a big blue and white striped marquee. "Something's going on," I thought (there's always something going on if you look for it), so off I went. It was a 'Greek Holiday', an Ionian-themed local celebration. Being something of a philhellene I thought this would be just the job as I am quite partial to a Mythos or Keo (yes, Cypriot I know – but Greek Cypriot). As the waiters were kitted out in national garb, I thought this must be the real thing, so you can imagine I was a little disappointed when I was told they didn't stock Greek beer. I was instead offered a Bud but by now I was in full on Greek Island mode and was desperate to have something authentic. I spotted a bottle of Demestica white wine (Domestica to its aficionados) and thought that would be my next best bet. Unfortunately, the opened bottle was standing on the counter and when I asked how cold it was I was informed by Demetri (I have no idea if that was his name, but in my experience it had a good chance to be) that it was 'room temperature', which wasn't great news considering it was a hot day and I was standing in what was effectively a big tent. The best he could offer was a glass of this with a couple of ice cubes in it, which soon put paid to savouring the taste of gorgeous Greek grapes.

There was not actually much to see at the river as it is heavily-lined with trees, at least that was the case with the bit I saw. To be fair, there are 41 miles of river-bank within Tulsa County, so I would imagine that once you get out of town it will open up nicely. There is apparently lots of wildlife, including bald eagles with a wing span of up to seven feet, so, if one fancied a taste of my Mars Bar, I could have been in for a bit of a tussle.

I set off back for town, conscious that I did not yet have a ticket for the evening bus journey. My next stop was to be Oklahoma City, which I was using as a stepping stone on my way to Wichita. The bus was due to leave at 6pm, so I had plenty of time to find somewhere to get a snack first. I came across a deli called 'the Greens on Boulder', on Boulder Avenue that is, one of the main thoroughfares in town.

The owners were the Green family, Ron and Susan. Over a sandwich and a coffee Ron told me that his great great great grandfather was Nathanael Green, who was a general under George Washington. This would mean that Ron is of esteemed lineage as the general was one of Washington's right-hand men and is remembered as a Revolutionary War hero and a great man who has statues, parks, naval vessels and towns all over the country named after him.

Ron then told me an interesting story about a guy he used to work with called Jock, who was not surprisingly a native Scotsman. After getting divorced, I think from an American woman (who took him to the cleaners), Jock came to the States, teamed up with Ron, won boatloads of Government contracts in the aircraft parts industry, somehow got payments in advance, absconded with the cash, and cost Ron his job. It was more complicated than that, but the fine details escaped me. I do recall that it involved South Africa, two Russian helicopters, Government Agencies, a business partner who had to sell all to get out of jail and that Ron would have been a millionaire had Jock not absconded. Oh, and Jock has a castle in Scotland (or more to the point had, I think it now belongs to his ex-wife).

But it all worked out well in the end because Ron and Susan now have a very nice deli and I would thoroughly recommend a visit if you're ever in town.

TALKING OF WHICH, I mustn't forget the reason for my visit to Tulsa. The words of the late Gene Pitney have immortalised the town, which I might never have heard of if it hadn't been for the Bacharach and David classic of the sixties:

'And I can never, never, never go home again'.

Was there ever a more memorable last line of a song? *Twenty Four Hours From Tulsa* is perfect for Pitney's plaintive voice and almost has you feeling sorry for his character in the story. Our sympathies should, of course, lie instead with the recipient of the letter he is busy writing. She has been dumped for someone the writer has just come across by chance at a motel while on his way back home from (presumably) his business travels.

I hope he is not really writing in his letter the words contained in the lyrics. If he is, he is likely to have a hatchet-wielding wife or girlfriend on his tail when she reads '. . . and I caressed her, kissed her, told her I'd die before I would let her out of my arms'.

Let's not take it too seriously – it's only a song. But one that made Gene Pitney famous across the world. It wasn't his first hit, but it was the one that made the big breakthrough for him in 1963 and paved the way for a brilliant career on both sides of the Atlantic. What many people don't realise, and I didn't myself until quite recently, is that Pitney, the 'Voice of Heartbreak', was first a songwriter and only had big success as a singer after writing songs such as *Rubber Ball*, a hit for Bobby Vee and *Hello Mary Lou*, which became a smash for Ricky Nelson.

He had been a talented student, studying electrical engineering at college, but had dropped out to follow a musical career. His first band was neatly called Gene and the Genials (typing errors best avoided), after which he had a partnership with a lady called Ginny Arnell (they were known as Jamie and Jane) and then he became known as Billy Bryan. When the record company declared they wanted to call him Homer Muzzy, Gene sensibly decided it was time to revert to his real name and the legend was born. His first hit was a self-penned song called *I Wanna Love*

My Life Away, on which he played piano, guitar and drums, overdubbed the vocals and generally demonstrated pioneering techniques in the recording industry using his electrical engineering skills.

Strangely, his own big hits as a singer were usually written by others and most famously by Burt Bacharach and Hal David who wrote *Twenty Four Hours From Tulsa*, as well as *The Man Who Shot Liberty Valance* (1962), *Only Love Can Break A Heart* (1962), which was his biggest chart hit, reaching number two in the States, and *True Love Never Runs Smooth* (1963).

The Bacharach and David numbers started to dry up when they concentrated their efforts on the up-and-coming Dionne Warwick, but Gene went on to record many other great songs such as *I'm Gonna Be Strong* (1964, Barry Mann, Cynthia Weil), *It Hurts To Be in Love* (1964, Howie Greenfield and Helen Miller), *I Must Be Seeing Things*, (1965, Al Kooper, Irwin Levine, Bob Brass), and *Looking Through The Eyes Of Love* (1965, Barry Mann, Cynthia Weil).

Great though these songs were he found the number one spot elusive and, very ironically, was prevented from reaching number one in the States with *Only Love Can Break A Heart* by his own composition *He's A Rebel*, sung by the Crystals and produced by Phil Spector. He did, though, become the first pop singer to perform at the Oscars when he sang *Town Without Pity* in 1962. This performance and song amazingly rescued the film of the same name, starring Kirk Douglas, which had been struggling badly at the box office.

It wasn't until 1989, when he had an unlikely teaming up with Marc Almond, that Gene finally got a number one. They re-recorded *Something's Gotten Hold Of My Heart* as a duo and it really took off, staying at number one in the UK charts for four weeks. Unexpected, belated, but well deserved.

Surprisingly, in his younger days, amid the Swinging Sixties scene, Gene had a fling with Marianne Faithful, though you would have thought they were miles apart – perhaps they were (it is said she later claimed he was boring, but there again by her standards I guess most people would be). Of course, think of Marianne and you think of the Stones and, again surprisingly, Gene struck up an immediate rapport with them, partly because they were impressed by his expertise in the studio, and he actually played the piano on their early hit *Not Fade Away*. He then recorded the Jagger/Richard song *That Girl Belongs To Yesterday*, which went to number seven in the UK charts and gave Mick and Keith their first hit as songwriters in the States.

But it is *Twenty Four Hours from Tulsa*, which reached number seventeen on the Billboard Charts and number four in the UK, that is probably Gene's best remembered song in Britain.

So why Tulsa? And where would he have been if he was twenty four hours away? Well he could have been anywhere within a thousand mile radius if he was travelling by Greyhound, or just as far if travelling by car as he would need to rest (at a motel, no doubt, which fits in with the song).

What does the man who wrote the lyrics say about it? Well, quite a lot actually, but nothing that provides the answer; Hal David is quoted as saying: "I wrote that to a melody that Burt wrote and that's what the melody said to me." "I don't think I have ever been to Tulsa." "When I hear music I very often hear a story. The fact that it was Tulsa, as opposed to Dallas is not very meaningful, but the sound of 'Tulsa' rang in my ear." "More often than not the idea just pops into my head – where it comes from I hardly ever know. Above all I try to create an emotion to which others can respond, otherwise I throw the lyric away."

He certainly created an emotion and, for a song that never reached the top in either the States or the UK, it has endured as one of the most memorable records of a memorable era.

Gene Pitney died on 5 April 2006 in the Hilton Hotel at Cardiff after a show during his UK tour. He was 66. There were no suspicious circumstances and he was lying on the bed, still dressed as he had come off stage. He had just performed a typically energetic show and had received a standing ovation – a fitting way to go for a man who was well liked and respected in the industry and who still has a host of fans all over the world.

Twenty Four Hours From Tulsa

Dearest, darlin', I had to write to say that I won't be home anymore
'cause something happened to me while I was drivin' home
And I'm not the same anymore
Oh, I was only twenty four hours from Tulsa
Ah, only one day away from your arms
I saw a welcoming light and stopped to rest for the night

And that is when I saw her as I pulled in
outside of the small motel she was there
And so I walked up to her, asked where I could get something to eat
And she showed me where
Oh, I was only twenty four hours from Tulsa
Ah, only one day away from your arms
She took me to the café, I asked her if she would stay, she said 'OK'

Oh, I was only twenty four hours from Tulsa
Ah, only one day away from your arms
The jukebox started to play and night time turned into day as we were danc-
in'
Closely, all of a sudden I lost control as I held her charms
And I caressed her, kissed her, told her I'd die
Before I would let her out of my arms

Oh, I was only twenty four hours from Tulsa
Ah, only one day away from your arms
I hate to do this to you but I love somebody new, what can I do?
And I can never, never, never – go home again

Words and music by Hal David and Burt Bacharach

Chapter Eighteen

"I hear you singing in the wires ..."

'MY NAME IS PLUMP, Timothy Plump — P.L.U.M.P.' The imposing and generously-sized bus driver, complete with black leather gloves, waistcoat and official cap, made sure he had everyone's attention before reading the rules which would apply if you wanted to travel on his bus. "No swearing, no drugs, no alcohol." the usual sermon, which I now knew by heart. He then got off the bus to finish supervising the luggage and that's when it all took off.

"Excuse me!"

"Excuse you!"

"Shee-it."

"Shee-it to you too."

I was sitting on the right hand side of the bus and this little exchange was taking place between two black ladies sitting to my left, one directly in line with me and the other one row behind. For the past hour or so, whilst waiting for the bus, I had developed the feeling that this journey was going to be fractious. I had arrived at the bus station an hour before the bus was due to leave for Oklahoma, only to be told it was fully booked and that there were eight people on the waiting list. The next bus would be at half past midnight and would arrive in Oklahoma City at two-thirty in the morning. This would have been a more than awkward scenario for me, as I had no accommodation booked, and I have to give credit to the young lady in the Greyhound station who averted the situation by somehow getting me on to this 6pm service, presumably as some people with tickets hadn't shown up. But it was tight, hence the commotion. It appeared there was some sort of dispute over seating arrangements, although both the protagonists of this little spat did seem to have seats.

"Bee-itch."

"F****** bee-itch."

I could see it was getting worse.

"Mother******* bee-itch."

"You're the mother******* bee-itch."

Both ladies were on their feet and squared up by now and a lady in a row in front had joined in. At this point Mr Plump got on the bus and hauled off the two main miscreants. They were followed by the third lady, who turned out to be the mother of one of them. Despite exhortations from myself and others on the bus for them to calm down and say nothing, it only took about thirty seconds after they got on to the tarmac before one of them was in the other's face. The inevitable happened and Timothy produced the red card and banished them from the bus altogether.

We then had to sit for half an hour while all the luggage was unloaded in order to get their cases off. Sporadic outbursts and flare ups between the women took place during this process and I shudder to think what the atmosphere would have been like for the next six hours in the depot as they waited for the midnight bus, if they were allowed to travel that is.

I couldn't help feeling sorry for the trio and just a little bit guilty as it turned out I had unwittingly been the cause of this contretemps. As I boarded the bus I had asked one of the ladies if the seat next to her was available and she had replied "no". I could see it had a bag on it and I assumed this must have belonged to another passenger, so I found another seat. Then the lady behind had accused the woman in front of 'blocking' the seat and lying about it being taken. This is what sparked the argument. There was nothing I could do to help as Mr Plump was definitely the type to enforce the zero tolerance policy and, as the ladies had continued the fight after his intervention, it was a lost cause. I came to the conclusion that trouble follows me around and closed my eyes to block out the world.

We arrived at Oklahoma around 8.30pm and I got a taxi to take me to an Econolodge on the edge of town, where I booked in before crossing the road and settling down for a truckers meal at the Iron Skillet, which was one of the few eating places around. All I wanted to do was to get some food and get my head down, as I would be moving on in the morning. That is until I saw the sign at the Windjammer hotel next door to the Econolodge. 'Free live country music – tonight!' it shouted out at me. Never one to miss a free offer I just had to investigate, particularly as the Iron Skillet wasn't licensed and there was now the chance of a couple of beers as well as some free music.

I had forgotten only one thing – this was out of town and was, should we say, a more rural venue than I might have encountered downtown. The fact that I was in shorts and T-shirt while everyone else, male and female, was dressed in cowboy hats, boots with big heels and buckles, checked shirts, bootlace ties and drainpipe jeans made me a little more conspicuous than I would have liked. Troy King and the Wild Eyed Country Boys were playing and never can a band have been more aptly named. To give you a better feel for the ambience I should mention there was a free beer draw for the ladies. I found myself a corner and, fortunately, there was waitress service, so I managed to keep a low profile while I listened to some Merle Haggard and Kenny Chesney. It was certainly better than retiring early to a boring motel room.

SATURDAY 7.30AM – A COFFEE and 'bun' and off I went into Oklahoma City to pick up the mid-morning bus to Wichita, which lies 175 miles due north in Kansas, not too far away from Dodge City. We went through some rolling countryside before hitting the plains – flat prairies with an otherwise monotonous landscape punctuated by those curious 'nodding donkeys' (officially called Pumpjacks), which were busily, and presumably profitably, in the process of sucking up their lucrative dark liquid.

The approach to Wichita brought me down to earth, the entry to the city being along an expressway with three lanes in either direction and a watercourse down the middle, surrounded by rail marshalling yards and industry. But this was nicely concentrated around the approach roads and once inside the city limits the commercial side of things was less apparent. What I hadn't realised was that Wichita has a distinguished past, and healthy present, based around the air industry and that having just left the 'Oil Capital of the World', I was now in the 'Air Capital of the World'. It transpires that the town was very instrumental in the development of powered flight and is now home to five aviation firms who between them produce an amazing 60% of the world's aircraft.

Like Tulsa and Little Rock, Wichita lies on the Arkansas River, this time with a slight elaboration as, right on the edge of town, there is the confluence with the Little Arkansas River, which is a major tributary. The town was founded by Wichita Indians in 1863, during the Civil War, and was incorporated as a city in 1870. It was given the nickname 'Cowtown' as it was the railhead destination for cattle drives from Texas and other points in the South West. It also gained a reputation as a hard-drinking, hard-living town as the cowboys understandably wanted to let their hair down after a long dusty cattle drive on what was known as the Chisholm Trail. This was just the place for cowboys and lawmen wanting to make names for themselves and, sure enough, Wyatt Earp turned up in 1874. He became a police officer before moving along the road to Dodge City, where he met Bat Masterson and Doc Holliday and became Assistant Sheriff. Whilst he went on to great things, and achieved legendary status, it could have been so different as a result of a little incident while he was in Wichita. The story goes that his gun went off as he leaned back in a chair, the bullet passing through his coat and into the ceiling, redefining my definition of a close shave.

The town became another major player in the oil boom when 'black gold' was discovered in 1914 and it was the prosperity gained from this that led to the development of the aircraft industry, with Walter Beech and Clyde Cessna being key figures. Both men based their companies in town, starting businesses which became world famous. Cessna, in particular, was a true pioneer of aviation and in 1911 he survived as many as twelve plane crashes teaching himself to fly and in attempts to get his machine off the ground. There was much initial public scepticism at that stage, but when he achieved his goal he was able to command substantial fees taking his flying machine around state and county shows.

Wichita played its part in World War II as, by 1945, 4.2 bombers were rolling off the production line each day in local factories. Today the industry maintains huge airplane manufacturing capacity in Wichita and employs tens of thousand of people through Boeing, Cessna, Raytheon (Beech) Bombardier (Learjet), and Airbus. As if it needed to establish any further credentials in this respect, Air Force One, the US Presidential aircraft, is maintained at the Boeing Wichita plant.

On a rather different theme, another famous business originating in Wichita is the ubiquitous Pizza Hut, the world's largest pizza operator. The business was founded in 1958 (in a hut naturally) at Wichita State University campus by two students Dan and Frank Carney. They were supported by a loan of $600 from their mother, who I'm sure couldn't have realised the enterprise would end up making so much, er, dough.

Once away from the industrial outskirts, Wichita is a pleasant, well laid out town and whilst this was a Saturday, and therefore there was probably less traffic in town, I got the feeling that it would be equally pleasant to walk around on a normal working day. The centre is separated from the historic Delano district by the river and, unlike Tulsa, the river has wide open aspects which I looked forward to exploring at the earliest opportunity. But first I needed to find accommodation.

I found myself outside the Convention Centre, a huge modern circular complex adjacent to the Hyatt Hotel. The main entrances were closed as it was a weekend, but, thinking that the Centre might house the Tourist Bureau, I persevered and found my way into the building through a circuitous route and what appeared to be the tradesman's entrance. I wandered about corridors, until I came to a plush carpeted area and eventually realised that I had found my way into the Hyatt. I was bit of a scruff with my pack on my back, not for the first time lowering the tone of things in nice surroundings. What was different about this occasion was that there must have been some executive training courses taking place and I soon found myself slaloming through tables and chairs with well-dressed, serious-talking young businessmen deeply engaged in what the training industry calls 'breakout groups'. I thought it was quite amusing, I'm not sure they saw it the same way.

The reception area was busy and I took my place in the queue until being attended to by a young chap, who soon confirmed that I would not be staying with them for the weekend. He very politely used a phrase something like "do you usually stay in hostels?" As I left he said I hoped I enjoyed myself in town, but warned that "nothing happens in Wichita".

Soon I found myself in the business area of town and as I was rather hopelessly lost I decided to stop a woman who was approaching me from the opposite direction. After a brief conversation I established that she had no better idea than me where to find a hotel and it seems she must have been heading for an open air religious gathering I had passed a few blocks back. She then asked me if I had found God, at which point I was very tempted to use the Forrest Gump line "I didn't know I was supposed to be looking for him," when asked the same question by Lieutenant Dan. Not wishing to be sacrilegious I kept my thoughts to myself and smiled accommodatingly when she dipped into her bag and presented me with a six page booklet entitled *Search For God.* One thing at a time. First I needed a hotel.

I called in an antique shop and the owner pointed me in the direction of the Old Town, which was just a short walk away. There I found a Marriott Courtyard hotel which in the UK I would have had to rule out on price. But again, with Wichita being a bit out of the way, it was within my budget and I had the luxury of a nice hotel for my Saturday evening stay.

After dropping off my bag and enjoying a quick tidy up, I set off to explore the surrounding area. I had earlier passed under a railway bridge and had spotted an old black steam train standing on the tracks above. I discovered this was part of a railway museum – the Great Plains Transportation Museum. I went in and, as it was about to close for the day, I had the sole attention of J Harvey Koehn one of the curators. Harvey told me that, like many other towns in the States, passenger trains are no more. The last one to stop at Wichita was in the 1970s, which is great pity because again there is a classic old Union railway station, big, brash and beautiful, and which is now used as a corporate headquarters for a communications firm.

This was just the opportunity for me to check out all my assumptions about those massive BNSF freight trains I first mentioned in Flagstaff. Were they really a mile long or was it just my imagination? Yes, they are in fact up to a mile and a quarter long; with up to 120 freight cars, which if stacked doubled would represent 240 containers per train. Harvey then educated me to the fact that there are 7,000 containers on a decent size container ship, so that's twenty-nine trains to distribute the goods from one container ship.

Harvey also told me that some trains have four engines at the front and two pushing from the back thus stopping the train breaking in half with the strain.

"But how do the engines all run at the same speed?" I asked, perfecting my wide-eyed 10 year-old school kid impersonation.

"Ah, that's because they're all controlled by one driver at the front with an umbilical cord, with 21 pin connector cables, linking all the front engines, and the ones at the back are controlled by radio," he answered confidently. So, now I know, I can relax while sitting on the bus at railroad crossings as the train rolls by and I will be able to turn to my fellow passengers and say, "Do you know how long that train is? And do you know how the engines talk to one another?" My popularity would be assured I feel.

I returned to the hotel and decided to relax for half an hour with a copy of the *Oklahoma Gazette*. I came across a column called *News Of The Weird*, which I thought might be worth a read. One item related the story about a 60 year-old man who was arrested after police found numerous homemade videos of him "having sex in public with traffic signs." I'm not sure how this works, but I'm also not sure how he filmed it. Or indeed, how the police got involved.

There were two cases of less-than-observational motorists. One was arrested for driving home with a pedestrian lodged in the front windscreen and the other was charged in connection with driving home with a (dead) motorcyclist lodged in the rear window. I decided I would be extra careful as I crossed the street from now on.

There was also an article which seemed to support my earlier comments on how we Brits are regarded by some of our friends in the States. Two British plane spotters were seen with telephoto lens taking photos of planes near Vance Air Force Base, just north of Oklahoma, and according to the paper, the security guards asked them if they "would be so kind as to realise they were in restricted area, eh, what?" And that they would like to have a "chat with the old boys". The article then stated that the men were last seen driving away from the site and ended with, "Cheers fellows! It's a long way to Tipperary." Strange, but I think in mitigation we need to recognise that less than 2% of people in the States leave the country in their lifetime and a much higher percentage enjoy watching old TV programmes bought in from the UK.

I was getting to quite like the wit of the journalists and TV newsreaders in the States. In the *Wichita Old Town Gazette*, the Bucky Walters column reported on the Larry Craig scandal currently rocking the country. Senator Craig (Republican, Idaho) had been found engaging in un-manlike activities in the Men's room at Minneapolis St Paul airport. Commenting on the fact that, like all good politicians, Senator Craig had his wife at his side as he faced the cameras at the press conference following the revelations, Walters said, "Did you get a look at that woman? If he wanted understanding from the public what he should have said is 'I am not gay! But look at her – what would you do?'" Amusing perhaps, but a bit cutting.

And then there's Jay Leno, the chat show host, who was reporting on another news item causing controversy i.e. the violent Tasering of a student who interrupted a speech by John Kerry at Florida University. Leno made the wry observation "It's the first time anyone's been electrified at a John Kerry speech."

Another case in the news was the latest O J Simpson fiasco where he was arrested on suspicion of armed robbery against two sports memorabilia dealers who he accused of having items belonging to him. The CNN presenter, Nancy Grace, opened the programme with the greeting, "Good morning O J, wake up and smell the prison coffee," before adding that he could face 93 years in jail. When her co-reporter mentioned "O J and his entourage" entering the victims' hotel room she corrected him "don't you mean the 'robbing crew'?"

Somehow I can't see the BBC or ITV getting away with that approach, although in the case of O J Simpson I would find it very amusing.

In the evening I plumped for Old Town, an area of converted red brick warehouses, old railway buildings and properties dating back to the late cowboy era. It was very vibrant and had lots of illumination, colour, atmosphere and plenty going on. The first bar I went to had a band playing in the yard (that rather quaint American term for garden – it could encompass an acre of lawns, trees and a lake and it would still be a yard), which was very pleasant on a nice warm evening.

The band was playing heavy rock – AC/DC, Black Sabbath and the like – and they were obviously very popular. I could only see one seat available, so I took it and ended up next to two girls who were a little aggrieved that the music wasn't heavy enough for them. They said they preferred a band who had been resident until recently. However, I soon came to the conclusion that they were away with the fairies, in view of their extreme and unrestrained reaction to numbers they did like. I put this down to the fact that they had mentioned they had come out much earlier (it was still only 8pm) and I thought they must have had quite a few of whatever they were drinking. But then the girl next to me started rifling around in her bag and the next thing I knew she was rubbing something into her gums. I decided it was time to move on.

I had something to eat, a few more beers, and ended the evening by standing in another yard listening to a band called Rain. I was surprised by how much the music harked back to the '60s and the British scene in particular. The band were playing Yardbirds and Stones (*For Your Love, Paint It Black*) followed by The Beatles' *Come Together* and I wondered whether the British '60s invasion had only just reached Wichita or whether it was a revival? Or whether it had arrived in the '60s and just never left? Whatever, it was interesting to see twenty-something year-old girls freaking out to the same music their parents would have been listening to in the days of LSD and Flower Power.

As I walked back to the hotel I spotted a sign advertising an event for the following week – '2007 Fall Old Town Pub Crawl, prizes at every stop, drink specials at every bar, begins at Oscar's Sports bar at 7pm.' All I can say to my friend back at the Hyatt is "get a life", or alternatively get him to tell me where he normally goes that makes this place seem so tame.

OUT FOR MY SUNDAY morning exploration of the river, just as I reached the riverside walk a chap coming from the opposite direction stopped me and said:

"Did you hear about the accident last week?"

"What accident was that?" I replied.

"At the sawmill, down the road – a man lost his left arm and left leg."

"That's nasty," I volunteered. "Did he die?"

"No, the latest news is that he's going to be all right."

It took me a moment or two to catch on. I like to think this was due to the element of surprise, and as the man walked away giggling to himself I thought, "well, that's made his day." So I smiled and went on my way, reflecting on the fact that people really do like to talk to you in the street in the States which is (on most occasions) rather nice.

The first thing I came to at the waterfront was the Kansas Veterans Memorial Park. This was a little garden area and consisted of various sections commemorating different conflicts. Prominent among these was the Korean War Monument, alongside which was a large stone, housing a brass map of North and South Korea. Down the side there was a list of all the actions and a year-by-year account of the campaign. I had noticed whilst in the States that the Korean War has a very high profile and I had observed in the Medal of Honor garden in Little Rock that a large number of awards, many of which were posthumous, had been awarded in respect of Korea.

This is hardly surprising considering the death toll, with 36,000 US troops killed. Year on year this is a higher attrition rate than Vietnam, as casualties in Korea were mainly over a three-year period – a much shorter time than the Vietnam conflict. It is sometimes referred to as the 'meat grinder' war, as total casualties on all sides ran into the millions. Apart from cult comedy series *MASH*, though, there doesn't seem to have been the popular recognition in terms of books and films, perhaps because it was never officially declared a war, but was instead a 'United Nations action'. It is still sometimes known as the 'Forgotten War' and that is certainly the case in the UK where you hardly ever hear of it, even though over a thousand of our troops were killed. The walk through the gardens confirmed my view that the Americans do show a lot of respect and recognition to the people who gave their lives for their country and the memorials are always impressive and well maintained.

Also in the Memorial Park, I spotted a torpedo on a plinth. This was a Second World War weapon and was part of a commemoration to the Submarine Corps. Specifically, it was in remembrance to the 77 crew of the submarine SS Dorado, which left New London, Connecticut, on its maiden voyage in 1943, never to be seen again. Although not conclusively proven, it appears that while on its way to Panama it was sunk by a US plane, suggesting that the controversy over 'friendly fire' is not a new phenomenon.

Further upstream I came to the convergence of the Little Arkansas river with the Arkansas. This is a very scenic spot, adorned with a modern pedestrian bridge and a 44 ft steel statue of an Indian chief, created by Blackbear Bosin, a Comanche-Kiowa artist. The statue, which depicts the chief offering a blessing to the sky, is called 'Keeper of the Plains' and, together with a display outlining the history of local tribes, forms part of a celebration of the Indian heritage of the area. Once again a rather belated acknowledgement of the culture, traditions and nobility of people who were considered 'savages' for so long. Still, late contrition is better than no contrition at all. I crossed the bridge and walked back to the hotel via the historic Delano district, arriving back in good time to get my gear together before departing for the 170-odd mile trip back to Oklahoma. I had enjoyed the walk and it had also given me time to reflect on the reason for my visit, namely the Glen Campbell song *Wichita Lineman*.

What was the song all about? Well it's another Jimmy Webb composition, so perhaps we should not expect any easy answers. As Winston Churchill might not have said, "Never in the field of human song-writing have so many been puzzled by so few". So few words that is; the whole song consists of just eight lines, plus two which are repeated. Some people think it's about an electric company worker, others about a telephone engineer. I did try to contact Jimmy Webb to ask him, but he was apparently tied up with Carly Simon, so I guess I didn't come high on his list of priorities. Come to think of it I would agree entirely with his judgement.

'I am a lineman for the county and I drive the main road
Searchin' in the sun for another overload
I hear you singing in the wires, I can hear you through the whine . . .'

Surely this so far indicates we are talking about telephone wires rather than electricity? On the other hand telephone companies are less likely to have a county lineman than electricity companies because of the way the businesses are organised. On balance of probabilities, I'm going for the telephone option.

Now the next question: is the 'Wichita lineman' the same person as the narrator? 'And the Wichita lineman is still on the line' – could mean that the narrator ('the lineman for the county') is listening in to a love rival who is the Wichita town lineman.

No-one at the hotel seemed to have a clue and I was getting some rather strange looks as I made my enquiries. In desperation I turned to the internet and needless to say the web offered me numerous solutions to the riddle. One 'blogger' suggested that the words refer to the drugs scene, as 'everyone knows' that Main Street in Wichita is the best place to get a 'line'. Another suggested the song is about Ouachita, a county in Arkansas. And Stephanie from Houston was almost orgasmic about the line – 'and I need you more than want you, and I want you for all time'. "I melt every time I think about it," she declared passionately.

Weighing all this up I had a ghastly thought – was I in the wrong place? Further investigation told me that there is a Wichita County, nowhere near Wichita the town. Then I discovered there are, in fact, two Wichita Counties, one in Texas and one in West Kansas. But here I was in Wichita Town, which is in Sedgwick County, south east Kansas. This was not good news as even the second Kansas location was 250 miles away, and the Texas option was on the other side of Oklahoma City, a distance of 339 miles. I was confident that I could discount Ouachita, but I was uncomfortable at not exploring the 'county' aspect as I didn't want to find out later that I hadn't visited the place the song was about, even if I couldn't get to the bottom of the lyrics.

More research revealed that Wichita County, Kansas, with its county seat Leoti, is so tiny as to be irrelevant to my quest as the entire county only has a population of two and a half thousand. You wouldn't need a county lineman to service that small number of people even if they all did have phones, I reckoned. Anyway it is a dry county, one of those still not uncommon counties within a state where you can't get an alcoholic drink, so I was less than keen on that option. The other Wichita County, though, could well be relevant, particularly as I had come across a report suggesting that Glen Campbell was inspired by his experiences in Wichita Falls, which is the county seat of Wichita County. Mind you, I reasoned that was probably erroneous information as firstly Glen didn't write the song and secondly it didn't say what the 'experiences' were. I decided I had to make a visit, one which would be a real pain logistically and which would cost me another planned rest day. But what the hell, all my other rest days had gone out of the window so why spoil a perfect record?

I TOOK THE BUS TO Oklahoma and arrived at 8pm. I summoned a taxi and asked the driver to take me up to the Windjammer. The taxi driver seemed to want to treat me to a tour, at my expense, diverting first to some big mural depicting the history of Oklahoma and then educating me on the history of a 137 year-old railway bridge that we passed under. As I had noticed the warning sign on the bridge, stating that maximum height clearance was 13 feet 7 inches, I realised he was making it up as he went along and told him firmly to get me to where I wanted to be. It was getting late and I needed some sustenance.

It turned out there was no music on at the Windjammer, and no food, so I ventured across the street and settled for Corky's Grill. In the morning I went to pay the hotel bill at the front desk only to be greeted by the sight of the receptionist clearly in some distress. She was holding her head in her hands and was muttering and moaning. When I asked her if she was OK she burst into tears and she was suffering from some sort of ear infection. She was clearly in severe discomfort and when I suggested she needed to get off duty and get a doctor she said she had made a phone call and was waiting for someone to turn up. But at the moment she was the only person on duty. I felt helpless as the pain was clearly getting worse and it was at the point where the poor girl couldn't function. In the end she had to call an ambulance and when this arrived the paramedics came and took her away while I kept an eye on reception. It was another of those 'what am I doing here' moments and I thought "I don't believe this – here I am running a hotel in Oklahoma and I'm actually only supposed to be passing through." I suppose this was better than passing out, which is what the unfortunate receptionist was doing by now. Fortunately, before too long someone turned up and I was able to hand back my responsibilities and get on my way.

Arriving in Wichita Falls I quickly got settled in at the Hawthorne Suites hotel and I started my exploration of the issue at hand. Wichita Falls is the county seat of Wichita County, and contains the bulk of the county's population of 125,000. The town gets its name from the Comanche word Wee-Chi-Tah meaning 'waist deep', referring to the river crossing, and the 'Falls' comes from a waterfall which used to exist up until 1886 when it was destroyed by a flood. After a hundred years of visitors asking where the falls were, the town eventually constructed a 54 foot man-made falls to replace the original. This now forms part of a quiet (except when you go under the highway) riverside walk extending to the 170 acre Lucy Park recreation area.

What I liked best about this town was the building known as the 'Littlest Skyscaper' which is a four-storey building dating from 1919 and which was the subject of a property fraud. It is only 10 feet wide, 18 feet deep and 30 feet tall, with access to the upper floors gained by shinnying up a ladder-like staircase. The property developers had persuaded unsuspecting investors to put money into the project and the blueprints apparently indicated the dimensions in feet. However, when it was built it was constructed in inches! The developers ran off with the money and were never heard from again.

Despite Witchita Falls being a pleasant enough town, I quickly established that I wasn't going to find out any more about the lyrics of *Wichita Lineman,* so the mystery remains over the meaning of a song which reached number three in the States and number seven in the UK and which was recorded, apart from Glen Campbell, by Ray Charles, Sammy Davis Junior, Johnny Cash, REM, and even Homer Simpson. I had paid my respects to a song whose longevity far outweighs its chart success and I was now ready to move on to my final destination – Amarillo.

Wichita Lineman

I am a lineman for the county and I drive the main road
Searchin' in the sun for another overload
I hear you singing in the wires I can hear you through the whine
And the Wichita lineman is still on the line

I know I need a small vacation but it don't look like rain
And if it snows that stretch down south won't ever stand the strain
And I need you more than want you and I want you for all time
And the Wichita lineman is still on the line

And I need you more than want you and I want you for all time
And the Wichita lineman is still on the line

Words and music by Jimmy Webb

Chapter Nineteen

"When the day is dawning . . ."

'I'M GOING BACK HOME to see Momma," said my young travelling companion. "It's the first time I've been on a bus."

This surprised me, because when I say young I don't mean juvenile young. I'm talking mid-late twenties.

"I haven't seen her for seven years," he added wistfully. When I asked why, his rather coy reply was that he had "been in some trouble", a phrase which was becoming quite familiar. The 'trouble' turned out to be 17 months in jail, which again surprised me as he seemed a pleasant and smart young chap. It seems Cedric had a liking for fast cars. Unfortunately they usually weren't his. Like Lachunté, the young lady on the bus to Nashville, he was now determined to stay out of trouble and the first step was to reconcile with Mum.

A chap in his forties who was sitting in the seat behind must have overheard this little conversation as he leaned forward and said to my friend, "So, you've been in the Texas Navy as well, then? Me too." I looked blank at the reference to the Texas Navy and, seeing this, they explained to me that prisons in Texas are referred to as 'the navy' because of their white naval-style uniforms.

I had been talking at some length in the bus station, during the hour the bus was delayed, to the newcomer to the conversation and hadn't suspected anything at all untoward.

"Three and a half years I've been in," he told us, "sentenced to five but got out early. I've been in the Falls Unit just throwing distance from the execution chamber, I've seen them come in walking and then go out in a coffin."

"Quite a sobering thought," I murmured to myself, and this turned out to be a rather appropriate phrase because this guy's problem was, in fact, drink and his sentence was a result of his ninth DUI (Driving Under the Influence) charge. He had been out for 46 days and hadn't touched a drop, apparently. Well, I didn't like to say anything, but I felt like suggesting they had both better get used to the bus as I didn't think they would be driving much for a while. Not unless they fancied another spell at sea that is.

If it was a scary thought sitting next to two guys just released from prison it paled into insignificance compared to the situation with the young man occupying the fourth seat in our little section of the bus. He was very agitated and a lady across the aisle seemed to be keeping an eye out for him, whispering comforting words like "perhaps it's time for your medication", which might have been comforting for him, but weren't very re-assuring for me or the other passengers! She apparently had no connection with the chap, but I had seen her attempt to calm the lad down in the bus station and she had been joined by a few others who were also trying to help. They had obviously been travelling with him on the journey before I got on the bus and were generously trying to help him sort himself out. The worry was that when he got agitated he started to get aggressive and he was very powerfully built. He settled down, fortunately, and my navy friends and myself spent the rest of the journey eating prison issue sweets, (used as currency in jail) and talking to the youngster who clearly had some mental problems. He kept talking about having to be back by a certain time and it was clear he was on a break (perhaps prematurely, I thought) from some sort of institution.

I discovered that living in an institution seems to be an occupational hazard if you are a resident of Texas. Being intrigued by the amount of people I had met who had served jail sentences, I did a little research and discovered that Texas has 106 state prison and jail facilities, as well as a further 268 county jails. These provide accommodation, for want of a better word, to a total of 232,000 people at any one time. When you compare that to the entire prison population of the UK, at around 82,000, it gives you an idea of the relative attitudes towards custodial sentences, especially when you consider that Texas has a population of around one third of the UK. If I was to be cynical I might link this to the fact that some prisons in Texas are privately run, with at least one company being quoted on the stock market, so it would seem there is money to be made in locking people up. One of my navy friends advised me that a

Japanese company is apparently attempting a takeover of one of the contracted companies. Now that would be ironic – American prisoners in American jails, owned by Japanese businessmen.

At 10 pm, after a four hour journey, I stepped off the bus, but not before bidding farewell to my three travelling companions and wishing them luck; they would all need it one way or the other. Although it was late and I was a bit on the tired side, I was quickly refreshed by a huge surge of adrenaline as I stepped onto the tarmac and looked up at the blue and silver Greyhound sign – 'Welcome to Amarillo'.

I had made it! After six weeks of travelling, more than five thousand miles, and numerous bus journeys across eleven states, I had reached Amarillo, Texas – my final destination! I couldn't resist a little clenching of the fist and an inaudible "yes" as I made my way to the luggage hall.

I SUPPOSE IT WAS ONLY human nature to have a little nagging in the back of my mind; a little concern that it would be a let down, the whole trip falling flat at the last minute. The inspiration for my trip had been the famous song about a place that was a mystery to me. Although I now knew where it was, I had no idea what it was like. What would I find in Amarillo? I really did not know what to expect.

My first job was to find the Quality Inn, which I had booked in advance, knowing that I would be arriving quite late. So into a taxi and a short ride with a lady driver called Jonisha. Somehow, in that short journey, we got into a rather deep and meaningful conversation. From out of the blue she said, "I've been getting visions of communication and art together, but I can't work it out – can you help me?"

"Just what I wanted at ten o'clock at night," I thought, after a long day and having been a captive audience to some rather dodgy company for the previous four hours. I rose to the occasion, though, and mentioned Marcel Marceau, the French mime artiste, who had died the previous day, and explained that there was an example of art as a form of communication.

"Wowee, that sends a shiver down my spine," responded Jonisha. Warming to the theme I then mentioned Elvis who "passed on a message through his liking for Gospel music" and this made her even more ecstatic. Then the clincher – "I'm writing a book and some would say that's a form of art and it's my way of communicating my experiences to people," I told her.

"Man, that's awesome – you've given me such an insight tonight and answered all my questions. My name is Jonisha – it means God is Gracious and he's put you in with me tonight for a reason – God bless you."

Looking back five weeks to Thelma and Louise, I now have no choice but to consider the possibility they could have been right – perhaps I am the preacher after all.

When I woke up in the morning my first thought was, like many other mornings over the last month or so, "where on earth am I?" as my brain struggled to assimilate its new surroundings. Then I again got the tingle of excitement when I realised I had woken in Amarillo. I decided to have breakfast while I worked out where to start, so I ventured across the road to an 'IHOP' restaurant. Despite the fact that it could be obtained for only $13.99, I settled for something less than the most heavily-promoted option: 'T Bone steak, 3 eggs, hash browns, and 3 butter-milk pancakes' – and this was the breakfast menu.

After a comparatively restrained double eggs and toast I found out the location of the Convention and Visitor Council and made my way to its headquarters in the Bivins Mansion, a historic building close to the town centre. I was introduced to Eric W Miller, Director of Communications, who could not have been more helpful. Eric told me a bit about the history of Amarillo, a town of around 200,000 people, which, among other things, is famous for marketing and transportation of cattle, with over 30% of the beef eaten in the US coming at some stage through Amarillo! One of the few towns I had visited on my quest that does not have a river, Amarillo has prospered because it forms a railroad 'crossover' and has always been an important marshalling point for cattle distribution.

I learned that the town is also known as the 'Helium Capital of the World' (yet another 'capital' to add to my burgeoning CV) as it sits atop vast quantities of one of the planet's rarer elements and for decades the US National Helium Reserve has been held in Amarillo. It is also the home of the American Quarter Horse Hall of Fame and Museum, the Quarter Horse being America's favourite equine breed. These horses are exceptionally powerful in the hind quarters and excel in distances of around a quarter of a mile, reaching speeds of 55 mph. This is a big money business and the American Quarter Horse Association also has its national headquarters in Amarillo

Eric went on to tell me about one of Amarillo's most famous landmarks, the Cadillac Ranch, a project undertaken by one Stanley Marsh 3 (not the third), a local eccentric millionaire. It sounded spectacular as the work consists of ten Cadillacs buried nose first in the ground at precisely the same angle as the Pyramid of Cheops. This was located six miles out of town and I put it on my short list for a possible visit.

Other notable things about Amarillo include the fact that the massive Pantex plant, 17 miles out of town, has been the nuclear weapon assembly/disassembly plant for the nation for many years and has for a long time been the town's major employer. Now that this industry is in decline a new saviour for Amarillo has come along, leading to the town's latest nickname of 'Rotor City', as it is now the final assembly centre for the Bell-Boeing V-22 Osprey 'tiltrotor' hybrid military helicopter/plane. This strange-looking invention takes off like a helicopter and then tilts its rotors and flies like a plane! It may be weird, but it has brought a lot of work to the town, so I'm sure it is very welcome.

When I asked Eric about Tony Christie's much-loved *Is This The Way To Amarillo* he became probably the first American I had come across on my travels to know the song. It was hardly surprising that he was familiar with it considering what it has done for the town in terms of heightening its profile outside of the States and also the fact that Tony Christie had visited in 1995 and had been awarded the keys to the city in a special ceremony. My experience in the States so far had been that most people, when you mention Amarillo and music, assume you are talking about George Strait and *Amarillo By Morning*, which was a number one country hit in the eighties and is still popular today. Quite rightly so, as it is a good number.

Among other things, Eric suggested I should have a trip out to the old Route 66 and visit the Golden Light Café, a famous watering hole on the route. He also suggested I should try the mountain oysters while I was in town. I thanked him for his considerable help and decided to first have a wander about the place.

The first thing I should say is that Amarillo is flat, very flat. So walking is easy and, as the town is laid out in a grid system, navigation is not difficult even for the easily confused like me. The roads running east to west are called avenues and are numbered, and the roads running north to south are called streets and are named after US presidents. The Bivins Mansion is on Polk Street, named after James K Polk, who was the 11th President of the United States as I'm sure you'll know. He might not be a household name in the UK, but Mr Polk's credentials as President in his one term between 1845 and 1849 are considerable, including a successful conclusion to the American–Mexican war and the acquisition of California.

Polk Street has been the main thoroughfare of Amarillo since the town was founded in the late 1880s and the Bivins house was bequeathed to the town by the family of that name who were one of the first ranching families in the area, owning a million acres of land! The building became the City Library before it was designated as the Chamber of Commerce and it is typical of the impressive mansions in the Polk Street Historic District where all the best houses were built on the west side of the street to catch the sunrise in the morning.

Not far away, in the commercial heart of the city, there are a number of eye-catching art deco buildings including the Santa Fe Building, the old 1930 skyscraper headquarters of the railway company which is one of Amarillo's most famous landmarks and has been recently refurbished at a cost of $12million, the old Paramount Theater, the Greyhound Bus Station, which is now partially office accommodation, and the Kress Building. This wasn't the first Kress Building I had come across on my travels as there were also art deco buildings with the same name in Tulsa and El Paso. Looking into this I discovered that S H Kress & Co. were a chain of 'five and dime' retail stores which operated across the States from 1896 –1981. These stores, selling goods at either five cents (a nickel) or ten cents (a dime) sprung up all over the country and were well known for their architecture. Although they stopped trading in the 1980s their memory is preserved through the many surviving historic buildings as well as the Kress Foundation, which provides continuing support to the world of art.

Having suffered economic deterioration over the years, the downtown area of Amarillo is now being revitalised, as evidenced by the Santa Fe Building, through the efforts of city management and various enterprise groups. One feature currently enhancing the ambience of the streets is the Hoof Prints of the American Quarter Horse project which involves the purchase by organisations of life-size, fibre glass, replica horses which are painted colourfully by local artists and then erected outside the company premises. At present there are nearly one hundred of these dotted around town.

After I had strolled my way through downtown, I decided it was time to take up Eric's suggestion of Route 66 and the Golden Light, so I hailed a taxi to take me out to the Old San Jacinto neighbourhood. This area used to be a favourite stopping off place for Mother Road trekkers, with Amarillo representing the half-way point on the journey from Chicago to Los Angeles. Nowadays the area consists mainly of antique shops and a few bars and restaurants. It was practically deserted this sunny mid-afternoon and I located the Golden Light, which appeared shut, before meandering further up the road till I came to the edge of town and the old Route 66 signs. I turned around, wondering where I might get a drink of some sort and as I passed the Golden Light, a small single-storey brick building, I thought there would be nothing to lose by trying the door handle. I'm glad I did because to my surprise the door opened. I walked in, to find myself inside an atmospheric, old-fashioned establishment, as you might expect from a place billing itself as the oldest restaurant in Amarillo, having opened in 1946, and the oldest continuously operating restaurant on Route 66. It was essentially dark inside, but the interior was illuminated by neon signs and, in places, by rays of sunlight coming through the windows.

I started chatting to some guys at the bar and one of them, who was in his seventies, told me the story of his dad being killed by Al Capone in 1932. Apparently Pop stole some liquor from Al, hi-jacking a truck in the process, and then tried to sell it back to him. This was not recommended behaviour, of course, and resulted in Mr Capone firing ten bullets at Pop, one of them hitting my new friend, Babiash, in the leg as he lay in his pram. Babiash, who is of Polish extraction, even went to the extent of rolling up his trouser leg to show me the wound. The bullet was still in the bone he insisted. Whether it was true or not I have no idea, but it was certainly a good yarn and worthy of another beer.

After a longer stay than I intended, the barmaid organised a cab for me and, over a discussion with the driver on the game of 'crocket', I was returned to the hotel for a well-earned rest and a review, before heading out for a meal, of the part Tony Christie had played in me ending up in Amarillo.

As I say, ask anyone in America, outside of Texas, about Tony Christie and *Is This The Way To Amarillo* and they will probably look blank and shake their heads. Ask anyone in the UK and they are likely to burst into song, whether you want them to or not, and give you a rendition of what must be the most iconic song in recent musical history. But ask them where Tony Christie comes from and they will probably say America. Me too until recently. It's a case of the world assuming that because the song was about some place in the States that the singer must actually be from there. Tony is, in fact, from Sheffield and in his early days served his apprenticeship on the northern club circuit. There is, however, a grain of truth in the association of Christie and the USA. After serving his time in the clubs, Tony's career took off in 1969 when he landed a contract with MCA records in America and began working with the legendary producers Mitch Murray and Peter Callander. He hit the charts in 1970 with Las Vegas and this was followed by *I Did What I Did For Maria*, which became number one in the UK in 1971, the same year that *Amarillo* reached number 18. He achieved phenomenal success in Europe and still has a massive following there, as well as in New Zealand and Australia where he toured regularly.

Having amassed more than 30 million sales over the years, Tony's other hits include *So Deep Is The Night, Avenues and Alleyways* (the theme song for the TV series *The Protectors*) and *Don't Go Down To Reno*. But it is *Is This The Way To Amarillo* which has guaranteed his place in pop history, reaching number one in Spain, Denmark, Sweden and Germany and, of course, more recently in the UK after its re-release, being given the full Peter Kay treatment to raise funds for Comic Relief.

A versatile entertainer, Tony sung the part of Migaldi on Andrew Lloyd Webber and Tim Rice's album *Evita* and was invited to play the role in the West End musical, which he unfortunately had to turn down because of other commitments. Another example of his versatility is his unlikely success in 1999 with *Walk Like A Panther*, which he recorded with Sheffield band The All Seeing I. The song was penned by Jarvis Cocker, who in his youth was apparently star-struck by Tony, who was something of a local hero in Sheffield. As Tony recounts: "I used to go into this pub in Sheffield and there would be this youth at the other end of the bar looking across at me." It turned out, of course, to be Jarvis, who went on to great things himself as lead singer of Pulp, inspired by his fellow Yorkshireman.

Panther brought back Tony to *Top Of The Pops* long after he thought he would never return to the scene of arm waving youngsters and he confesses he did find it somewhat bizarre at this late stage in his career. But all good fun. When Tony could not appear for a second week on the show due to tour commitments in Germany, Jarvis actually stood in for him, thus completing an unlikely but uplifting chain of events.

In 2005 *Is This The Way To Amarillo*, which had been featured a few years earlier in Peter Kay's Channel 4 comedy drama *Phoenix Nights*, was used for the Comic Relief event and, thanks to an hilarious video which featured a host of

Britain's comedy stars walking alongside Peter on a travelator simply took off. It hit the top of the charts, far exceeding the song's original success 34 years earlier. It stayed at number one for seven weeks, selling over a million copies and became the best selling single of 2005. Although Peter Kay fronted the video, the song was actually a straightforward re-release of Tony's original hit.

Amarillo was written by Neil Sedaka and his writing partner Howie Greenfield, who had many hits in the '60s. The lyrics to the song, unlike some of my Jimmy Webb featured songs, are easily decipherable, quite simply being about a love-struck man travelling to Amarillo to be with his intended. Why Amarillo? According to legend it is the only place Sedaka could think of that rhymed with pillow and willow. Such is the science behind the world's great musical success stories.

Tony, now in his sixties, continues to perform energetically and having had the chance to meet him after one of his performances recently I can con-firm that he is in good shape, a real nice guy – down to earth and a keen foot-ball fan. He must have been over the moon then when Amarillo was played before the World Cup Final in Berlin in 2006. Not bad for a Doncaster Rovers supporter!

I HAD HEARD THAT THE Big Texan was the place to go in the evening and I discov-ered that they provide a complimentary limousine service, so this looked a very good option. When the limo, a Cadillac, turned up at 7.30pm I was surprised to see it had a massive pair of steer horns sticking out of the bonnet. I was shown into the back of the car and felt quite important having the vehicle to myself. When I con-sidered the 'Texan Longhorns' adorning the bonnet, and having read the reports of drivers taking people home in the windscreens of their cars, it was not hard to imag-ine the potential for the impaling of some hapless pedestrian. I hoped it would not be tonight.

The Big Texan is a Route 66 legend and its huge long-legged cowboy sign is a major landmark. The kitchen there has served tens of thousands of travellers huge steaks cooked over open fires, but it had to move with the times and conse-quently re-located to the Interstate 40, the 66 replacement route. It is particularly famous for its 72 oz Steak Challenge which, if eaten in under one hour, is free to the diner. I introduced myself to the manager, a lady called Tish who humorous-ly calls herself the 'Little Texan' (she is 4 foot 6 inches in her shoes). Tish is a real Amarilloan character and she sat down with me and explained that Klondike

Bill, the wrestler, is one of the people who have successfully met the steak challenge and that the record for devouring the beast is held by Cincinnatti Reds ex-pitcher Frank Pastore, who wolfed it down in nine and a half minutes. I forgot to add that the accompaniments have to be eaten too, but they consist of a mere baked potato, salad, dinner roll and shrimp cocktail.

Frankie, who has had a lot of practise in this area, having succeeded in the feat seven times, achieved the record through his technique of butterflying the sirloin, making it one and a half inches thick, and putting the accessories in the middle so that he could eat it like a taco. His achievements, mountainous as they may be, are perhaps surpassed by the eight stone lady who ate the steak in 35 minutes, danced with the band and enjoyed strawberry cheesecake for dessert!

Tish keeps two snakes — one Rattlesnake and one Bullsnake, the latter being one of the few snakes capable of killing a rattler. I didn't ask how big the Bullsnake was, but I know they can grow to six feet long. She told me she feeds it live rats to keep it happy and said that if I would like to take up another of their challenges, usually only offered as part of their Hallowe'en celebrations, of staying for a specific time in the same area as the Bullsnake, she would make sure she fed it beforehand.

I declined Tish's kind offer and asked for her help with the menu instead, telling her that I was looking forward to the mountain oysters that Eric had recommended. I said I was in a seafood mood and that I would follow the oysters with a salmon steak. At this point Tish looked at me a little quizzically and clearly thought she needed to enlighten me on my culinary knowledge.

"You do know what mountain oysters are?" she asked as politely as she could, but I think she knew the answer before she asked the question. I hadn't a clue. In fact these delicacies are not from the molluscular world, but rather from the testicular domain, of a bull that is. Or was it a buffalo? Whichever, it was too late now — how could I face a four and a half foot Texan lady who keeps deadly reptiles and tell her this macho Englishman didn't have the stomach to sample the gonads of their finest bovine specimens? So it was salmon with gonads, sorry mountain oysters, as a side dish that found its way on to the order pad. I rapidly ordered another beer in a desperate attempt to accelerate the anaesthesia process.

When the meal arrived I breathed a sigh of relief that Tish left me to my own devices, but that didn't mean I was going to chicken out. I was also relieved to see that the 'oysters' were cooked in batter and that I had a spicy sauce with which to smother the offending articles (they have big bulls in Texas by the way). I am proud to say I made a brave attempt and whilst I didn't clear the plate I devoured a healthy portion, eating enough to avoid the waiter having to ask "Is there a problem with the oysters sir?", in which case the word 'bollocks' may well have featured in any reply.

Setting off back to the hotel in my return limo I felt quite pleased with myself and reflected that I had probably made not too bad a choice as, if I had gone instead for the Howlers (sliced jalapenos), I might have regretted it in the morning as they are sub-titled on the menu with the alternative designations of 'Blazin' Saddles' or 'Ring of Fire', descriptions which don't leave too much to the imagination.

I awoke the next morning with no ill effects and when I came round fully it dawned on me that that this was my last day – in the evening I would be setting off back to Oklahoma and the plane home. I felt sad, and elated, and pleased, and worried. Sad that the adventure was coming to an end, elated that I had achieved my objective, pleased that I would soon be enjoying the luxuries of home and worried that I had not really come up with enough the previous day to end the trip on a high. But what could I do – you can't just decide something is going to happen. Or can you?

Poor Eric Miller probably thought he had seen the last of me the day before, but I turned up on the doorstep of his office just after 9am.

"He's in a meeting," said the receptionist.

"I'll wait," I said, and didn't waste any time in accepting the invitation to take a seat in the sumptuous surroundings of the entrance hall of the Bivins Mansion. An hour later Eric was still in his meeting. But no sweat, I was a man on a mission – where to was anybody's guess.

When Eric surfaced he invited me into his office and seemed genuinely pleased to see me again. I explained that there didn't seem to be much going on of an exciting nature in Amarillo at the moment and that I was looking for ideas. He suggested the Quarter Horse Center or the Don Harrington Discovery Center and gave me top contacts for both. Whilst I am sure both centres would have been very interesting I wasn't so sure either was what I was looking for, so I kept talking. There was the Palo Duro Canyon, the second largest canyon in the States, but that was 25 miles out, or the Polk Street Historic District, which I had already seen. All good stuff, but then the Cadillac Ranch came up again: "Stanley Marsh – he's regarded as the most eccentric character in Amarillo, certainly the most colourful, and definitely the most controversial."

Eric explained that Stanley Marsh 3 is a millionaire who loves public art and his work either excites or annoys the local population depending on their taste.

"I need to see the Cadillac Ranch," I declared, thinking out loud, even though I knew it was six miles outside town. "And I wouldn't mind a chat on the phone with Mr Marsh if there is any chance of that."

"I can give you his secretary's number," Eric offered. "She's called Melba and I've always found her very helpful."

Eric explained that Marsh Enterprises is based in the 31 storey Chase Tower, the tallest building in Amarillo, just ten minutes walk away from his office. I decided that fortune favours the brave and rather than ring I would go and knock on the door. So off I went.

On arrival at Chase Tower I went through the revolving doors into the ground floor and found myself in a huge banking hall full of people going about their financial business. I found a quiet corner and phoned the number that Eric had given me for Melba. I got through and asked if I could possibly speak to Mr Marsh.

"I'll check with Mr Marsh to see if he's free to speak to you," she replied.

"So far so good," I thought. When Melba came back she took me by surprise when she said, "would you like to come up to the 12th floor, Mr Marsh will see you now"!

I was amazed at this as I had not even asked to see him at this point, just to have a chat. Off I went to find the elevator, feeling, I have to admit, a little nervous about the prospect of dropping in unannounced on the highest profile figure in town.

When I got out of the lift I expected to see Melba, but instead I was greeted by a man in his sixties who shook my hand and introduced himself as Stanley Marsh.

"Come and meet my secretary Melba and the rest of my team," he said. So here I was, as the man himself introduced me to his secretary rather than the other way round, my head spinning from this unexpected turn of events. It dawned on me that I had not even got a clue what sort of business Marsh was in; all I knew was that he is famous (and indeed infamous) for his sponsorship of extravagant street art.

This was a bank building remember, so the sight that greeted me as I walked in to his office was totally surreal. Everywhere else in the building appeared to meet the expectations of a normal banking environment, but floor twelve was a real eye opener. I knew as soon as I saw the plastic ride-on tractor in the middle of the floor that this was going to be something different. The layout was open plan, but it wasn't filled with desks, just lots of space, and there was an area sectioned off where I could see a number of young people at work. Not banking work, though – far from it. They seemed to be making artworks, painting – much of which, I think, could be best described as 'contemporary'. There was paint spilt on the floor and the scene generally represented a surprising image, to put it mildly, for the unsuspecting visitor.

Mr Marsh – Stanley, he insisted, invited me to follow him to a seating area around the corner and I was surprised to see what looked like a lounge/dining area containing a dining table and a three piece suite, on which were perched two youths in their twenties, dressed in jeans and T-shirts. I sat down on the sofa next to Stanley and told him the reason for my visit. He introduced me to his young colleagues, one of whom was called 'LBK' ('Long Board Kid' apparently, as he is some sort of skateboard champion) and the other was called 'Skippy', for reasons I never did discover. As I glanced up I was surprised to find myself looking at a huge screen on the wall showing a spreadsheet of stocks and shares and I saw that the screen was linked to a laptop, which was being operated by one of the youngsters.

"It's a hobby," said Stanley. "I like to dabble, but I'm getting pretty boring these days, mostly utilities and the like."

I got out my notebook, hoping to squeeze a few words out of my host. I needn't have worried because half an hour later he interrupted his flow for the first time to ask "would you like to stay for lunch? And then afterwards I'll get someone who's available and who wants an afternoon out to take you to my ranch and to see some of my work, including the Cadillac Ranch. With a bit luck you might meet my beautiful wife, but beware – she'll want you to stay for tea."

I was completely stunned by this, but also extremely grateful. It would mean I would get to see the Cadillac Ranch without messing around with taxis and it would be at the invitation of the patron of the project. This was getting better and better.

Stanley told me that his wife, Wendy, who used to be the girl next door is "very rich as well as beautiful", being the grand-daughter of the man who invented barbed wire. Apparently her family ranch was the first to be fenced with the 'Devils Rope', which changed the face of the West. I discovered later from an Amarillo

Globe News report that she is also a 'tireless civic worker, social activist and philanthropist in the Amarillo community.' Quite a lady by all accounts.

It became apparent that I didn't really need to go anywhere else to find out all about Amarillo as Stanley was a fascinating host. He told me that he was born in Amarillo during the depression, when Amarillo was in the 'Dustbowl' – that disastrous period when hundreds of thousands of people had to move west to escape the deprivations of the drought and its consequences.

"Only the greedy and the nutcases stayed," as Stanley put it. Although he didn't say in which category he would place himself, we might get a clue from the quote he apparently once made to a reporter who enquired about some of his more bizarre activities: "Art is a legalised form of insanity and I do it very well."

Stanley is now 69 years old, and although he came from an oil dynasty, he was himself a successful businessman, owning and operating a number of TV stations in Texas for 37 years. When he turned 65 he sold his media empire and started to use his time to indulge himself in other activities such as "enjoying making things". Though he has never been near art school and has not sold one work of art he has surrounded himself with aspiring artists and clearly enjoys their rebellious company as he is renowned as something of a prankster and extrovert himself. I had already learnt that he once disrupted a TV weather report in wintry conditions by getting out of his car and doing an Indian snow dance in front of the cameras. Clearly my host was not the shy and retiring type.

When I mentioned that I was aware that Amarillo was famous for helium and that I had intended to visit the Harrington Center, which incorporates a steel Helium Monument, Stanley declared that he could tell me everything I needed to know about helium and proceeded to do just that. Basically it is an inert gas that won't burn, it is quite rare on earth, and much of what there is lies under the ground in close proximity to Amarillo. It became much sought after during the Second World War and the underground Amarillo supplies had to be heavily guarded. Stanley reckoned the "dirty Japs" and "rotten Nazis" were going to land in Baja California to come across and destroy the helium reserves. He also told me that helium blimps were used in the Caribbean to locate submarines on the shallow sandy bottoms and that it was used in barrage balloons, including those over London during the Blitz. He was clearly and justifiably proud of the contribution his home town had made to the war effort.

Interestingly, the advantage of having helium available rather than other gases was demonstrated by the Hindenburg disaster in May 1937. There was a military embargo on sales of helium to Germany at that time, so the giant airship had to be filled with hydrogen, which is actually slightly more buoyant than helium, but, of course, flammable. So when the craft crash-landed it burst into flames, tragically killing 36 people.

These days helium is used in deep sea diving equipment, to assist in welding and in cryogenics. But we all know that the best use of helium is by breathing some in from floating balloons at parties and making your voice go all squeaky. In case you're wondering why this happens it's because sound travels three times quicker in helium than it does in air, so there's another useless piece of information for you to impress the kids with.

Next, Stanley promoted the Amarillo beef industry by telling me that it is more nutritious than meat from other places like Scotland and England (I suppose it would be nutritious if you ate 72 oz of the stuff). He put this quality down to the rich soil and grass. According to Stanley most of the ranches in Texas were founded by English people, who got Scots to manage them. The accuracy or logic behind that I'm not sure about but it's an interesting observation.

At this point Stanley looked at his watch and informed me that very soon we would be joined by 'Yellow Man', who had just flown in from London and was heading straight down to the Chase to join us for lunch. Yellow Man is the artistic name of Matthew Williams, an ex-employee of Stanley, who is from a ranching family in Amarillo. Matthew is a graduate of the Royal Academy of Arts in London and has "immersed himself in the colour yellow". I haven't yet mentioned that Amarillo is the Spanish word for yellow and that yellow is the official colour of the town. Apparently this is because of the colour of the soil along the banks of Amarillo Lake and Amarillo Creek, although there are other theories, such as the one which suggests it is because of the proliferation of yellow wildflowers. Whatever, it appears that Yellow Man paints only in that colour, which I was also advised is the colour of communication. I couldn't help thinking that Jonisha the taxi driver would have been impressed at this further link between art and communication.

About forty minutes later, in walked Yellow Man right on cue. I thought at first it was someone in a banana outfit, as he was dressed top to bottom in a bright yellow tracksuit. Matthew would be in his thirties, I guess, with a sparse covering of dark wispy hair, dark stubbly beard and big red glasses. He joined in the conversation and expressed great interest in my visit and, despite the fact he had just got off a transatlantic flight, he decided he would like to come on the afternoon tour.

Lunch arrived and I enjoyed a real treat of delicious sandwiches and an unhealthy portion of nicely fried chips.

After lunch it was time to say goodbye to Stanley and I thanked him for his hospitality which far exceeded anything I could possibly have expected. He may be a controversial figure but I found him very friendly, incredibly open and a generous host. I think he just decided not to grow up!

Down in the basement, Skippy, LBK, Yellow Man and myself jumped into a four wheel drive, colourfully painted in the Stars and Stripes, and took off for the Marsh ranch, known as Toad Hall. Unfortunately for me, when we arrived there was no sign of Wendy, but I can understand why she was not around when I consider the impressive list of honorary positions she holds and the amount of charitable work she performs. At least it meant I didn't get sidetracked by an offer of tea, which I would have been unable to resist. Perhaps another day.

We got back into the truck and took off along a bumpy track with LBK at the wheel. Without warning, a mile or so along this trail, LBK shouted "offroad" and swung the wheel to the right, or was it the left; I was so surprised I cannot be sure. What I do know is that no-one, LBK included, could see where we were going as we were ploughing at speed through grass which must have been eight feet high.

"Watch out for the lake," came a shout from the back and at this point I wondered whether it was a good ploy to have my seat belt fastened or not. But I should have had faith in the Kid as all of a sudden we came into a clearing of sorts. We were still in long grass, but at least I could see a route ploughed through it, in the shape of a circle. We drove around it and I could see dozens of road signs lying at regularly spaced intervals around the perimeter. I was informed we were now in the Graveyard of Signs. This is the resting place of 'retired' signs from one of Stanley Marsh's best known projects, his Dynamite Museum, which consists of hundreds of mock road signs which spring up, at Stanley's instigation, all over Amarillo in the form of diamond-shaped road signs similar to their municipal counterparts. The difference being that Stanley's signs are highly colourful, with pictures, and they carry weird messages such as 'Road does not end' (parodying the municipal signs of 'Road ends in xx yards'), 'What's cookin' good lookin'?', 'Ostrich Crossing', and 'What is a village without a village idiot?' Yes, you're right, this is as bizarre as it gets, not least because at this very moment I was in a home of retired road signs which were seemingly arranged in the same way the Dakota Indians bury their dead!

We proceeded on our way past the lake that I was so pleased not be making closer acquaintance with. I was advised that on the island in the middle there are a number of breeding monkeys which Stanley has acquired from the zoo. I decided I would not get out of the vehicle in case there was something worse lurking in the pampas.

Back on the main road we headed off to the Cadillac Ranch, probably Stanley's most iconic venture. This was created in 1974 in conjunction with the Ant Farm Group, a collective of underground architects and designers from San Fransisco, working on the 'fringe of architecture'. Supported by Stanley, the Ant Farm team planted ten Cadillacs nose first in the ground in one of his wheat fields, the angle of burial being precisely that of the pyramid of Cheops at Giza. The model of cars used ranges from 1949 to 1964 and the monument celebrates the rise and fall of the Cadillac tail fin. It is also a 'shrine to the Americans' love of the open road'.

Visitors are welcome to enter the field and are even encouraged to bring their own spray cans and paint whatever they like on the vehicles. Every now and again Stanley sees to it that the vehicles are sprayed one colour again, providing a new canvas for the would-be artist.

The fame of the Cadillac Ranch has spread far and wide; it has been featured on *Blue Peter*, its website has received almost one and a half million hits and homage was paid to it in the Disney/Pixar film *Cars* in which the town of Radiator Springs is described as bordering the Cadillac Range. In the film, the landscape behind Radiator Springs is modelled on the profile of the Marsh Cadillacs – quite a tribute.

Perhaps just as famously *Cadillac Ranch* was the title and topic of a Bruce Springsteen song on his 1980 album *The River.*

'Well there she sits buddy justa gleaming in the sun
There to greet a working man when his day is done
I'm gonna pack my pa and I'm gonna pack my aunt
I'm gonna take them down to the Cadillac Ranch'

'James Dean in that Mercury '49
Junior Johnson runnin' thru the woods of Caroline
Even Burt Reynolds in that black Trans-Am
All gonna meet at the Cadillac Ranch'

'Well buddy when I die throw my body in the back
And drive me down to the junkyard in my Cadillac'

There are many stories about the creation of the ranch and the *Amarillo Globe News* in 2004 quoted Stanley Marsh as saying, 'They are a monument to the American dream, when we all thought we could hit the road, get a blonde, break the bank in Las Vegas and be a movie star.'

Chip Lord, one of the original Ant Farm group, goes into more detail in an article for the Cadillac Ranch website saying that a Cadillac was a status symbol, signifying that a person had arrived at a comfortable level of accomplishment in life. He maintains that the growth of tailfins on Cadillacs, eventually reaching 42 inches off the ground, was a marketing tactic by General Motors to get the motoring public to accept the design concept of tailfins on cars generally.

When Stanley met the Ant Farm group in the 1970s he liked their radical ideas and invited them to put forward proposals for some sort of installation on his ranch. He liked their idea of the Cadillacs and, with the artists, he went out and bought the cars, mainly from used car lots in town at an average price of $200. One seller, though, wanted $700 for his silver 1949 fastback and, bearing in mind this was 1974, the team considered this to be exorbitant. Stanley resolved this by paying the money and then getting revenge by having the front end smashed up with sledgehammers in front of the horrified previous owner!

The cars were transported to one of Stanley's wheatfields and a bemused backhoe operator was hired to dig holes eight feet deep and ease the cars into them with his tractor bucket while a mixer truck poured in concrete. An opening party was held with 200 guests and gin and tonics were served while the lead car was christened with a bottle of champagne.

Since the launch the Ranch has been used for countless TV and newspaper advertisements and has been the subject of a feature film, released in 1996, and named appropriately enough *Cadillac Ranch*. This stars Christopher Lloyd as the bad guy in a road movie involving three sisters and a stash of money hidden at the Cadillac Ranch site which, for this film, was actually re-created in Austin Texas.

But, fittingly, the last word must go to its creator Stanley Marsh who says, "It's fun to go out there, I'm continually drawn to it. I've never seen a politician go there to shake hands and that means it must be blessed."

There are many other examples of the Marsh sense of fun, art, and mischief around Amarillo and its outskirts, not least being the 'Floating Mesa', a flat top hill, around which Stanley has wrapped a white band, giving the impression in certain light conditions that the top third of the hill is floating in the sky. And then there is the giant pool table, which is only visible from the air, or the thirty foot high roadside pair of legs inspired by the Percy Bysshe Shelley poem *Ozymandias*:

'I met a traveller from an antique land
Who said: Two vast and trunkless legs of stone
Stand in the desert . . .'

I could have gone on to look at these creations, but time was getting short. I had a bus to catch, my journey was over and it was time to say goodbye.

As one, we decided the best way to do that was over a beer.

"Let's go to Hooters." I'm sure it was Yellow Man who made the suggestion. So I ended up back in the world of orange hot pants, a fitting conclusion to the most bizarre day I can remember. If I had brought with me a bizarreness monitor it would have been in meltdown at today's events. I had never set foot in a Hooters bar since my first destination, Las Vegas, six weeks earlier. Was it just pure coincidence that I was ending my trip this way, I asked myself, or was there a greater force at work? But philosophical considerations slipped from my mind when Betty Lou sauntered across to take our order.

We discovered that the beer can be ordered in large jugs, so the farewell drink turned out to be just a bit more than I had reckoned on and we had a great laugh as I recounted my many experiences over the last few weeks. An hour or so later, as we climbed back into the truck, I heard Skippy say "that song – you know, the one by that English guy. I know the tune but not the words."

"I just happen to have a copy of the lyrics in my pocket," I replied, passing them over my shoulder.

A few moments later, as we took off down the highway, I heard the cue from the back seat, "All together now; one, two, three . . ."

'Sha la la la la la la la
Sha la la la la la la la
Sha la la la la la la la . . .

An incredible end to a fantastic adventure. Awesome in fact.

Is This The Way To Amarillo

Sha la la la la la la la
Sha la la la la la la la
Sha la la la la la la la

When the day is dawning
On a Texas Sunday morning
How I long to be there
With Marie who's waiting for me there
Every lonely city
Where I hang my hat
Ain't half as pretty as where my baby's at

(Chorus)
Is this the way to Amarillo?
Every night I've been hugging my pillow
Dreaming dreams of Amarillo
And sweet Marie who waits for me
Show me the way to Amarillo
I've been weeping like a willow
Crying over Amarillo
And sweet Marie who waits for me

Sha la la la la la la la
Sha la la la la la la la
Sha la la la la la la la

There's a church bell ringing
With a song of joy that it's singing
For the sweet Maria
And the guy who's coming to see her
Just beyond the highway
There's an open plain, and it keeps me going
Through the wind and rain

Chorus

Sha la la la la la la la
Sha la la la la la la la
Sha la la la la la la la
And Marie who waits for me

Words and music by Neil Sedaka and Howie Greenfield

ABOUT THE AUTHOR

GEORGE MILLER

GEORGE MILLER IS A management training consultant and freelance writer based in the North East of England. His interests include fell walking, playing tennis and the masochistic pastime of supporting Newcastle United.

His first book *One Night at the Palace* featured as Sunday Times Sports Book of the Week and in the Independent's Top Ten Sports Book chart.

After a casual expression of interest in the musical history of the USA it was inevitable that his lust for travel and adventure would lead him into the escapades described in this book.

Having survived the rigours of thousands of miles on the Greyhound bus, normal service has been resumed on the tennis courts of Northumberland while he dreams of his next unlikely episode.